THE LAST OF THE FEW

THE LAST
OF THE FEW

Forty-two Years of African Safaris

Tony Sanchez-Ariño

SAFARI PRESS INC.

The trademark Safari Press ® is registered with the U.S. Patent and Trademark Office and in other countries.

Sanchez-Ariño, Tony

Second Edition

Safari Press

1995, Long Beach, California

ISBN 1-57157-168-X

Library of Congress Catalog Card Number: 95069974

10 9 8 7 6 5 4 3

Printed in China

Readers wishing to receive the Safari Press catalog, featuring many fine books on big-game hunting, wingshooting, and sporting firearms, should write to Safari Press Inc., P.O. Box 3095, Long Beach, CA 90803, USA. Tel: (714) 894-9080 or visit our Web site at www.safaripress.com.

TABLE OF CONTENTS

ACKNOWLEDGMENTS

The author would like to thank the magazine *Caza y Pesca* (*Hunting and Fishing*) for its contribution to these pages. This magazine has been a supporter of the author since 1955 through three generations of Joaquin Españas, beginning with its founder, Colonel Joaquin España Cantos, his son Joaquin España Paya, and his grandson Joaquin España Aguado. Several chapters of this book first appeared as articles in this respected magazine. The reproduction of some of these articles has been fundamental in the creation of *The Last of the Few.*

To my dear friend Ramón Tatay who was with me at the age of twenty-two when I took my first elephant. To the memories of those great hunters John A. Hunter and George Rushby who kindly advised me when I was a young man full of illusions and empty of experience. To the memory of my beloved parents who always did everything possible to make me happy. Always in first place, to my wife Isabel, the accepting partner who puts up with my frequent absences when she has to be both mother and father to our children. To my dear sons Antonio, Jorge, and Carlos so they can see how I spent the past forty-two years of my life.

Some years ago, when I began to formulate the idea of doing a new book on Africa, I was lucky enough to catch Tony Sanchez-Ariño at his home in Valencia and spoke with him for the first time. He says that after this first, lengthy conversation his wife, Isabel, asked who he'd been talking to. Tony answered, "With a lunatic from Seville who thinks he's going to put together the book nobody has dared to do about Africa."

This was the beginning of our friendship, and although years have passed our friendship has grown stronger over time. When we began planning this book, we wanted to commemorate Tony's forty-two years as a professional hunter and to recognize the experience and knowledge of this incomparable master.

I confess that my initial joy in the project was replaced by admiration and fear when I realized what was entrusted to me. I held in my hands the exceptional work of the man who, better than anyone else today, can tell us about that great part of the world known as Africa. I had always dreamed about Africa, and by a strange twist of fate I now had the duty and obligation as publisher—a job I wasn't sure I was up to—to present the legacy of a man who for forty-two years has been the professional hunter most admired and respected throughout Africa.

Several months went by, and, with all the material arranged, selected, and prepared for printing, I received a letter from Tony, sent from Cameroon in May of 1992, which said, among other things, "About the prologue to my book. I think you should do it, OK?" It might seem silly, but the pride this gave me cannot be surpassed, and the responsibility I felt became greater than ever. So what can I say about someone considered to be the last great hunter of the old school?

There are many admirers of this hunter, yet if you were to meet him on the street you would probably not associate him immediately with professional hunting because of his charm, his eloquent manners, and his courtesy. Moreover, this "great white hunter" is a mature man whose looks defy his age . . . even though he has spent more than four decades under the broiling African sun. For me, Tony is a person rarely found in the real world, accessible to everyone and engaging you with his erudition and culture, his discretion, his loyalty, and his great sense of friendship. No one has described him better than the German gunsmith Harald Wolf in the German hunting magazine *Jaeger*.

"With his looks, education, and manners, Tony is the image of a Victorian gentleman around whom the hurries of the modern age ricochet without making a dent."

To me, there are three aspects of Tony definitely worth noting: First, I believe that he is one of the best professional hunters ever. Few have been in the field more years and, above all, he has experienced firsthand the two greatest arenas of African hunting—the real arena of sporting safaris and the mythical and nostalgic arena of the ivory hunter. Second, I believe that Tony personifies the ideal professional hunter in the classical sense—the professional hunter who is a likable character, adventurous, romantic, a little crazy, who appears to us for a time as a god capable of solving all our problems. In Tony's case, this description doesn't begin to capture the person. Before anything else, he is a gentleman in the most complete sense of the word. The circumstances of his birth, his university career, his affinity for culture, his love of literature, his stamp collection, and so much more make him stand out from the rest.

And last, as young people colloquially put it, he's a "good guy," as all of us who know him can attest. Unlike other celebrities who like to stay up on their pedestals, Tony is always ready to give a hand to anyone who needs it. These, I think, are the traits that make Tony, for me and for so many others, one of a kind.

On top of it all, he has a tremendous knowledge of large-caliber rifles backed with plenty of personal experience, and his name is always associated with the best and most famous gunmakers. With his steady nerves, he is a first-class shot even under the most difficult circumstances, and his record as an elephant hunter is almost impossible to beat. It is also important to point out that in forty-two years of hunting, neither Tony nor his clients nor his staff have ever suffered a scratch. Perhaps the most eloquent words said about Tony come from Norman J. Carr ". . . he is one of those precious ones who are the last great hunters of Africa. He is *The Last of the Few* remaining of our old, beloved, and agonized profession."

Finally, I'd like to mention some of the many honors awarded to Tony as well as his many achievements over the years:

1. He was the first Spanish member of the elite Professional Hunters Association of East Africa, which is like being a member of the "Royal Academy of Hunting."
2. He is a founding and lifetime member of the International Professional Hunters Association and served as vice-president from 1981 to 1993.
3. His book, *Ivory*, written originally in Spanish, was translated into English.
4. He was named Honorary Member of the Official Hunting Association of Spanish Guinea for being an "exceptional elephant hunter," as it states on the diploma.
5. He holds the record for having hunted elephants in twenty-three countries and territories in Africa.
6. He never has had a single problem with any hunting department in the many territories where he has hunted.

7. He is the Spaniard to take the greatest number of trophies in Africa—a record probably impossible to beat considering the negative scenario for hunting now and in the future.

8. He is part of the small group of distinguished elephant hunters.

9. His book, *On the Trail of the African Elephant*, became a textbook for hunters who hunt elephants or those who plan to in the future.

10. His African assistants, clients, and Tony himself were never touched by a dangerous animal . . . because of Tony's knowledge and experience in the hunting field.

11. He has killed twenty-eight elephants with tusks of more than 100 pounds each.

12. He has shot twenty elephants in an hour and fifteen minutes.

13. He has had a film made about his life and experiences in Africa by Game Conservation International as a testimony for the future.

Tony, I hope, and I say this wholeheartedly, that the story you tell, the life you live, and the profession you love, please God, never die.

With a warm embrace,
Antonio Reyes de los Reyes

CHAPTER I

Africa or Bust

I was born 16 February 1930, in the beautiful Spanish Mediterranean city of Valencia. I've spent forty-two years, more than half my life, in Africa. For everyone, there is that moment of nostalgia in looking back over a lifetime of memories, and this is it for me. I see myself arriving in Africa at the age of 22, younger then than my youngest son, Carlos, is now. I was full of optimism and with all five senses on full alert so as not to miss one bit of this dream that had finally become reality. I was set to match the adventures of "Karamojo" Bell, James Sutherland, and Frederick Courteney Selous . . . if not go them one better!

I've forgotten how many times I've been asked how I became a professional hunter in Africa. To begin with, I have to say that no one in my family had ever been hunters, nor was there anyone to introduce me to the sport. Actually, it was exactly the opposite. My father, a famous surgeon, was opposed to all violence, guns, and the killing of animals, and he had a great hostility toward all hunters, whom he labeled "barbarians." Who could have told the poor man that I, his eldest son, would devote myself body and soul to these occupations to the point of making them my profession? My dream of becoming a professional hunter was diametrically opposed to the profession he had chosen for me. My father wanted me to follow in his footsteps and take up the profession of medicine. For my father, medicine was everything, and he completely devoted his life to it until the day he died.

For some unknown reason, I had a great inclination toward hunting. This was not something that could be explained by anything in my early life, surrounded as I was by white doctors' coats, the smell of disinfectant, by parents who could not have been less interested in hunting. Even though I was raised in the heart of a nonhunting Spanish family of that period, my parents tell me that from the time

I was very small I was crazy about wild animals, primitive tribes, hunts, and explorations and that these dominated my games and reading.

I remember that during the '30s there were lots of movies with African themes, especially for children. Admission was forty cents—not always easy to get hold of—and off to the movies I went every holiday for the 3:30 show, breathless with anticipation. With a little imagination, the traditional afternoon snack of bread and chocolate became a repast of elephant or rhino meat, just like in the fantastic adventure stories of Emilio Salgari, who was my favorite author in those days.

It seems like only yesterday that I organized my first safaris along the weedy banks of the Turia River near my home in Valencia with my brother Rafael, my cousins Sebastian and Mari Cruz, and my friend Alberto Thous filling in as "native porters." In single file we blazed trails through the thickest vegetation following elephants' tracks and avoiding Masai ambushes. It is impossible to describe how much fun we had on these expeditions through unknown territory, which always ended tragically when we had to go home, covered with mud and with holes in our clothes.

I remember with great pleasure the innumerable hours spent perusing maps, old books of African geography, and a Mauser catalog, which I almost knew by heart. These were happy times, full of excitement, and I doubt anyone could have enjoyed planning a trip to Africa, with its forests, and, most of all, its elephants, more than I did. I tirelessly searched cut-rate bookstores seeking anything there was about Africa. I read again and again everything I could find about hunting, animals, and explorations and practically memorized the Count of Yebes' *Twenty Years of Big Game Hunting* reading the chapter about guns at least a thousand times. *Yambo, Safari in the Jungles of Tanganyika* by Jose Maria Oriol was hardly out of my hands for a minute as I debated which area I'd choose for my first safari. I endlessly and with total pleasure calculated how much money and what kind of supplies I'd need for that trip—and I wasn't even ten years old yet.

In 1940 I began high school in Valencia along with Molina and Alberto Thous, two of my buddies who shared my African dreams. Our trio came to an end when Molina confessed that as well as wanting to be an elephant hunter he wanted to become a soccer player, which was seen as such a betrayal of our principles that we kicked him out of the club, so only Alberto and I were left. We took advantage of Latin and Religion classes since the old professors couldn't control us, and we would sit in the back row and plan our expedition, adding and subtracting things from our list of necessities. No one bothered us, and we were left to dream in peace.

As I recall, the budget for our first safari came to 15,000 pesetas (around $150.00 today), which was an astronomical figure in those days. We decided to combine forces and put our savings into a common piggy bank. At last after enormous sacrifices we collected seventy-five cents from change we'd managed to squeeze out of the most susceptible adults—grandparents, aunts, uncles, and godparents. With this money, we bought our first pieces of equipment, investing in twenty meters of hemp rope, a hammer and nails, an axe, a lantern, and an old colonial helmet, that made us feel like we were almost in Africa already. I only took a little bit from my sparse funds to invest in stamp collecting, my other passion. Little by little my stamp album filled up with stamps from the Belgian

The record rhino for Angola, 31 ³/₄-inch horn, shot on safari with Jorge Roque de Pinho, 1964. It was shot near the Luiana River in the Cuando-Cubango area.

Congo, Ubangi-Shari, as well as Borneo, and I only had to hear their exotic names to feel shivers of pleasure and have visions of the most marvelous adventures.

From the time I was about eight years old, I knew without any doubt that I wanted to be an elephant hunter, and the longer this dream persisted, the more securely it hooked me. Of course, at home I was looked on as a sort of harmless fool surrounded by maps of Africa, hunting books, and gun catalogs. But because I was harmless, they left me alone to daydream.

Bad winds blew for everybody following the Spanish Civil War that ended in 1939, times when everyone had to tighten their belts to the last notch. But I regarded these hard times as a sort of training period, figuring that elephant hunters have to endure all kinds of hardships with good humor. I did the best I could with what I had and found that my two peseta weekly allowance, carefully administered, still allowed me to buy an occasional book on my favorite subjects from the used bookstore, add stamps to my collection (especially ones from the Belgian Congo), and go to the movies if a jungle adventure was on the bill. I was a big fan of Tarzan and his chimpanzee Chita.

Time passed, as it does. (It's only now that I realize how quickly the years pass!) I got through the difficult times with faith in the future. I completed high school and entered medical school, planning to follow in my father's footsteps. But even through all those university years, I never gave up the idea of becoming a hunter in Africa and nobody could make me change my plans. I remained firm in my commitment, faithful to my childhood dreams.

At last the moment came to make a decision. I was up to my eyeballs in medicine, working on my father's surgical team and alternating several girlfriends. I have to confess that what attracted me almost as much as elephants was a beautiful face with blonde hair and blue eyes, I being a great admirer of the feminine sex. I'm afraid that in that period when everything was a sin, I should have been condemned from head to toe. Anyway, one day I examined my conscience, telling myself that I had to make a decision. It wasn't very difficult, to tell the truth. On one side was the option of an easy life, safe and secure, but without any enchantment. On the other side was an exciting existence but a difficult one, uncomfortable and uncertain.

I thought that to focus my life around the sole adventure of making money was nothing to be proud of, especially since I thought that there is nothing more vulgar in the world than making money for the sake of making money. So I calmly chose to follow my vocation, starting from zero and putting my whole heart into it. It wasn't easy to cut myself off from everything that surrounded me, which included my family, possessions, security, and protection at every level. With faith in God and confidence in myself, I took the big step toward finding my promised land . . . something that was considered nothing less than sublime foolishness in those long-ago, peaceful, ordinary days of 1952.

At the age of twenty-two I realized my dreams when I killed my first elephant on an island in the middle of the Campo River, where it flows between Cameroon and what used to be Spanish Guinea. I was with my good friend and fellow Valencian Ramón Tatay, an aeronautic engineer who at the time was in charge of building the new airport at Bata.

This experience was decisive for me, cementing my desire of becoming a professional elephant hunter in Africa. I went back to Valencia, and, plucking up my courage, went into my father's office to explain my hopes and ideas to him. He heard me through without a word of reproach, which only made it worse for me. When I finished, he answered by saying that if I had decided this was to be my real vocation he couldn't object. He went on to say that in this life, whatever one decides to do, the important thing is to do it with dignity and honor. He could not have said more with twice as many words.

With a loan from an uncle, I went back to Africa where I ran into every possible difficulty and problem including malaria attacks. But with an iron constitution and a lot of effort, I was able to realize the fantasy of my child-hood—a fantasy in which I envisioned myself at the head of an expedition returning to Mombasa with a cargo of ivory and other wonders. Today, looking back after so many years under the African sun, I see that only Divine Providence saved me from any number of disgraces landing on my young and enthusiastic head, allowing me to emerge healthy and unharmed from many scrapes, which might have cost me dearly considering my inexperience. I never had the chance to learn directly from anyone, unlike many others who began as assistants to this or that famous hunter in East Africa who taught them the tricks of the trade. I had to learn by myself, and I made plenty of mistakes along the way, while I learned my lessons for the future the hard way. The path that I chose so long ago has never lost its wonder.

The truth is that at the beginning I had to work very hard so as not to be left behind. It was a titanic effort in the beginning to get ahead in a profession that is distinguished by its hostility. I had to compete with local hunters who for the most part had been born there. They didn't give an inch to upstarts like me, whom they saw as possible competition, which is a perfectly logical, human, and understandable attitude.

Slowly but surely I moved ahead, always remembering the advice my father had given me and adding my own promise to play fairly with the world. This resulted in winning the affection, support, and friendship of such famous hunters as John Hunter, Phil Percival, Bob Foster, and George Rushby, to name a few of those who we refer to as "the greats."

Once I got more or less settled, I dedicated myself completely to ivory hunting, sometimes by myself, other times working for different game departments to reduce the number of elephants in certain areas. With infectious enthusiasm and the physical ability and stamina that enabled me to perform almost any physical activity, I threw myself into pursuing the hunt, traveling through nearly every African country where there were elephants. I took elephants in twenty-three territories, which is something of a record.

For better or for worse, I've been a witness to a 180-degree change in Africa's evolution. Without a doubt, Africa has advanced more than any other part of the world in the forty-two years I've spent on the continent. This progress was not without cost, however. It has been the rich and varied fauna that has paid the price. I had the luck to arrive in time to see and to enjoy it at its best, when there were endless possibilities of achieving your dreams.

I remember when I was the only established hunter in the Sudan. Only an hour's drive from Juba one could find the most incredible hunting, with animals as far as the eye could see, including thousands and thousands of buffalo, which along with lions could be hunted freely. Once, during Christmas of 1959, my good friend General Taher, commander of the Army of the Southern Sudan asked me to provide some meat for the holiday celebration for the thousands of soldiers at the garrison. Obviously, I couldn't refuse, and I shot eighty-three buffalo for this purpose.

In those days it was a marvel to travel along the Boma Plateau in eastern Sudan near the Ethiopian border. It was a wild land, untouched and hard to get to, where the white-eared cob could be seen for miles and where there were lions everywhere. It would have been a crime to destroy such a paradise. It makes me laugh to read occasional articles where the author claims to have been the first to go there in 1970-something. Without wanting to sound presumptuous, I visited the Taboasas area beyond Loeli at the end of the 1950s. In those days there was no radio or anything, so we were like the old explorers. There were lions stretched out in the shade of acacias in broad daylight. Since they'd never been hunted, they didn't pay attention to anybody. Their peace and tranquility was a gift to the spirit.

Today's hunters cannot even begin to imagine the number of elephants in the old Belgian Congo, especially in the northern part. It was incredible. The areas of Watsa, Aba, Niangara, and Epi had been literally invaded by elephants. You only had to follow the road between Nagero and Gangala-na-Bodio (where the "Elephant Hunting and Training Center" was located) to find the tracks of these animals everywhere, easy to get to and with magnificent specimens among them. In 1959, with a Belgian friend who was later killed in the strife that followed the Congo's independence, we used our .416 Rigbys to shoot ten elephants, with ivory averaging ninety pounds per tusk. In January 1989 I visited the area again as a guest of President Mobutu and saw the tracks of only one medium elephant—an elephant that never stopped during the many long hours we followed it.

In Kenya it was the same, with thousands and thousands of elephants in what was called the North Frontier District along the Tana River, Lorian Swamp, Uaso Nyrio, and the Voi area. I can remember safaris on horseback, leaving Mararal in search of the large male elephants that were to be found in the Mathew Range, where you could always expect to take trophies of between 80 and 140 pounds per tusk. This now sounds like a myth.

Tanganyika (now Tanzania) in the old days was a wonderful country, beautiful and with innumerable head of animals. It was where you found the most impressive lions with the most magnificent manes. As well as splendid trophies of lions, the area was teeming with leopards and rhinos. We sought elephants in Tabora, Kizigo, Rungwa, Mehenge, Liwale, and Tunduru—places where elephants are no longer seen or remembered. Then there were elephants everywhere, and tusks weighing 60 or 70 pounds were commonplace.

Another country that enchanted me was what used to be Italian Somaliland. There one could find abundant lesser kudu, beisa oryx, *hirola* or Hunter hartebeest, and everywhere lions—although most were without manes because the lower region is very hot. The average elephants were always good trophies and 100 pounds per tusk was not unusual, especially in the marshes of the

A record Nile buffalo taken by the author in the Sudan, 1962.

Uebi Scebeli, northern Afmadu, and along the Guiba River. Unfortunately, the Somali poachers have closed off every corner of the country after so many years of chaos.

Northern Rhodesia was the most amazing hunting area in the world, with an abundance of all species, and this lasted for many years after independence, when the country was renamed Zambia. I hunted in the Luangwa Valley between 1966 and 1974, and I never saw in all Africa such a density of the "big five" as in my concession in Chibembe, which everyone knows as "Fort Spain" where I made my main camp. Many times I took elephant, leopard, lion, rhino, and buffalo in the same safari within an easy radius of two kilometers of the aforementioned camp. I imagine that if any of my old friends who were there on safari with me read this, they'll remember it with the same fond memories as I do because it really was a hunter's dream.

Another beautiful territory was Nyasaland (Malawi), where to hunt two elephants in those long-ago days cost £45 and a rhino only £15. There were hordes of them on the Nyika Plateau, and there were leopards all over the country.

In 1962 I had the privilege to be one of the first to enter and hunt in south-eastern Angola (Cuando-Cubango), playing a double role of hunter and explorer in an area then known as the "land at the end of the world." On the plains near the Cuando River, the herds of red lechwe were so vast that they made a red stain as far as the horizon. Countless thousands of them peacefully grazing as

Elephant killed in the Nile Valley (Shambé, the Sudan, 16 February 1960), the day of my thirtieth birthday.

if the grass would never end is something that I'll never forget. There were rhinoceros all over that part of Angola, and once near the course of the Kandonbe River I saw thirty-three of them in a single day.

The old French Equatorial Africa was made up of the federation of four countries—Gabon, the Congo, Ubangi-Shari, and Chad with the general capital at Brazzaville, and it offered every kind of terrain a hunter could want, ranging from equatorial forests to the deserts of northern Chad. Each particular area was a hunter's dream. The Rafai, Zemio, and Obo districts in Ubangi-Shari were famous for their huge elephants, with hundred pound tusks our bread and butter. It saddens me to report that today this part of the Central African Republic has been completely picked clean by damned poachers. It was there that I got some of my best trophies, over thirty years ago.

French Equatorial Africa was one of my favorite hunting places, and in those days it was still a hunter's paradise with its glorious, untamed wilderness. Many parts of French Equatorial Africa were still unknown, and it had enormous hunting potential.

I have hunted everywhere in Africa except Mozambique. There they had a strange regulation that did not allow anyone who was not a permanent resident of that country for at least five years to work as a guide, a circumstance that did not apply to me. I visited northern Mozambique several times and it was beautiful. I also took several short vacations at the lovely hotel Polana, in Lorenzo Marques, where you could eat seafood until it was coming out your ears.

Mozambique was where my old friend, the great elephant hunter Harry Manners, took a super-monster in 1957, near the Nyasaland border in the Milange district. The tusks weighed 185 and 183 pounds each, and it was the second largest elephant ever killed by a European. Powell-Cotton shot the largest in 1906 in the Congo Free State (which became the Belgian Congo in 1908) on the shores of Lake Albert. The tusks weighed in at 198 and 174 pounds respectively.

One of the places that impressed me most during my African travels was the Republic of Liberia, a small west African country created by the Americans in the nineteenth century for freed slaves who wished to return to the land of their ancestors. When I arrived there in 1955, the capital city of Monrovia was very small and still ramshackle. The road from the airport, as I remember, was worse than awful, dotted with holes full of water, rocks, and multicolored lizards basking in the sun. Most of these were minus tails as a result of having been chased by the local kids, as abundant in these latitudes as ants.

When I arrived in Monrovia, I felt that I was living in a novel by Emilio Salgari. The atmosphere was tremendously colorful and exotic, with natives from the interior, frankly primitive, sitting against the walls of the houses selling leopard skins and elephant tusks carefully arranged in piles. If I remember correctly, the regular price for a leopard skin was $10 and ivory went for $5 per kilo, although if you haggled you could always get a better price. Sailors in port were the prime targets for the merchants of this picturesque market, made all the more colorful by the multitude of wild animals, mostly monkeys and birds.

In those days, hunting in Liberia was unrestricted, and you needed only to get a permit from the Ministry of Agriculture. This permit cost $250 per year and gave the hunter an unlimited license, which permitted the hunting of every sort of animal in the country, including elephants. Then elephants were everywhere, especially in the eastern part toward the border of the Ivory Coast, with the greatest number in the area of Tchien. There were also a lot of bongo, which remained in acceptable numbers until only a few years ago. Unfortunately, the same cannot be said of the elephants, which have been practically wiped out everywhere in the country due to poaching and the endless civil war.

West Africa never offered the hunter the number and variety of fauna that were to be found in the central, eastern, and southern part of the continent. This was mainly due to the large human population and its negative effect on wild animals, but if you looked carefully you could find corners here and there that would reward your effort. Until 1962 you could still hunt two elephants in Sierra Leone for only £5, and there were still a good number of tuskers in the forested mountains of the north. There were also many in old French Guinea, the Ivory Coast, and Upper Volta (now Burkina Faso.)

In the Ivory Coast along the Cavally, Bandama, and Sassandra Rivers, there were huge elephants. It was not unusual in those equatorial forests to find ones with tusks weighing between 60 and 110 pounds. I shot some big bulls in the areas of San Pedro and Grabo. In Upper Volta you were always sure to find huntable elephants in Gaua and east to the border of Niger as well as in Pama and Arly. Although in Burkina Faso there is still generally good hunting, the number of elephants has decreased dramatically. The same is true in the Ivory Coast, where a minister said that if things keep on as they are, they'll have to change the country's name because there won't be any ivory left.

I also hunted elephants in the northern part of the Gold Coast (now Ghana), where I became a good friend to Dr. Morris, a British army physician who held the elephant record for the Gold Coast, having taken a bull with tusks of ninety pounds each with a single shot from his .404 Jeffery rifle. It was a pleasure for both of us to meet again in Uganda shortly before the independence of that country, where Dr. Morris had been sent in his latest posting as a military doctor. After independence, he returned to England, and we stayed in contact through the years, exchanging Christmas cards until his death. He was much older than I.

Another good place was northern Dahomey (now Benin) along the Mekru River, where, besides a few modest elephants, there was a good number of lions, buffalo, etc. Unfortunately I haven't been to this part of Africa for many years, and the information I receive isn't totally reliable, but I fear that the situation in West Africa for wild animals is very precarious and in rapid recession, helpless before the human population explosion. At least I was lucky enough to have visited these lands during the "good old days" that are now history. The memories of my visits are priceless.

A country for which I feel a special affection is the old Spanish Guinea, perhaps because it was the first place in which I set foot in Africa, seen through the impressionable eyes of a twenty-two year old. Since then there's been a lot of water under the bridge, but after forty-two years of traversing the four corners of Africa, deep in my heart I have a special place for the tiny and beautiful land of Guinea, where I had the opportunity to hunt elephants and enjoy myself as I don't think anyone else ever has. I read with sadness the bad political reports about Guinea, and I am always hopeful that everything will be straightened out. I am also hopeful that, if God wills, I shall return to see my old Guinean friends and walk again on the beaches of Hanye, climb the Churu Mountains, watch the wonder of thousands of green pigeons flying over the River Utonde, hear gorillas making their beds in the forests of Nsoc, go fishing in Bolondo, and do so many other things that make me feel younger just to think about.

One area of my activities that I never discuss and hardly ever refer to are my hunting expeditions outside Africa. Most of my stories revolve around my beloved elephants to whom I've dedicated my life, but I've gone around the world and hunted on five continents, in such diverse areas as the Arctic, Central Asia, Eastern Siberia, Australia, and places in between.

Australia was always a marvel . . . that is, until recently when the government decided to eliminate the innumerable water buffalo in the Northern Territory in favor of domestic cattle, which for me robbed the place of its main attraction. When I hunted south of the Daily River in Arnhem Land, it was easily accessible from Darwin, where I had my base, and it still contained large and small game in incredible numbers. I was once charged with eliminating a certain number of buffalo on one of the ranches and took advantage of this to test the ballistic possibilities of the 9.3x64 Brenneke. This gun is one of the unsung heroes of the arms world, not as popular as it should be but extraordinary in every sense. I took seventy-one buffalo with eighty bullets, which I think is outstanding. I also shot twenty-four lions in Africa with that rifle, close to a hundred buffalo, several leopards, and about fifteen elephants without any problem, or better to say, in a very satisfactory manner. I decided not to continue using it only because I didn't want to have to carry several different types of ammunition and I wanted to focus on my .375 H & H Magnum, which was my preferred tool of the trade.

One of my most interesting memories was of the visit I made in 1978 to the private hunting museum of His Royal Highness, the Sultan of Johore in Malaysia by his kind invitation. Even after all these years I still want to return to make a videotape of his collection to show to my friends because his museum contains the best Malaysian trophies in the world. The passage of time has made me forget everything but the highlights, but if I remember correctly, besides industrial-sized quantities of tiger skins and heads, some mounted whole by Rowland Ward, there were scores of seladang heads (a seladang is a Malaysian gaur), banteng, rhinoceros, something like twenty-five pairs of elephant tusks, black panthers, and so on. It was a most impressive sight—all of that combined with the most strange and exotic scents.

If you add to that large numbers of yellowed photographs with the sultan's father and grandfather surrounded by more than 100 tigers, rhinos, and elephants, there is nothing that could evoke more strongly what Malaysia was like before 1939—a real hunter's paradise. Like the rest of the world, the Malay peninsula has suffered the effects of blasted "civilization," so much that the fauna of its immense jungles has been reduced day by day to the precarious state where it is now. For example, of more than 3,000 tigers found in 1950 there were at the most only between 400 and 500 in 1989, and this after the complete protection they have enjoyed for many years.

One of the biggest satisfactions I've had in my life was to meet many of the great and famous hunters of the good old days, enjoy their friendships and listen, mouth agape, to stories of feats performed before I was born or while I was still in diapers. When I think about it now, I see how very lucky I was to have this unique opportunity since all of them have vanished with the passage of time. Thankfully, I have lots of notes and photos that one day I hope to gather together in a book so that this breed of supermen, magnificent yet unassuming, will live forever.

I remember John Hunter, with his easygoing nature, who was such a great conversationalist that we would talk ourselves hoarse whenever we got together. It was a pleasure to hear him and I'd pepper him with questions whenever we met. He lived in a chalet beside the hotel he owned, called "The Hunters Lodge," in Makindu on the highway between Nairobi and Mombasa. I passed many pleasant hours there in his company. John Hunter always preferred large-caliber weapons, and one of his favorite sayings was "never give a boy a man's work," which was his way of scoffing at small rifles. He would only use a .30-06 to get meat for the camp or to shoot some leopard. For everything else, and especially for dangerous hunting, he used mainly .475 No. 2 Nitro Express, .500 3" Nitro Express, and .577 Nitro Express. For bolt-action repeating rifles, he preferred a .416 Rigby, especially for lions and a .505 Gibbs to control elephants. At the end of his professional career, his preference was for a double .500 3" Nitro. I remember that he offered me his last .500 3" Nitro, an Evans with an Anson & Deley system, along with 300 cartridges when I spent Christmas of 1960 with him at Makindu. His asking price was £300, a pittance today, but in 1960 it was more money than I could possibly afford. It broke my heart not to have that gun, and was one of the few disappointments I've had in my life. Every time I pass through Milindi, on the Kenyan coast, I see John's son David Hunter who lives there, and the memory always surfaces of his father's rifle and my sadness at losing it.

Robert Foran was one of those few, lucky people who hunted in the legendary Lado Enclave. Between 1904 and 1909 he illegally hunted elephants in what was then the Congo Free State, thumbing his nose at the Belgians. He was marvelous to talk to and for me the hours passed like minutes, listening to his adventures in the Enclave, where he took more than 400 elephants, most of which had large tusks. Then old and retired, he lived in Nanyuki, Kenya, at the Sportsman's Arms Hotel. I stopped by whenever I could to hear his tales of long-ago adventures with such other hunters as Pete Pearson, "Deaf" Banks, Bill Buckley, Billy Pickering, Quentin Grogan, the Craven brothers, and John Boyes. Perhaps influenced by Robert Foran's stories, there began my interest in that lost corner of central Africa that was the Lado Enclave, where the largest elephant hunts at the beginning of the century took place, turning me into a kind of biographer for that exciting spot where so many adventures took place.

Philip Percival was one of the most famous "white hunters" and so perfect a gentleman that all the young hunters tried to copy him. With big bags under his eyes and a humorous face, he always smiled at my hundreds of questions, answering them in a quiet voice that was sometimes hard to hear. He was quite deaf from a client's wild shot with a .505 Gibbs that not only just missed his head but also missed killing him by a whisker.

When I met him, he was already retired and living in his ranch at Machakos, about an hour's drive from Nairobi. I often went there to see him and chat and to go hunting with his son, Dick. At the time there were plenty of Thomson gazelles and hartebeest nearby, and the meat was always well received by the

Large lion shot in Angola, 1962.

native workers on the ranch. Percival went on his first safari in 1909 as an apprentice, in charge of the horses, oxen, and carts for former U.S. president Theodore Roosevelt's great expedition.

The event lasted eleven months and encompassed the virgin territories of British East Africa (which became Kenya in 1922), Uganda, and the Anglo-Egyptian Sudan. The safari began in Mombasa and ended thousands of miles later in Khartoum. Percival had plenty of stories about Roosevelt and the professional hunters who accompanied him, such as Cuninghame and Tarlton, with help from Foran and Grogan in Uganda and the Sudan and the great Selous in charge of organizing the enormous operation. I guard my notes from his commentaries along with the photos as though they were gold. These stories heard firsthand have tremendous historical value.

Tony with his pet chimp, "Pirracas," in Spanish Guinea, 1955.

Moving along, there were many other famous hunters who honored me with their friendship, like Bob Foster, who near the end of his life got no less than sixty-nine elephants with tusks of more than 100 pounds each and with whom I had the privilege of hunting in Uganda. Bill Pridham was another, who took some 2,000 elephants and who also lived in Uganda. I remember the day with pride when we hunted together and I stopped a wounded buffalo that was attacking us at less than ten sands, with a single shot from my .416 Rigby. Pridham was always a fan of the .416, too, but his gun jammed at a crucial moment that day we were hunting. With the great veteran Pat Ayre, I had the pleasure of several fishing trips on the Indian Ocean. He lived seventy miles north of Mombasa, very close to where I used to visit Commander Blunt, who was also a respected figure from the old days. It always amused me to note that Pat Ayre, who was completely baked by the tropical sun reflected off the ocean, had incredibly snow white feet. He always wore tennis shoes and the contrast when he took them off was something to see. He was the one who usually took the American photographer Martin Johnson and his wife Osa around East Africa in the 1920s, making the movies that made them famous.

George Rushby was one of the greatest elephant hunters in the late '20s and early '30s, known for having killed about 400 of them between the Belgian Congo and Ubangi-Shari (today the Central African Republic) with his .577 Nitro Express. Later he went to the Elephant Control Department in Tanganyika where he hunted another 1,400 using his .375 H&H Magnum and .416 Rigby. I met him in Tanganyika in 1958 and we remained good friends until his death in Simonstown, near Cape Town in South Africa, where he had retired. Rushby liked to talk to me because I was hunting in what had been his old stomping grounds. He was the one asking me questions about this and that in the places he'd adventured twenty-five and thirty years previously. Jim Sutherland was a good friend of Rushby's and thanks to him, I have lots of unedited information about the man we could call the "dean of elephant hunters."

Finally, I also knew John "Pondoro" Taylor when he lived in London and was having a rough time financially. He was the author of *African Rifles & Cartridges* which I'd read so many times that I probably knew Taylor's book as well as he did. This gave us a base for many juicy discussions about this or that caliber and we discovered that we both favored the same calibers: .375 H&H Magnum, .416 Rigby, and the .465 Nitro Express Holland & Holland with which each of us had shot many elephants.

The memory of these legendary greats of African hunting and the kindnesses they showed me when I was young and idealistic are my greatest treasures. And to tell the truth and philosophize a little, I don't want to leave this world without writing down everything I know about them for the pleasure of the younger generation of hunters who won't have had the good fortune to know them as I did.

After forty-two nonstop years of hunting, travel, and exploration, I think the time has come to take stock of whether it was worthwhile to spend most of my life traveling from one end of the earth to the other with a large-caliber rifle on my shoulder. Let me say that I am satisfied with my activities, and, if conditions were the same as they were, I'd do it all over again. Unfortunately the panorama of today has completely changed. . . . Today we live in a climate that is negative and unromantic, and where the noble art of hunting has been politicized by ignorant, useless, and stupid politicians who want to impose their own mistaken values on everyone.

For me everything always went well, and I can count myself among those few happy mortals who could translate their passion into a profession. On top of everything else, I've had the great good fortune to find someone as exceptional as Isabel who, as well as a wife, has become my best friend and collaborator. I have three sons, Antonio, Jorge, and Carlos, who are as strong and tall as oaks and who fill me with pride and satisfaction. It has been my delight to have them occasionally accompany me on safari. I also have many friends all over the world and ended on friendly terms with ninety-nine percent of my clients. Some of these clients have even become lifetime friends.

I've been asked many times what hunting is to me, if it is a passion, a necessity, or a mania. The truth is none of the above, and I want to say that I've always been a moderate, easygoing, and balanced person, and not someone to fly off the handle easily and without cause. As for the thousands of animals I've taken, there was always a reason for hunting them rather than the simple act of killing. For me the hunt is more than merely shooting at some poor animal. It's the combination of circumstances around it, like the distance, the remoteness of the place, the exotic landscape, the people of the area and what are, for us, their strange customs, the difficulty in getting there and finally, the noble and dignified struggle between man and beast. If you get the desired experience, and maybe a trophy, you are filled with the kind of satisfaction not found since man first walked on earth.

I've often been asked how many animals I've hunted, especially among the dangerous "big five." Not wanting to sound like a braggart, I've always avoided giving out figures, but now that the facts will never change for better or worse, I guess now is the time to count up this thing that has everyone so curious. So, here is the exact number of each species taken by me as of 9 January 1994. Please note that I shot many of the following animals for control purposes or because the natives in a particular locale needed protection from a marauder. The elephants, for the most part, I shot for their ivory.

	Shot by Tony Sanchez	Taken with clients on safaris
Elephants	882	372
Buffalo	1,446	553
Lions	159	169
Leopards	64	84
Rhinoceros	60	72

This makes a total of 1,254 elephant, 1,999 buffalo, 328 lion, 148 leopard, and 132 rhino.

Everything in the world is changing and fads have hit hunting as well. Before, big-game hunters were celebrated in books and movies and were popular heroes, but now we're the bad guys. I want to say that the string of nonsense thrown out by those ignorant hysterics has affected me very little and that we hunters have been and are the greatest protectors of animals. In order to preserve them, their value must be recognized. If an animal ceases to be valued by the community, that is its doom.

We can use the rhinoceros of Kenya as an example. In 1975 there were at least 8,000 head in that country, a high number by all accounts. Alarmists, seconded by textbook experts, convinced the government that they were in danger of extinction and banned all hunting; at the same time they put strict protective measures into effect. By 1989, after fourteen years of theoretically correct measures, official Kenyan figures count no more than 400, a decrease of "only 7,600." This disaster should convince anyone of the foolhardiness of complete prohibition. I fear that if the dreams of some antihunting fanatics come true and hunting is banned and no boundaries are set, in a few years not only the rhinoceros but also other big-game animals will become extinct, gone forever.

Many ask me when I'm going to retire. The truth is that I haven't even thought about it yet. While I still have the energy and enthusiasm that I have now, I don't see any reason to give up what is, when all is said and done, the essence of my life. Besides having the perfect family and profession, I have time for other pleasures like Italian opera—the works of Puccini and Verdi most of all—and stamp collecting. I'm a real addict of stamp collecting, and I specialize in the old African colonies, especially in stamps from the Belgian Congo up to 1908, while it was still the Congo Free State and the private property of King Leopold II.

I've always been very keen for big-game weapons, about which I've written multitudes of tracts and articles. After so many years of having fired practically every one in existence, I've found that the ones I like best and the ones with which I hope to finish my hunting days are these:

A. The .300 Holland & Holland Magnum for all sorts of antelopes. According to the tables, it doesn't have the same impressive numbers as the .300 Weatherby or the .300 Winchester, but I guarantee that it kills like the best and with the added advantage of light recoil and lower chamber pressure.

B. The .375 Holland & Holland Magnum. This is the perfect all-purpose weapon and one with which I've taken everything from gazelles to elephants with no problem.

C. The .416 Rigby. The rifle and caliber are magnificent for all types of dangerous hunting and after forty-two years of using it, it has become an extension of my right arm.

D. The devastating .500 Jeffery, which is the most effective caliber I've ever seen for high-risk situations with elephants, regardless of terrain or circumstances.

The truth is that I have been blessed in my life and in my chosen profession, and I only have reasons to be satisfied with my life. The reality of my adult life has far surpassed my most cherished childhood dreams. . . .

Before everything else I was always a tireless elephant hunter. I have followed the footsteps of many bulls across the whole of Africa, including the remotest parts. I arrived at a good time to enjoy the *belle epoque* of hunting and to take advantage of the opportunities that these "good old days" offered. It was only when the chances to hunt elephants commercially were reduced that I phased out of this activity little by little, turning toward my operation of taking paying clients out on sporting safaris.

My start in Africa was not a bed of roses as I had to learn to survive in the strange and hostile place that Africa was to me. But slowly and after many hardships, I got what I had dreamed of, which puts me where I am now, thank God. Unfortunately for the future, I do not feel that hunting newcomers will be able to enjoy the sport in the same way that my generation did. The challenge is to adapt to the new set of circumstances and make the best of them, forgetting the good old days and looking ahead to the future and what it has to offer.

•••

CHAPTER II

My First
African Trophy

In July 1952 I was in Bata, the capital of what used to be Spanish Guinea, finally setting foot in Central Africa. I gawked at everything, daydreaming and enjoying myself as I doubt many had before. At last I had reached my promised land. After a few days in Bata, which is on the coast, I headed for the interior with the hopes of hunting elephant, something I had wanted to do since I reached the age of reason. I was twenty-two years old and enthusiasm seeped from every pore.

I was armed with a 10.75x68 caliber Mauser, lent by a generous friend who had also given me nine cartridges. Even though I had never fired a shot with it in my life, I left Bata, full of enthusiasm, on a rusty, dilapidated bus for the tiny town of Mikomeseng, located about 100 miles inland. It sat in the middle of the beautiful equatorial forests and I had a letter of introduction to the captain of the colonial guard, which administered the territory at the time.

I suppose that this gentleman, very polite and hospitable, must have thought I was crazy. At least that was my impression since he started off the conversation by asking me whether it was true that I'd come all the way from Spain to hunt. At my enthusiastic affirmation, he kindly offered to take me to Otto Krohnert's farm twenty miles away in a place called Akom, which was loaded with elephants and gorillas. He invited me to spend the night at his home, saying that he later would take me to Akom in his Willis Jeep, which was wonderful for me.

Otto Krohnert was a German, born in the old South-West Africa, today called Namibia. From the time he could hold a rifle, Krohnert went hunting with his father, an old professional hunter of ivory, skins, and "biltong," or dried meat. From those distant lands, young Otto left his family and went into the interior of Africa to hunt elephants and deal in ivory. After many years he moved to

Guinea and wandered in Angola, the Congo, and Gabon. In Spanish Guinea, Otto Krohnert was a living legend. When I realized that I would not only have the honor of meeting him but that I would also go to his house, I got goosebumps just thinking about it. I had heard so much about him from other hunters that I was starstruck.

We finally arrived at Akom and found Otto Krohnert and his administrator Domingo Kretchman, another German who had lived for many years in German Cameroon and had moved to Spanish Guinea after the loss of the colonies in

To protect the local plantations, the author shot this rogue gorilla with a 12-bore shotgun, Spanish Guinea, 1955.

Tony with a big gorilla shot for crop protection, Spanish Guinea, 1959.

1918. We met them strolling along the road, and, when we stopped the Jeep, they greeted us in a friendly way. When the captain of the colonial guard explained who I was and why I was there, they welcomed me warmly. Because it was late, the captain rushed back to Mikomeseng, leaving me and my equipment with my new acquaintances. While some natives collected my things, we took a walk down a long avenue flanked by oil palms toward the central patio where the offices and living quarters were. I was welcomed to the home as though I was a guest of honor.

When we got to the door of what turned out to be a living room full of trophies and Otto Krohnert's other souvenirs, I explained my hopes and plans. Otto Krohnert told me that there weren't any elephants in the area at the present, but there were plenty of gorillas. He went on to explain that the gorilla was a real curse to the natives because they constantly raided the villagers' farms. Otto had a request from Agustin Nve, chief of a village called Beayop, asking him to help rid the area of gorillas. Otto told me that this would be a great opportunity for me because, besides getting the chance to hunt, I would be helping the villagers.

The truth is that with elephants as my holy grail I'd never thought much about gorillas, but since the tuskers weren't available, I wasn't going to sneer at gorillas. From that moment everything centered on the possible hunt of those marauding animals. Otto asked me if I knew anything about those animals and I gave him something of a lecture on them. All theory, of course, but he was impressed, and offered to put me in charge of the battle against the gorillas since he was very occupied with the plantation and couldn't get away.

With all the cockiness of a twenty-two year old, believing myself to be another Karamojo Bell, I agreed, saying that it would be easy as pie for me. Only later, after the first euphoria had passed and I was alone in my room, common sense stepped in and I asked myself what I had done. But I'd already said yes, and it was too late to go back. I would have to keep my promise despite my dry mouth and clenched stomach.

In the morning, after breakfasting on huge cups of coffee with condensed milk, Otto said that he would take me himself the six or seven miles to Beayop in one of the trucks. My gorilla lecture must have been a good one because his demeanor exuded total confidence in me as a gorilla expert. Of course, his trust in my ability immediately raised my already high anxiety level.

All too soon, I found myself getting off the truck in front of the little village of Beayop, where a multitude of grinning natives all tried to shake our hands at the same time. Otto Krohnert spoke with the chief, Agustin Nve, and explained that although he would not be able to take part in the battle against the gorillas, he was leaving me, a great specialist, to do the job. With that, he climbed up into the truck, wished me luck, and took off in a cloud of red dust, which left us all gritty.

I watched my last hope of escape vanish from sight. With a drooping spirit I followed Agustin to the hut I had been assigned. It was the best in the village, and I arranged my small amount of equipment, clothing, and arms. Afterward we sat awhile in what was called the "house of the word," the place where the men hung out to talk and pass the time. It consisted of four wooden walls and a roof of palm leaves to keep out the rain. We began organizing our strategy. The first problem to overcome was to find these marauding gorillas, which would be a challenge because those clever primates never raided the same farms twice in a row.

Although I was only twenty-two, my height and breadth caused the natives to give me a consideration and respect that was out of proportion to my actual real-life experience, treating me as if I was something special. This helped me recover my confidence and stop being so pessimistic, although to tell the truth, I would still have been very happy to discover that the gorillas had moved over the border to Cameroon.

Time passed in conversation as we waited for the men sent out by Agustin to locate the gorillas. One by one they returned with no news, and I was inwardly cheering when one of the guys on shift returned all excited to say that he'd discovered a big band of gorillas preparing to spend the night no more than a couple of miles away. The others rejoiced at the news, but it fell on my ears like the proverbial ton of bricks.

The author with a Babinga pygmy in the Congo, 1965.

I want to clarify at this point that gorillas have never been considered big game in a hunting sense, and the only reason for taking them was to supply scientists and museums. But they were a plague in those distant days in many areas, and farmers were constantly fighting them to protect their crops. I've taken a number over the years but always to help native farmers survive. I've never taken any pleasure in hunting these animals, and I support the recent efforts made by governments and organizations that are now doing everything in their power to protect the gorilla.

After the "happy" news that a tracker had located a band of gorillas, we really began in earnest to devise our plan for the next day. The villagers put everything in the hands of the "gorilla expert," but I made sure that Agustin got to offer his input, and agreeing with him, we came to certain decisions.

It was very simple. At 5 A.M. we would leave the village under the cover of darkness and hike to where the gorillas were sleeping. We would creep up at first light and take as many as we could, which would guarantee those that escaped wouldn't come back to the area for quite some time. In theory, this was pretty simple, but in real life, things rarely are.

Our way was lit by torches that gave off only a minimum of light. This is a common occurrence in Central Africa where batteries seem to come from the factory with minimal power or completely empty. Silently we marched in single

In the "happy old days" hunting for ivory in Equatorial Africa, 1957.

file through the cold, damp darkness. I had loaded my 10.75x68 Mauser with four expanding bullets, saving the five solids for elephants. I doubt I had slept five minutes in a row that night due to a major case of nerves. Through my head ran every story I'd ever heard about how gorillas were monsters, how they attacked without provocation, and how they enjoyed popping off the head of a human as if it was a bottle cap. So much for silly, impressionistic stories. Fortunately, my sense of survival calmed me as we approached the gorillas, and little by little I began to look forward to seeing the gorillas and taking action.

The guide signaled that the gorillas were close at hand. Silently in the half light, we tried to hear the gorillas' sounds. Finally we heard some of the classic noises made by females and youngsters when they leave the nest of leaves and branches they had made for the night. The males are too heavy to sleep in trees, so they pass the night on the ground. They were a stone's throw away, and the moment of truth had arrived. Agustin, with his 12-gauge shotgun loaded with buckshot, and I with my 10.75x68 Mauser, stepped forward.

In theory the plan couldn't have been simpler. The natives said that all we had to do was get close enough to see the gorillas and fire away, but I didn't really get a good picture of the plan of attack because it was hard to see anything in the thick underbrush of that shadowy predawn darkness.

With my heart thumping painfully, I moved forward slowly with Agustin beside me. I didn't do much more than move my neck as I tried to make sense of the shadowy world in front of me. All I could do was hear the gorilla sounds as well as a kind of snore, perhaps made by an old sleeping male. Suddenly, when we least expected it, we heard voices to our left, coming from some women from another village heading to work on the local yucca plantations.

All the gorilla noises stopped, including the snores. I turned to Agustin to say that the animals must have fled when a huge shadowy form lumbered toward us. I don't know who was more surprised, the gorilla or I, but I still had enough presence of mind to raise my rifle and fire. At the sound of the shot all hell broke loose with gorillas screaming and running around trying to escape. I reloaded and shot one racing off to my left. It fell near Agustin, who was watching all this with the calm face of experience. He had left it all to me, the "gorilla expert."

Then, as quickly as all the noise began, it stopped. In the profound silence, I saw two dead gorillas and a happy African smiling with joy and slapping me on the back. The nightmare fears vanished, to be replaced by the most happy of realities. Agustin called the others, and as he told them what had happened, they looked at me admiringly, touching the gorillas and shaking my hand solemnly. I have no idea what Agustin told them in the Pamue language, but our return to the camp was like the "Triumphal March" from *Aida*. I don't need to tell you that once I returned to Bata I spun this story out for all it was worth, giving everyone the impression that I was the greatest gorilla hunter of all time.

•••

CHAPTER III

Traditional Rifles for African Hunting

At a hunters' convention years ago, a professional of the new generation—which is to say, at least in many cases, someone who knows elephants little better than by account—was seconded by his contemporaries in vehemently arguing with me about the best caliber of weapon for hunting elephants in any terrain or circumstance. They took it as dogma that their erroneous theories were the right ones and that we, the old ones or the "mummies," were totally ossified and out-of-step with our big-caliber weapons. If they knew the wise old saying, "experience is the basis for all science," they certainly had forgotten it.

Experience is a great teacher, and this so-called expert with minimal experience behind him insisted that a caliber 7x57, with a bullet of 175 grains and initial energy of 2,490 foot/pounds, is as fatal to elephants as anything between the .375 H&H Magnum and the .577 Nitro Express. He said that he had taken a large number of elephants with a rifle with these characteristics as his only weapon. I don't want to scoff at anyone, but I suspect that those "large numbers" he mentions, given the age and length of time this man had been in the profession, would equal about four or five elephants at best, hunted with clients. This new "Karamojo" Bell was born too late to be able to hunt as many elephants as were we "mummies" who still have the pleasure of being in this world.

Only an ignoramus or someone completely crazed would say that the perfect weapon for elephant hunting in any situation is the tiny 7x57. I can just imagine the incredulity on the faces of the clients when they see the mighty hunter who is supposed to cover their backs and protect them with this toy in his hands! I am willing to bet that more than one client broke out in a cold sweat despite the heat!

There's no doubt that a 7x57 can kill an elephant, but to think that it is the best caliber at any time for the purpose is inexcusable. The essential requirement in an elephant rifle is that it be able to stop a charging animal in its tracks, which is why the English call these rifles "stoppers." You get this kind of result only from rifles firing projectiles of not less than 400 grains at an initial velocity of not less than 2,000 feet per second and an initial energy of not less than 4,000 foot/pounds, all of which are far from the capabilities of the modest 7x57.

As I've said and written many times, please take with an enormous grain of salt the theory that a bullet of 100 grains can have the same effect as one of 1,000 grains. In the concrete case of elephants with their huge size and weight, firing a bullet at the exactly correct spot does not mean that it will hit the mark in light of the obstacles it has to overcome along its path to the vitals. You must also take into consideration the power of the cartridge that fired the bullet, its diameter and weight, the distance from which it was fired and the position of the animal in respect to the hunter. Do not forget, also, that small-caliber solids were not designed for hunting elephants. Small-caliber solids lack the necessary resistance to impact and penetrate those huge bones, where they easily can break or be deflected.

Naturally, the opinion of an inexpert hunter is no reason to use a lot of space in retort, but I find it surprising that even after the many books written on the subject there are still doubts on the part of many sportsmen. I still get asked questions that leave me with my mouth hanging open, without the energy to enter into another discussion, much less dogmatize.

I'll now talk about the rifles and cartridges used by the most respected elephant hunters over the years so that the reader can come to his own conclusion. Those hunters have taken at least 400 elephants apiece. Hunting "by mouth" is the easiest thing in the world, and, as the tales are being told, those numbers can go up and up out of all proportion. I personally don't believe a word about the numbers supposedly taken by some of the younger hunters. Considering their age and the restrictions that have been in effect all over Africa since they began their careers, it is physically impossible to have shot as many animals as they claim.

The hunters included in the following list cover the period from approximately 1900 to 1975, when elephant hunting went into a tailspin because of poaching. Since most of the new regulations only allow elephants to be hunted by clients on safari, this leaves most of the new professionals out of these figures. Of all those included on the following list, only two of these hunters are still alive: Harry Manners in South Africa and yours truly, who is writing this in Spain. Of course, during so many years of hunting elephants, many different calibers have been used, but these are the ones preferred above all others by each of the following hunters:

1. Deaf Banks — .577 Nitro Express double.
2. Pete Pearson — .375 H&H Magnum bolt action and .577 Nitro Express double.
3. Mickey Norton — .404 Jeffery bolt action and .577 Nitro Express double.
4. Bill Buckley — .500 Nitro Express and .577 Nitro Express, both doubles.
5. Billy Pickering — .450 Nitro Express and .577 Nitro Express, both doubles.
6. Robert Foran — .350 Rigby bolt action and .450 Nitro Express double.
7. James Sutherland — .318 Westley Richards bolt action and .577 Nitro Express double.
8. George Rushby — .375 H&H Magnum and .416 Rigby, both with bolt action; and .577 Nitro Express double.
9. Marcus Daly — .416 Rigby bolt action.
10. John Hunter — .505 Gibbs bolt action and .500 Nitro Express double.
11. Samaki Salmon — .416 Rigby bolt action and .470 Nitro Express double.
12. Harry Manners: — .375 H&H Magnum bolt action.
13. Tony Sanchez-Ariño — .416 Rigby bolt action and .465 Nitro Express double; since 1986 the .500 Jeffery bolt action as well.
14. Andy Anderson — .318 Westley Richards bolt action, .470 Nitro Express and .577 Nitro Express, both doubles.
15. "Karamojo" Bell — .275 Rigby and .318 Westley Richards, both bolt actions.
16. Eric Rundgren — .416 Rigby with bolt action.
17. Bill Pridham — .416 Rigby with bolt and 600 Nitro Express double.
18. John Taylor — .375 H&H Magnum, .416 Rigby bolt action, and .465 Nitro Express double.
19. Bert Schultz — .450 Nitro Express and .450 No. 2 Nitro Express, both doubles.
20. Bob Foster — .470 Nitro Express double.
21. Bill Bennet — .450 Nitro Express double.
22. Theodore Lefebvre — 8mm Lebel bolt action.

As can be seen on this list of twenty-two hunters, only two use calibers less than .375 magnum. One, the famous "Karamojo" Bell, who hunted before the 1914 war, was an exceptional shot with an excellent knowledge of elephant anatomy, which allowed him considerable success with small calibers. However, in neither his books nor stories does he say how many took off wounded. The Frenchman Theodore Lefebvre hunted in the old Ubangi-Shari around 1907 using a Lebel 8mm military rifle strictly for economic reasons, he said. Inexplicably, he got good results with this weapon, hunting a large number of elephants and rhinoceros.

Again I say that any small or medium caliber can kill an elephant under such favorable circumstances as firing at the animal broadside. For example, James Sutherland and Andy Anderson, both of whom used the .318 Westley Richards with a 250-grain bullet, always took along another larger, and more powerful, caliber just in case. Things can get tricky fast and only these "stoppers" can resolve the situation in a manner favorable to the hunter.

For the future hunter who hopes to make a clean kill on elephant, a disinterested piece of advice is this: No matter what the hunter hears or reads, never use a rifle of a lower caliber than .375 H&H Magnum. Even a .375 doesn't fulfill the three requirements of an elephant rifle because its bullet is only 300 grains instead of the minimum 400 required; however, the penetration is so good that it can be used against elephants if caution is used. Another piece of advice: Leave the 7x57 at home for Sunday target shooting.

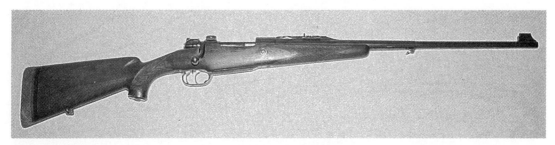

.375 Magnum.

THE .375 HOLLAND & HOLLAND MAGNUM

Without a doubt this caliber is the most useful and popular, worldwide, for big-game hunting in Africa, North America, Southeast Asia, and India. Although there is no hunting in India today, in its time the .375 H&H Magnum was frequently used there to hunt tigers, leopards, and bears. A notable example of this is the Maharaja Joodha of Nepal, who, between 1933 and 1940, killed 433 tigers, mostly with a .375 magnum with a Mauser action, especially made for him by John Rigby & Co. of London.

During my African hunts, I never ceased to see .375 magnums everywhere, from Khartoum to Bulawayo and from Dakar to Mombasa, in the hands of professionals, visiting sportsmen, local hunters and representatives of various game departments. Personally, I have nothing but praise for it.

The .375 H&H Magnum is a glorious veteran with eighty years of experience. It was designed between 1909 and 1910 and after the necessary tests and trials, the famous London firm of Holland & Holland had it on the market in 1912. It is a shame, almost an injustice, that the name of the specialist that developed the most advanced caliber of its period has disappeared completely. I verified this during my visits to the firm of Holland & Holland, of which I am an old client and friend.

Whoever he was, the designer had a grand vision of hunting for the future and created something totally different from the series of the .400s and .500s that dominated the hunting world at that time. Selecting a medium-caliber projectile, .375 (9.5mm), he gave it a large-capacity case, reinforcing it with a belt around the back part in order to avoid problems of extraction with the new and elevated charges of smokeless powder. And so was born the very popular .375

magnum, which in theory was designed as the closest thing to an all-round rifle. There were a few limitations to this new cartridge, such as the lack of trajectory necessary to hunt sheep in the mountains with shots of more than 300 meters and the power to stop an elephant in a thick forest with low visibility. In the last situation it is easy to understand that a heavier projectile than the 300 grains of the .375 is needed. Except for those very particular cases, this is certainly the most versatile rifle that can be found, covering 90 percent of the situations a hunter can expect to encounter. Of course, it's not all in the arm chosen. Common sense and a little experience are of primary importance.

Originally, the .375 magnum was created to be used in Mauser bolt actions and, with a rimmed counterpart, double rifles. Today, after so many years, it continues to be a modern cartridge and king of the all-rounds. Rifles produced over the years to compete with it such as the .350 Rigby Magnum, the .338 Winchester Magnum, and the excellent 9.3x64 Brenneke (.366 in English measurements) have barely dented its popularity. I have used the .375 for many years as a tool of the trade, as well as my .416 Rigby and .465 Nitro Express, and I can say that I am completely satisfied with this rifle. What I'm saying is based ninety-eight percent on experience and a modest two percent on theory.

The .375 magnum was devised to be used for everything by those hunters who want to employ only one rifle in their activities. For that reason there were different bullet weights capable of dealing with all game, including all big game, with almost the same point of impact up to 200 yards. This achievement added to its success. The different bullet weights were 235, 270, and 300 grains.

A. For small and medium animals with thin skins, at long distances, a load was created with a 235-grain bullet, an initial velocity of 2,800 feet per second, and energy of 4,100 foot/pounds. For many years the British continued regular production of ammunition loaded with the 235-grain projectiles until Winchester introduced a better load. As a result, the 235-grain bullet was used less and less until it disappeared. Its uses have been supplanted by the 270-grain bullet, which duplicated and improved on it. Unless I'm mistaken, commercial ammunition hasn't been loaded with 235 grains since 1945.
B. For large, thin-skinned animals usually shot from a medium distance and occasionally long range, the 270-grain bullet is perfect, with an initial velocity of 2,740 feet per second. This is only sixty feet per second less than the 235-grain bullet, with energy of 4,500 foot/pounds.
C. Finally, the projectile to be used against dangerous animals at short distances is the solid, with 300 grains of weight. I would use this for elephant, buffalo, rhinoceros, and hippopotami. I would use the expanding form against lions, tigers, and various bears, which gives an initial velocity of 2,550 feet per second and 4,330 foot/pounds of energy.

The .375 magnum, when employed with common sense, can be used with total confidence and satisfactory results. No animal in Africa, America, or Asia exists that cannot be cleanly killed with the proper type and weight of .375

bullet. The killing power of the .375 magnum is awesome and with the solid bullet it has one of the greatest penetrations known. On good terrain and with medium visibility, it is excellent for hunting elephants. The bullet will hit the mortal points from nearly any angle. Since the British firm of Kynoch stopped making metallic ammunition in 1967, American ammunition by Winchester and Remington has led the world, followed by the German RWS, which is also excellent, and the Norma from Sweden.

Something I personally never do is to load my own ammunition because, among other reasons, the seven or eight months of the year I spend on safari doesn't leave me much time for these things. Let us not even begin to discuss the legal problems in the majority of African countries when trying to transport the components, especially gunpowder. All my life I've used commercial ammunition with no problems. But for those who want to load their own, there exists a great range of projectiles for the .375 magnum, all commonly sold in the United States. Some of those are the Speer semi-spitzer 235-grain bullet, the 270-grain Hornady Spire-Point, the 285-grain Speer Grand Slam, the 300-grain Sierra Spitzer boattail, the 300-grain Monolithic, and many more.

Personally, after forty-two long years shooting with the .375, I prefer the solid bullet manufactured by Remington for hunting elephant, rhino, and buffalo, while for expanding bullets the Winchester Power Point with 270 grains is my favorite for general use. The 300-grain solid Remington bullet has a magnificent steel covering that allows it to keep on course without becoming deformed when it hits the largest bones or perforates the firmest and most compact muscle groups. The solid Winchester and RWS bullets are also excellent, but each one has its caprices and because of that I'm inclined toward the Remington.

Many years ago when the German firm RWS absorbed DWM and launched a new solid bullet on the market, a well-known gunsmith asked me to try out the cartridge and projectile to see how they performed in the field. After all, this is what is important to us. So, when I had to shoot a number of elephants that had been trampling farms, I decided to use the opportunity to try out this ammunition. Using my .375 magnum rifle with Mauser action, I began the double job of testing the ammunition and eliminating the wretched elephants. Since I wasn't sure of the results, I carried my old .416 Rigby just in case. Having it along enabled me to do things in my own way, which is to say calmly and quietly. I took my time so that I could shoot these elephants from different angles, which gave me the chance to really see the true effects of the shots. To my satisfaction, all six elephants were killed with a single shot each. In truth, the only thing I didn't like about the RWS ammo was that it often took a lot of force to extract the fired shell. This also happened with the 8x68. I never had this problem with American ammunition, which worked like a charm.

Winchester manufactures the 300-grain Silvertip expanding ammunition, which in theory permits more penetration before opening and deforming itself into a mushroomlike shape, but in my experience I found more killing power in the aforementioned 270-grain Power Point. I saw the results over the years when I faced a total of six lions wounded by clients, and on all these occasions this projectile got me out of trouble and left the lions dead on impact.

The long-gone German firm of DWM carried ammunition of 300 grains with the expanding TUG (Torpedo Universal Geschoss) bullet manufactured by Brenneke, which was a marvel against large, thin-skinned animals. Fortunately, RWS has again begun to manufacture this ammunition, and it is now readily available.

Loading by hand, never commercially, they've sometimes experimented with the .375 magnum with a 350-grain bullet. I never had occasion to use them, but I hear they were stupendous. I take this with a grain of salt because, if they were the panacea they were touted as, all the munitions companies would have incorporated them into their regular production. To this day they haven't done so.

As a point of curiosity, I will say that Holland & Holland, as well as the other European weapons manufacturers, used Mauser actions of normal length for .375 magnum rifles and very rarely used the long magnum Mauser action, which was $^3/_8$ inch longer than standard and cost much more.

My .375 magnum was manufactured in 1960 to my specifications by the firm Mahillon of Brussels (Ancienne Maison H. Mahillon), with a double trigger and variable telescopic sight. It was designed to be used in special elephant hunting conditions, such as when a good bull is in the middle of the herd and there is no way humanly possible to get close enough for a normal shot. Then, using a tripod and situating myself against the wind, I would wait patiently until sooner or later some member of the herd would move and I could see the animal's shoulder. When distance and light were perfect in the sights, I would then put a solid bullet in its heart. In this way, I was able to shoot elephant that in any other way would have been impossible.

Unfortunately, the firm Mahillon no longer exists. Its rifles were always high-quality products, among the best, and the company had years of experience in provisioning hunters throughout the colonial period in the old Belgian Congo. They made many .375 caliber rifles, which were very popular among the resident hunters of the Congo. The few to be found today on the second-hand arms market are much sought-after and command high prices.

My .375 Mahillon comes with its corresponding open sight, and between this and the scope it is so practical and versatile that I always keep it at hand. The Mahillon carries five rounds in the magazine, has perfect balance, and is a pleasure to handle. Its Mauser action is magnificent and has the best reliability you could hope for. The full-length extractor grabs the empty cartridge firmly, guaranteeing its expulsion without problems. This is ideal in extreme conditions, as much in cold as in hot weather. The telescopic sight is a venerable Khales from 3-9X and works as well now as it did the day I got it, with German mountings that allow it to be taken off or put on in only a few seconds, according to necessity.

I've read armchair experts in magazines advising the use of fixed-power scopes, with a magnification of only 2.5X on the .375 magnum. In my opinion, this is a grave error. The .375 magnum has exceptional ballistic capabilities that can benefit from variable scopes, adding greatly to its versatility. For the other part, I consider the fixed sight highly inadvisable, at least on rifles that will be used against dangerous animals. Nor do I buy the theory that against a wounded animal a low-powered scope is as quick to focus as an open sight. For a charging animal or one that's trying to escape, common sense says that an open sight is much easier to center on the target. With a telescopic sight, an animal moving in and out of leaves and branches goes out of focus very quickly, making it very difficult to follow.

In Africa, except in desert hunting, the average shooting distance is between 75 and 150 yards, rarely 250, and exceptionally 300. I fear when certain gentlemen talk of shooting and knocking down animals at 400 and 500 yards that this is pure fantasy. If they took the trouble to measure the distances, they'd be surprised to see how much these distances had shrunk. Those who bring a .375 magnum on safari to Africa will find that it serves for all necessities, if used with common sense.

Virtually every arms manufacturer in the world makes rifles of the .375 magnum caliber. The best are Holland & Holland, John Rigby, Purdey, the Belgian Francotte and Dumoulin, and so on. This isn't to say that less blue-blooded rifles cannot be used with total satisfaction and good results. The old F. N. Belgians are economic, magnificent, and still available on the second-hand market. I advise buying one if the chance presents itself. American-made Winchester and Remington, the Finnish Sako, the Austrian Mannlicher, and the Czech BRNO are all good rifles at accessible prices.

I put Uganda's Pete Pearson in first place among the hunters who have used the .375 magnum and who have achieved top results. Pearson was one of the greatest elephant hunters in the history of African hunting. He adopted the .375 magnum in 1914 along with his heavy .577 Nitro Express. He was a real enthusiast of the .375 magnum and took hundreds of elephants with his rifle, based on a Mauser action manufactured especially by John Rigby of London.

My old friend George Rushby, who hunted ivory in the Belgian Congo and Ubangi-Shari and who was in charge of elephant control in Tanganyika until he retired in 1956, also felt a great predilection for the .375 magnum. By the end of his tenure, he had taken 800 head through the necessity of reducing the number of animals in this or that district.

Two other friends of mine, Wally Johnson and Harry Manners, took more than 1,000 elephants each as professional ivory hunters in Mozambique, which was during a time when the enormous animals did not enjoy proper protection in that country. Curiously, they principally used the ordinary, low-priced Winchester Model 70 .375 magnum with spectacular results. The old pre-1964 Winchester action with its long extractor similar to the Mauser's was up to anything, especially combined with their enormous experience as elephant hunters.

The famous John "Pondoro" Taylor, author of, among other things, the book *African Rifles & Cartridges*, also had a great affinity for the .375 magnum. He told me that he had fired some 5,000 cartridges during his hunts in Mozambique, Nyasaland (now Malawi), and Northern Rhodesia (now Zambia). During the period of commercial meat hunting in Mozambique, many professionals used only the .375 magnum to feed the employees of the huge farming or mining companies and never felt the need to use a larger caliber. It was funny to listen to John Taylor talk about the .375 magnum. So great was his enthusiasm for this caliber and he claimed to have fired so many shots that I sometimes felt as though I was listening to the most fantastic stories about battles instead of about hunting. In between laughs and jokes, he finally would say that it could have been like this. . . .

Another friend vanished with time is the "white hunter" of Kenya, Syd Downey. He always recommended that his safari clients bring the following equipment: A .300 caliber rifle for antelopes, and a .375 magnum for dangerous game, both with telescopic sights that can be attached and removed quickly. I heard this opinion plenty of times over the years when we would have long talks in Nairobi—opinions which were backed up by his long years of practical experience.

Before the creation of the .375 Holland & Holland Magnum, the company had the .400/.375 Holland & Holland Express on the market. It also had the belted case, but the ballistics were much inferior and the cartridge soon disappeared into oblivion. In those days, the word "magnum" designated ammunition with greater initial speeds than 2,500 feet per second. Today it is primarily a marketing tag, with its reference to the Latin word *magnum*, meaning big.

At the same time as the creation of the .375 belted magnum, the Holland & Holland firm brought out a flanged cartridge for use only with double rifles. Many of these were manufactured until 1939. The production of double-barreled .375 magnums continued after the war, but these used a system of extraction that allowed the use of ammunition without rims. With this, the flanged cartridges lost popularity until they practically disappeared. Today all double-barreled rifles manufactured in .375 magnum use regular rimless ammunition with the aforementioned special extractors—not only those manufactured in England but in Belgium, Germany, Austria, Italy, and Spain. The Czech company BRNO also offers them in an over/under model.

After eighty years, the .375 magnum continues to be the most popular large-caliber rifle in the world. Generation after generation of hunters—from the most naive novices to the most experienced Nimrods—have used it with full satisfaction and optimum results. Given the hunting limits placed on the major species, the destruction of the elephant by poachers, the disappearance of the rhinoceros, and the general condition of the hunting world, the .375 magnum is everything the safari sportsman needs. As a result, this cartridge is experiencing a demand the like of which it hasn't known in many years. The professional needs more powerful rifles, like the .416 Rigby, .470 Nitro Express, .500, and so on, to protect clients in certain circumstances, but again, the sportsman who occasionally goes on safari doesn't need any complicated battery of sporting rifles. The sportsman will be perfectly armed with the .375 magnum as he doesn't forget the weapon's few limitations.

An example of those limitations would be confronting elephant and buffalo in dense forest with poor or little visibility where a heavier, more powerful projectile will be necessary to avoid possible risks. This ten percent negative is counterbalanced by the ninety percent positive ranking that will give the best service to the hunter of today and tomorrow, the same as it did to Pete Pearson, John Taylor, George Rushby, Harry Manners, and myself. The .375 magnum was, is, and will be the unrivaled king of all-purpose arms. Along with glorious calibers like the .416 Rigby, .470 Nitro Express, and .577 Nitro Express, it wrote the most important pages in the history of African hunting.

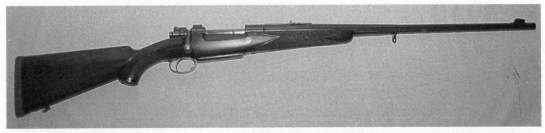

.416 Rigby.

.416 RIGBY

The proof of its extraordinary ballistic capacity can be found in the fact that, after eighty years, the .416 Rigby continues to be the most appreciated, respected, and accredited cartridge by hunters of dangerous game who want to use Mauser repeating rifles for their activities. The .416 was created in 1909 by the famous John Rigby of London and put on sale in 1912 after three years of testing in the African hunting arena.

It became nothing less than the regulation weapon for elephant hunters. An outstanding example of this was the case of Captain Samaki Salmon, head of elephant control in Uganda. Elephants had become a serious threat to farms and people in some areas and his job was to reduce the excessive number of elephants in places where this was happening. Over the years, Samaki Salmon killed 4,000 elephants with a pair of .416 rifles, including a record seventy in one weekend. He shot twelve of those with twelve shots in less than two minutes.

The .416 Rigby was unanimously given the title of "African weapon *par excellence*" and it is rare to find an African hunting book that doesn't use such positive or glowing terms in describing the gun. From the first moment, it became the ideal rifle for elephant hunting in any terrain in an era when there were more than twenty magnificent calibers to choose from for this kind of hunting. In bolt-action rifles, it became number one on the list by means of the superlative results achieved by those who used it. In those days, advertising was done via the practical results of field trials rather than through handsomely illustrated catalogs, as it is today. After the .416 Rigby's success, other arms manufacturers introduced calibers more or less similar in order to compete, but one after the other they disappeared, victims of the .416 Rigby's hold on the market.

The secret of the .416 Rigby that secured its reputation as an elephant rifle was the enormous penetration that allowed it to reach the animal's vital organs from any angle or position, something very important in this type of hunting. This was achieved thanks to the perfect combination of several factors. One factor included a projectile that was very resistant to deformation on impact against those huge bones; its resistance was the result of its reinforced steel jacket, weighing 410 grains and with an excellent sectional density, projected by 71 grains of Cordite that gave it a speed of 2,371 feet per second and an initial energy of 5,100 foot/pounds. This is the ideal combination for elephants and, of course, any other kind of hunting involving dangerous game.

I have some notes about the penetration tests performed against a material that had about the same resistance as an elephant's body. These notes show that the .416 Rigby beat all other rifles. The shots were fired fifteen yards from the target:

.577 Nitro Express	41 inches
.505 Gibbs	43 inches
.470 Nitro Express	41 inches
.465 Nitro Express	44 inches
.458 Winchester	42 inches
.416 Rigby	50 inches
.375 H&H Magnum	46 inches
9.3x64 Brenneke	45 inches

As you can see, of all the solid bullets fired from these eight rifles, the .416 Rigby was four inches ahead of its closest rival, the .375 H&H Magnum, four inches which, in a tight situation, can make a decisive difference.

Personally, through my years as an African hunter concentrating on elephants, I've used practically every rifle between the 9.3x64 Brenneke and the .577 Nitro Express. By the natural process of elimination, the .416 Rigby remained my favorite in the bolt action. Never have I used a rifle with fewer working problems than this one—none up to now, to be exact. It is a pleasure to see how smoothly it loads and how it expels the empty shell with equal smoothness. Let me clarify that I attribute these virtues to the original rifle manufactured by John Rigby & Co. of London. There are many Belgian, Austrian, and American manufacturers that also make .416 rifles, but even though these are excellent rifles, they lack the velvet handling of the original Rigby.

Throughout my life I have used several .416 Rigby-caliber rifles—an original Rigby, plus three of Belgian manufacture and one of Austrian. I calculate that I have shot several thousand rounds using these rifles. I got good results with the non-original Rigbys, but for smooth handling, ease of aim, and general use, they couldn't compare with the marvel made by John Rigby. There is simply something about my original Rigby that puts it head and shoulders above the rest. I've used my old and beloved John Rigby rifle for so long that it's now like a member of the family. I wouldn't trade it for its weight in gold—it would be like losing my right arm.

I've used the .416 Rigby in operations to control the number of elephants and buffalo, as a backup rifle to cover my clients on safari, and to get ivory. My .416 has given me the greatest satisfaction even when my travels took me to so many different territories: from the equatorial forests of Central Africa to the endless savanna of East and South Africa, through the Nile swamps and forests of bamboo. I have taken hundreds of elephants and buffalo with it as well as a goodly number of rhinos and lions. Its expanding bullet is excellent for such thin-skinned animals as lions, tigers, bears, moose, and elk.

An added advantage the .416 Rigby has over other calibers is evident in its flat trajectory up to 200 yards. Its 410-grain bullet falls only four inches in that distance. That is the same as many other smaller calibers using a bullet with only half the weight. Of course, shots fired while hunting dangerous game, especially with elephant, are made at short distance. Sometimes, however, it is necessary to fire over a longer range, such as in the case when elephants are standing along a riverbank, in a marshy area where it is hard to get close, in the midst of a herd, or when a wounded animal is trying to escape at what can be surprising speed. In these cases, its superior flat trajectory is very important and gives it a versatility that other large calibers can't even hope for. The .416 Rigby gives the same excellent results when confronted with a charging elephant or with a shot at 100 yards under difficult circumstances, such as when the animal is wounded and attempts to get away.

The longest distance where I've used the .416 Rigby was in the Sudan, shooting at an elephant 175 yards away that was escaping through a clearing. I was able to support myself on a tree limb and shoot him in the heart. He fell only a few yards away after tumbling head over heels like a drunk. The shortest distance was only ten feet, when a bull came on top of me in the rain forest. When I shot him between the eyes, it felt like I was actually touching him. A horrifying experience, and one I wouldn't want to repeat.

In the hunting world, the .416 Rigby has always been considered a professional weapon, but this is not to say that it wasn't used by famous sport hunters around the world, who preferred it to many other kinds of guns. There have been many impressive kills with it. The .416 Rigby was threatened with extinction by the doomsayers of the time in 1967 when Kynoch, exclusive manufacturer of large-caliber cartridges, suspended production of all metallic ammunition. This caused a panic among .416 Rigby owners who feared that they would no longer be able to buy ammunition. Many sold their .416 Rigbys in favor of other calibers which did not have ammunition problems.

I wasn't worried because I was sure that sooner or later there would be more ammunition for the .416 Rigby. A caliber with such a glorious past could not simply disappear, so logically, one had only to wait. To the disappointment of those who had put it aside, the Swedish firm of Norma agreed with John Rigby in 1970 to load 50,000 solids for the .416, to become available in January 1971. Rigby sold 22,000 between February and October of that year, so great was the demand. After putting the ammunition on the market, they saw that by mistake, the bullets weighed only 400 grains instead of the classic 410, but this does not alter the ballistics of the .416 Rigby.

Another small problem was that sometimes when the bullet hit the great bones of the elephant, its back part became somewhat deformed because the steel had not been adequately reinforced. I spoke many times about this with my friend David Marx, one of the directors of John Rigby & Co. in London, and between the two of us we came up with suggestions for redesigning the .416's projectile for the next lot of ammunition. We increased the walls of the steel sheath to be the same for all the length and strengthened the back as well as reinforcing the tip.

At last the ammunition made by Norma ran out, and Rigby contracted with the U.S. firm Brass Extrusion Laboratories, Ltd. in Illinois, which specialized in the manufacture of all the great and classic British calibers. I had the opportunity to meet proprietor James J. Bell in London to discuss possible improvements. After many studies and trials, his company began manufacturing a much-reinforced projectile that was 410 grains in weight. Many years later, other manufacturers, like Federal, followed in producing ammunition for the .416 Rigby and now it can be found everywhere. The new ammunition uses anticorrosive caps and a new type of gunpowder, excellent for the conservation of the barrels, to replace the old-fashioned Cordite.

Not even in the most uncertain moments was the .458 Winchester, its closest rival, able to overcome the reputation and prestige of the .416 Rigby, even with its advertising blitz. In fact, as soon as the initial panic was over, hunters who had gotten rid of their Rigbys tried in vain to get them back. Now after so many years, the old and respected .416 Rigby continues as the undisputed star among repeating rifles for hunting dangerous game. It pleases me to say that because of my influence, more than twenty hunting friends of mine have adopted the .416 Rigby as their backup rifle and I'm still waiting for one of them to complain to me about it. Perhaps in a modest way I have contributed to its popularity.

Actually, Rigby manufactures several models in the .416 caliber. The classic had a magnum Mauser action and square bridge, which are now taken from old rifles. Reconditioned, they are exclusively reserved for best-quality rifles. Other modern actions that have the same length as the magnum Mauser

($^3/_8$ inch or .95 centimeters longer than the normal 98 Mauser action) have become available and have permitted a notable reduction in the price of the finished rifle, while still being magnificent in all aspects. Rigby finishes each individually by hand, giving each the finishing touch that makes each one a select piece of complete reliability. The length of the barrel can vary according to taste from twenty-one to twenty-four inches, but I prefer the longer barrel. The first rear sight is set at 100 yards, with two more rear sights regulated at 200 and 300 yards in the typical shape of an open "V" to aim and shoot rapidly. The magazine has room for four cartridges. Just to hold these rifles is a real pleasure. Thanks to perfect balance they handle easily despite the caliber, with grand precision and moderate recoil.

Among the famous hunters who preferred the .416 Rigby—besides Samaki Salmon with his 4,000 elephants, next to whom we are all midgets—was Commander Blunt. Commander Blunt was not only a good friend but also one of the pioneers of "elephant control" in Tanganyika. My old friend John A. Hunter, the great professional guide of Kenya, preferred the .416 to any other caliber for hunting lions. He was using a .416 one night when he shot eighteen cattle-killing lions in the Masai zone. Bill Pridham in Uganda hunted the majority of his 2,000 elephants with a .416 Rigby. Once when we were hunting together many years ago in the Semliki Valley I saw that the bluing of his rifle had almost disappeared from use.

The veteran South African ivory hunter Marcus Daly was another grand enthusiast of the .416 and used it to shoot hundreds of elephants, including an immense bull with tusks of 203 and 207 pounds in what used to be Ubangi-Shari. The Frenchman Cormon also hunted about 500 elephants in Ubangi-Shari with his .416 Rigby. More recently, the most famous professional hunters of Kenya and Tanganyika used the .416 Rigby as a backup weapon in preference to any other, hunters like Tony Dyer, John Lawrence, Harry Selby, and Eric Rundgren, who has 800 elephants to his credit, thanks to the .416.

The caliber .416 Rigby was created to be used solely on bolt action repeating rifles, but by special order they can be made in double barreled rifles using special extractors that hook rimless ammunition. John Rigby & Co. has only made a few double rifles in the .416 caliber in all its history, but I have had the occasion to see examples of .416 doubles made in Belgium, Austria, and Spain. The owners seemed fully satisfied with their rifles, and I tried one, which had been made in Spain, with good results.

Due to the enormous popularity of the .416, in recent years a series of new cartridges have appeared in the United States in this caliber: the .416 Hoffman, .416 Taylor, .416 Remington and the .416 Weatherby, all which are ballistic copies of the .416 Rigby. But the reputation of the veteran is so grand and so deserved that they have never eclipsed it, and it will continue to be number one as long as there's a single elephant to hunt in Africa. I imagine that Samaki Salmon, from the Happy Hunting Grounds, would be in agreement with that point.

To wind up this commentary, I will use again the words of John Taylor, "Pondoro," who wrote about the .416 Rigby this way in his famous book *African Rifles & Cartridges*: "You certainly could not get a better or more reliable magazine rifle for general work amongst dangerous animals. It is tremendously popular throughout Africa and deservedly so. It is a great killer." Ballistic data on the .416 Rigby include:

Weight of the bullet .... 410 grains
Powder load .... 71 grains Cordite (original)
Muzzle Velocity .... 2,371 feet per second
Muzzle Energy .... 5,100 foot/pounds
Trajectory at 200 yards .... drop, four inches
Weight of the original Rigby rifle .... between nine and ten pounds

If for some reason I would be forced to use only one rifle for the rest of my life, without a doubt it would be the .416 Rigby!

.500 JEFFERY

.500 Jeffery Mauser

Contrary to what has been said in numerous articles, books, and tracts specializing in ballistics, this caliber is German, where it was originally known as the 12.5x70 Schuler, after its German creator.

When the famous British firm Jeffery saw the potential of the African market for large-caliber weapons in the repeating Mauser system, it decided to get into the market, too. After studying the situation, instead of developing its own caliber as everyone else had, it adopted the German 12.5x70 Schuler, with its ballistics ahead of its time, renaming it in English measurements as the .500, and adding the name Jeffery as the designation of the gunmaker. This is how the ".500 Jeffery Mauser" appeared on the repeating-arms and large-caliber market. Many believed that Jeffery created it, a misunderstanding that exists to this day. Jeffery only manufactured the rifles and used ammunition loaded in Germany by the Schuler company. This was in 1926, when the .500 was first introduced.

Unfortunately, the .500 Jeffery suffered a series of reverses, especially when new regulations put an end to the unlimited hunting of elephants. This meant that the Jeffery never gained the popularity or reached the kind of following it deserved. Something similar happened to the magnificent British .505 Gibbs. The production of arms was never huge in either caliber, and as a result it is very difficult to find original .500 Jeffery Mauser or .505 Gibbs rifles today.

From adolescence I had "three loves:" the .416 Rigby, the .500 Jeffery, and the .505 Gibbs, and I dreamed of having one of each one day. At the age of twenty in 1950, I got *African Rifles & Cartridges* by John Taylor, who later became a friend, and I remember reading over and over the sections on these three rifles. Luckily, I got my .416 Rigby shortly thereafter, which, as I always say, has become like an extension of my right arm after so many years. Later I got a .505 Gibbs but the Jeffery continued to elude me.

I first used a .500 Jeffery in 1960. It was the property of a missionary in the Sudan who also had another unusual rifle, the .333 Jeffery. He lent the .500 Jeffery to me to hunt meat for the various schools in his charge, something I did with great pleasure. In those days there was very good hunting everywhere, and one could shoot an unlimited number of buffalo, as they were considered vermin. From the start the .500 Jeffery impressed me with great results even though the ammunition was very old. They had stopped manufacturing it in 1939 and never started production up after the war.

Along with the rifle, the Combonian father gave me twenty-odd cartridges, solid and expanding, and I remember that every time I shot at a buffalo, regardless of the kind of projectile I used, it fell. It was with a sad heart that I returned that rifle when the job was done, knowing there was no way to buy it. The experience left me obsessed with the idea of getting one, something that only happened many years later. I had the good fortune to meet the German gunmaker Harald Wolf who also suffered from ".500 Jeffery Mauser Syndrome." He specializes in manufacturing rifles in traditional African calibers as well as ammunition for them. We became good friends.

Harald Wolf Mastergunworks is one of those increasingly rare gunsmiths who enjoy creating the finest rifles with innovations that work. He builds Mauser repeating system and double-barreled rifles, in any caliber existing. He moved from Wassenberg, Germany, to near Liege, Belgium, to improve his work opportunities. As a German, he is infinitely methodical, aided by his wife, Monika, who is an exceptional metal engraver.

After we became friends, Harald told me that his golden dream was to resuscitate the old, glorious and defunct .500 Jeffery Mauser and that he was already doing some tests with ammunition for it. On top of that, he already had a number of potential clients in Germany who were interested in acquiring a rifle of this caliber. He asked me if, when the time came, I would help him with some field trials. Of course, I said, "yes."

The original ballistics of the old 12.5x70 Schuler or .500 Jeffery were sensational and, as I mentioned before, well ahead of their time. Take a look at this: 535-grain projectile, initial speed of 2,400 feet per second and energy of 6,800 foot/pounds, with a low and safe chamber pressure.

The problem was getting the same ballistics with the new gunpowders without dangerously increasing the pressure. At last, after many tests, studies, and estimates, he found the exact duplicate, with a pressure that was more than acceptable for tropical climates. The cartridges were made of an especially resistant brass and could be reloaded seven times within the margin of safety.

What remained to be resolved was the question of the projectile. The old solids for the .500 Jeffery were not as strong as could be hoped, like those loaded by GECADO during the thirties. There are illustrations of five bullets taken from elephants and buffalo in John Taylor's *African Rifles & Cartridges.* One is fine, but the others distort unacceptably. After trying various bullets, I decided my definite choice was Australia's Woodleigh Bullets, which were outstanding in all aspects and practically indestructible, which I confirmed not only with the .500 Jeffery but the .416 Rigby. They produce the entire range of calibers up to the .600.

Once everything was ready, Harald Wolf made me a basic prototype of the .500 Jeffery Mauser along with 100 cartridges with expanding bullets and solids to do various tests. The results of the field trials were better than our greatest hopes for its killing power. So much so that as a joke I baptized it with the name "Peacemaker," due to the fact that any elephant or buffalo it hit was knocked flat—irreversibly so.

Just for comparison, the .460 Weatherby is more potent than the .500 Jeffery, with 8,095 foot/pounds of initial energy thanks to its greater speed of 2,700 feet per second at the muzzle. But this is also its greatest drawback. At the short distances in which elephants are usually shot, that excessive speed causes the bullet to swerve from its path more often than is desirable, and when the bullet hits a resistant body such as the skull, the result is often negative. The .500 Jeffery's heavier bullet with less velocity is much more effective. I want to point this out to those who only know calibers by the ballistic tables and are impressed by numbers—theory is very different from practice!

Everything I've shot with the .500 Jeffery up to now has been stopped in its tracks. Most notable of these was a really gigantic elephant, which lifted its two feet on the side where it had been hit into the air so that it lost its balance and collapsed on its flank, as if a giant hand had shaken it and later knocked the poor animal to the ground with a blow. When we later cut it up, I saw that the projectile had entered the right shoulder, passed through the heart and continued through the left shoulder. It had remained under the skin on the other side of the huge body, giving impressive penetration and remaining in perfect condition. You could have loaded it up and used it again.

Contrary to what John Taylor says, the .500 Jeffery doesn't fire smoothly with little recoil. It is easy to imagine why this is so if we keep in mind that the projectile weighs 535 grains and carries a charge of 95 grains of powder. Personally, the recoil never bothered me, but for those whom it does, Harald Wolf makes the .500 with a muzzle brake. It always makes me smile to read articles where the author considers the kick of the .375 magnum to be little better than fatal.

As a final point about the .500 Jeffery Mauser, we can say that its rebirth is a fact. I contributed to it in a modest but enthusiastic way and it was worth the trouble. It would have been a great loss if this magnificent rifle had disappeared because it is exactly what we need more every day in Africa—a "safety belt" for confronting elephant and buffalo that become more irascible and more aggressive season after season.

THE AFRICAN BATTERY IN THE 1990s

It is strange that now, when big-game hunting is declining because there are few elephants, no rhinos, and limited buffalo within reach of sportsmen, there is a demand for large-caliber rifles the like of which has never before been seen. It is really surprising. After consulting some gunsmiths I know, I've been able to verify that most of them were bought for nostalgic reasons and only a few will go to Africa to be used against buffalo or elephants. These rifles sit in the homes of dreamers impressed by the stories of Jim Sutherland, George Rushby, and John Hunter. This despite the campaign against hunting by a badly informed sector where hysteria and emotional pressure carry more weight than evidence and reason.

Like everything in this world, the field of arms is also subject to fashion. There has been a rethinking about which are the recommended calibers, some of the review done by arms manufacturers with the clear intent of making money. But in the end common sense clicks in and things return to normal, with some calibers returning to the preferential place they deserve, only temporarily eclipsed by brilliant and phony advertising.

My contentions are backed up by many years of hunting in Africa. I have no axe to grind, and I don't intend to try to change anyone's opinion about his favorite caliber—nor do I have any desire to begin discussions on the subject. I only want to explain the trends in African hunting in 1994, selecting what we could call the cream of each distinct category of calibers. Given the strict conditions under which the present-day hunter has to operate, he has to use the proper rifle—a rifle usually chosen through a process of natural selection. A rifle's performance is what counts at the moment of truth, not what can be read in handsomely illustrated gunsmiths' catalogs where elegiac copy touts a rifle's virtues with nothing more than sales in mind. Practical results can only be estimated by gaining the experience necessary through hunting and more hunting, not theorizing over ballistic tables of speeds and energies, which may or may not be exactly correct.

Despite the opinion of many armchair theorists whose experience consists of shooting three or four measly animals on some private ranch, the truth is that with two well-combined weapons all African species can be taken. Forget about those batteries of four or five rifles, which they recommend as indispensable. Another point I'd like to clear up is that African animals have the reputation of being more resistant to wounds than animals on other continents. This is true up to a point, but the exaggerations you hear are completely ridiculous and absurd. No creature on earth can flee into the tall grass with its heart destroyed by a bullet. I repeat that these are fantasies. If a hunter aims properly, he will see how easily an animal will fall at the first shot . . . and without life-threatening complications.

Wild animals are feeling the squeeze, not only in Africa but throughout the world. Their natural habitats are disappearing every day from a thousand different causes. The increasing difficulty of the hunt is nature's way of conservation: species we would define as trusting have become very wary, and dangerous animals have become especially aggressive. These circumstances have produced a turn toward high-impact calibers that promise the maximum power. This puts an end to the absurd practice begun in 1948 when certain gunsmiths with revolutionary ideas launched a series of rifles that shot small projectiles at very high speeds with the idea that shock was the actual killer. Over time it has been proven just how wrong this theory was, vindicating those who advocated using a heavy bullet at a moderate speed. In truth, those who used the heavier calibers were the only ones who continued killing cleanly and effectively, as they have always done.

One point I would like to discuss is the quality of weapons to be used on safari. I insist that these be the very best the wallet can afford. I have never understood why people who spend a lot of money to go on safari will bring a poor-quality rifle to hunt with. These people must forget that the rifle they bring with them will be the tool they use to bag the longed-for trophies . . . and that a poorly made rifle may cause them to lose the unique opportunity of achieving their goals. For reasons I cannot fathom, many modern rifles are getting worse and worse, which is quite unbelievable considering the technological advances in the area of arms manufacturing. I've seen recently produced rifles become a mountain of problems for their owners.

Due to professional ethics, I will not name any particular make, but I find it completely unacceptable that the magazine comes open upon firing, spilling the cartridges and leaving one unarmed. With double barrels, the situation can take on almost tragic proportions . . . as when rifles won't close after loading; when both barrels go off at the same time; when barrels come loose due to weak soldering; when stocks break after a few shots—occurrences not uncommon in both action types. It seems as though some manufacturers' rifles to last only a few years, like cars for example, so that the user has to repair his arsenal because of its gradual slide into uselessness. Because of my profession, I have had the opportunity to see, study, and experiment with rifles from many manufacturers and many places. As a result, I feel I can voice these criticisms with confidence, given my knowledge gained from a lifetime of experience in the field.

Of course there is that group of gunsmiths who, true to the tradition of quality, have always been reliable. The fame that follows is justly deserved. The British hold first place, followed by the Belgians and the Germans. Their products are the dream of every dilettante hunter. Let us now look at the recommended calibers, which we shall divide into two groups, for covering the full range of big-game animals in Africa:

A. All purpose calibers for plains game
B. Calibers for hunting dangerous game

ALL-PURPOSE CALIBERS FOR PLAINS GAME

This designates the calibers most frequently used by hunters. As a general rule the majority of these calibers range from .300 to .375, or from 7.62mm to 9.5mm. They fire a projectile of between 180 and 300 grains at a minimum initial speed of 2,500 feet per second and energy of 3,000 foot/pounds. Keep in mind that under ordinary circumstances in Africa, it is rare to have to fire at a range of more than 200 yards and that most animals weigh between 150 and 650 pounds. Any ammunition within the minimums described will give the hunter an ample margin of safety even in stressful situations. Today the most popular calibers are the following: .300 Holland & Holland, .300 Winchester, .300 Weatherby, 8x68S, 9.3x64 Brenneke, and .375 magnum.

There is no animal that will fail to succumb to a shot that has been well aimed, if the right projectile for distance and the animal's weight has been taken into account. The ballistic stats of the calibers already reviewed are:

Caliber	Bullet Weight (grains)	Initial Speed (feet)	Initial Energy (foot/pounds)
.300 H&H	180	2,920	3,400
.300 H&H	220	2,620	3,350
.300 Winchester	180	3,070	3,740
.300 Weatherby	180	3,245	4,201
.300 Weatherby	220	2,905	4,123
8x68S	187	3,280	4,460
8x68S	198	3,190	4,460
8x68S	224	2,653	4,041
9.3x64 Brenneke	285	2,750	4,790
9.3x64 Brenneke	293	2,640	4,550
.375 magnum	270	2,740	4,330
.375 magnum	300	2,550	4,532

The rifles in any of these calibers must include a telescopic sight, preferably variable from 1.5X to 6X. Several calibers that used to be very popular but which are now not often seen except in South Africa and Namibia are the 7x57, 7mm Remington Magnum, .30-06, and 9.3x62 Mauser. These have been replaced by the calibers listed above.

Of the "three .300s," you can apply whatever you want to say about one to the other two. If the ballistics vary on the tables, they vary little in practice. The first on the market was the .300 Holland & Holland Magnum in 1925, followed by the .300 Weatherby in 1948 and finally, the .300 Winchester in 1958.

When the famous British company of Holland & Holland created the .300, commercially designated as the "Super 30," it was popular from the start and continues to be used by all the famous hunters to this day, resisting the competition of more or less similar calibers that were introduced later.

The .300 Weatherby Magnum, based on the old .300 H&H but with a larger capacity for gunpowder, is in my opinion the best of the Weatherby line and the one that made its creator famous. It is an excellent caliber, immensely popular in the big-game hunting world, especially in the high mountains where its great trajectory is needed for long distances. The same can be said of the .300 Winchester, the most modern of the group.

Curiously, the original .300 H&H Magnum has again so grown in popularity that the well-known American company Federal recently incorporated the manufacture of this cartridge into its "Safari" line of ammunition in view of the demand.

The German 8x68S has extraordinary ballistics and I have seen it make clients and professionals capable of all sorts of deviltry with incredible shots. It is a versatile caliber, a great killer, and one of the favorites in Africa.

It is incredible and a shame that hunters in general are not more familiar with the magnificent 9.3x64 Brenneke, one of the greats of the world, manufactured by the well-known German company RWS. It has a high profile in the African hunting field due to its outstanding results. Created by Wilhelm Brenneke, based on the old 9.3x62 designed by Otto Bock in 1905, the 9.3x64 is extraordinary. When it uses expanding "TUG" ammunition with 293 grains, it is ideal for all soft-skinned African big game. With it I took twenty-three lions in a short period of time, which is a lot. Be sure not to confuse the 9.3x64 with the 9.3x74R, used only in double barreled rifles and of inferior ballistics, which are useless for Africa.

Within this all-purpose group, we finally arrive at the unbeatable and ever-popular .375 H&H Magnum, the king of all-purpose calibers. It is equally capable of cleanly killing a Thomson gazelle or an elephant, depending on the bullets. After over eighty years, the .375 Magnum has satisfied generations of hunters, and it is ideal for sportsmen, professionals, and game wardens.

CALIBERS FOR DANGEROUS GAME

First of all, we have to make two classifications in this category:

A. A division for thin-skinned dangerous animals
B. A division for dangerous animals with thick skin and large muscle masses

The first group includes the big cats. These animals can be hunted with all-purpose rifles, and despite the danger from the possibility of a charge, they can be stopped by bullets between 250 and 300 grains, at least in good visibility. In scrub or thick forest with little visibility or when tracking wounded animals, the situation changes and the risk increases enormously, making it absolutely necessary that hunters use the most powerful weapon they have. Of the 153 lions I have shot, about 70 were taken with the 9.3x64 Brenneke and the .375 Magnum; these hunts were all problem-free. I've only needed something stronger four or five times, and I can tell you that in those moments a .577 Nitro Express seemed too small.

In the second category we put the pachyderms (elephant, rhinoceros, and hippo), followed by the great bovines like the buffalo, which also have thick skins and large muscle masses. These species are characterized by being animals of great size, weight, and resistance. To hunt them safely, heavy calibers with high impact must be used. Theoretically, projectiles should not be less than 400 grains, initial speed not less than 2,000 feet per second, and initial energy of at least 4,000 foot/pounds. This is only possible in calibers of .400 and above.

It has been the heavy calibers that have created the most controversy. It has become fashionable recently to return to tradition and continue with the classic big bores, cartridges that have proven themselves a thousand and one times to be perfect for the uses they were designed for.

Today, the most popular calibers for hunting dangerous game in Africa are the following:

Caliber	Bullet Weight (grains)	Initial Speed (feet per second)	Initial Energy (foot/pounds)
Repeating Rifles:			
.404 Jeffery	400	2,330	4,840
.416 Rigby	410	2,371	5,100
.458 Winchester	500	2,040	4,622
Double Rifles:			
.465 Nitro Express	480	2,150	4,930
.470 Nitro Express	500	2,125	5,030

An unusual case is the .458 Winchester, which was very popular when introduced but which has been swept aside by the .416 Rigby. The .416 Rigby has become very popular again due to the fact that there are now no problems getting ammunition. It is being regularly manufactured by various firms, such as Federal in the U.S.

The basic problem with the .458 Winchester was always its erratic results as well as its lack of penetration in shots to elephants' heads. This robbed it of its appeal for me. The opposite can be said of the .416 Rigby, which has never failed to live up to expectations in the forty-two years I've used it. The .404 Jeffery continues to be, as always, efficient and safe, especially when loaded with ammunition from RWS in Germany, designated as 10.75x73mm there.

In double-barreled rifles, the old favorites, .465 and .470 Nitro Express, continue in their deserved popularity. The .470 is especially popular now that Federal manufactures the ammunition. These two calibers continue to be seen everywhere in the hunting fields of Africa. Even though they are nearly ninety years old, nothing yet has been able to take their places.

•••

CHAPTER IV

Elephants

FIRST ELEPHANT, 1952

It seems strange to think that in 1930, the year I was born, the great James Sutherland was at the top of his professional career, hunting unlimited numbers of elephants in Ubangi-Shari. Only nineteen years before, the Belgians had handed over the mythical Lado Enclave, paradise of ivory poachers in what was then the Anglo-Egyptian Sudan. At that time the Masai of Kenya and Tanganyika were still hunting lions with spears, as if it were the easiest thing in the world.

Times change, but memories stay fixed and unerasable. Among those memories, as clearly as if it were yesterday, one stands above all the rest: the day I took my first elephant. On that day, at the happy age of twenty-two, an elephant changed my life forever. After this monumental event, I gave up an easy, comfortable, and secure life in medicine for the difficult, uncomfortable, and insecure one of an elephant hunter. I've never looked back. In fact, I'd like to roll back time to be able to live this unforgettable era over again, something which unfortunately cannot be done.

At twenty-two I was a sort of "King Kong," being six feet, four inches tall and weighing 210 pounds. I was also in rude good health and filled with immense enthusiasm for the ultimate African adventure, the elephants. Nothing could keep me from realizing my dreams beneath the equatorial sun, especially when I had the great good luck to have had parents who adored me, something which gave me incredible courage.

So, there I was in that faraway time of 1952, chasing my dream in Africa at last. I had just finished my "career" as a "gorilla expert" in the interior of what used to be Spanish Guinea, thanks to the generous help of my friend Otto Krohnert. Full of the hunting spirit, I returned to Bata where I stayed in the home of fellow countryman and Valencian Rámon Tatay. My friend was an aeronautic engineer in charge of building the new international airport at Bata. As well as his professional qualifications, Rámon was, and is, a fine hunter and we became good buddies. In those days I listened, mouth agape, to his incredible adventures of having taken several elephants in Guinea. I took mental notes of his advice, for me like holy writ.

I remember that in 1952 Rámon Tatay lived in a house on the beach side of the road between Bata and the airport, surrounded by a garden and the calm sea. Because his wife Julia was in Spain, Fumbo the cook looked after us. Fumbo was quite a drunk, and, indeed would drink almost anything. While I was there, he even drank my aftershave and practically keeled over, as you can well imagine.

One day Rámon said that he had just heard from the Ayamaken chief and local hunter Tobias Makoa that a number of elephants were in the area and that he had thought of going after them the next weekend. Would I like to go? I couldn't believe my luck at the news and, of course, I said, "yes!"

Two others were to come along, a pharmacist by the name of Manolo Gomes-Moreno and a businessman whom Rámon always referred to as "the Sporting Canary." They wanted to do some hunting, so we decided that I would leave two days early along with the cook and his assistant to carry the camping equipment. We would wait for them in Ayamaken.

I left Bata on an African Transport bus. It took me as far as Ncombia, by the Mbia River, where the road ended. We had to make the last few miles along paths through the equatorial forest to Ayamaken. With the help of Fumbo, his aide-de-camp, and several local people, we made it to the village in a couple of hours. Tobias received us cordially and we became good friends. I later hunted with him for many years.

They organized the campground for me, which meant cleaning the biggest and best hut and arranging the beds. These were simple foam mattresses, the kind you see at the beach.

Tobias was an expert elephant hunter, and the time flew as I listened to his stories until the day the others arrived. Shortly after lunch, I heard the sound of motors and Rámon appeared on a motorcycle with Manolo riding behind, followed by "the Sporting Canary" astride another. They had left Rámon's Ford truck at the Mbia River with the chauffeur in charge, crossing the river by loading the motorcycles onto *cayucos*, which are canoes made of hollowed-out logs. They crossed the river and made good time to Ayamaken. After asking me how everything was, Rámon and Tobias began planning the next day's activities. I didn't miss a word.

Thanks to Rámon, one of the great Guinean hunters, Juan Durall, had done me the honor of lending me his gun while he was on vacation in Barcelona. Durall's gun was a .475 No. 2 Joseph Lang double, and he also gave me four cartridges—ammunition was scarce at the time. Rámon had a .475 Sarasqueta and three cartridges, which meant that we had seven rounds between us. Rámon had another rifle, which he'd gotten in the Cameroon, a 10.75x68 Mauser. Tobias, who only had an old 12-gauge shotgun, quickly took possession of that one. Once we'd gotten all that straight, we ate the dinner that Fumbo had prepared. We had to suspend the after-dinner conversation because the mosquitoes were eating us alive, so off we went to bed, wrapping ourselves up tightly in mosquito nets so that nary a bug could get through. We joked and laughed

I shot my first elephant on the Campo River, 26 August 1952, when I was 22 years old. The Campo is the border between Spanish Guinea and Cameroon.

until we fell asleep. I was as nervous as a cat thinking about the next day—after all, I was at long last very close to realizing my dream.

It was still dark when we were awakened, and we quickly got dressed, leaving the hut as it began to get light and fighting off the stinging "gen-gens"—little flies that at dawn and dusk pursue one in the woods. A smiling Tobias appeared and told us that during the night the elephants had started grazing close to the village and were still nearby. We breakfasted quickly, grabbed our guns, cameras, and food supplies and took off. Our party was we four Spaniards, Tobias, a pair of Bayeles trackers and some porters from the village.

We immediately saw the elephants' tracks when we reached the yucca plantation. There were three of them, all good-sized bulls. The ground was so soft and damp that it was easy to follow their huge tracks, which were headed in the direction of the Campo River only a few miles away near the border of Spanish Guinea and Cameroon. There was the risk that they would cross the border

The author age 22 years in 1952 in Equatorial Africa.

into Cameroon, which for political reasons would place them beyond our reach. We stopped a moment and Rámon told me that if we saw the elephants, I was to have the first shot, that I should pick the best one I could see and go for it. I thanked him with all my heart.

We followed them about an hour more and at 9 A.M. we reached the banks of the Campo River. There, on an island about sixty yards away, was a magnificent elephant giving himself a shower with water from his trunk. I stared at the sight like an idiot until Rámon and Tobias returned me to earth by saying that I had better shoot fast before the elephant disappeared into the forest.

There were some rocks in front of me, and without giving it another thought I sat on them, crossed my legs and with no more support than my arms, raised the .475. I did a quick mental review of everything I had read or Rámon had told me. I had never fired a rifle of that caliber nor had any idea of its kick, but, aiming at the elephant's head, I fired the right barrel. I felt an enormous bang and was tumbled backward over the rocks from the great recoil of the rifle. I got up right away, sat down again, and saw to my astonishment the elephant lying in the water. At the same time I heard the others congratulating me. I didn't believe it, but there was the elephant as proof that it wasn't a dream. Rámon and the others hugged me while Tobias and the trackers pounded me on the back and I cried tears of joy.

I'd like to say otherwise, but that was a one-in-a-million shot. Hitting an elephant in the head at sixty yards while badly situated on a rock and while firing an unfamiliar gun is about as likely as winning the lottery. I have no doubt that Saint Hubert gave me a big helping hand that morning: first, by seeing that the elephant stayed put on his island even though his companions had already disappeared, and second, by carrying the 480-grain bullet of the .475 No. 2 to its mark. Of all the 859 elephants I've shot, I don't remember a more unlikely shot than that one. The long and beautiful tusks weighed over fifty pounds each. From that moment, my life changed completely. . . .

WORLD-RECORD TUSKS

References to the largest elephant tusks ever taken in the history of African hunting crop up occasionally in books and in magazines, but these publications are always short on details. I'd already been collecting bits and pieces of information about these fabled tusks when I got access to the notes of an American ivory dealer stationed in Zanzibar at the end of the last century. Because of these notes, I now feel that I am in a position to tell the full and complete history of those incredible tusks, the most fantastic hunting trophy ever taken.

Before we get to the tusks, I think that it's important to give a little history about the people who were directly involved in the hunting and subsequent commercialization of ivory in order to properly set the story. Without a doubt, the top hunters and merchants of ivory of all time were the Arabs, who had been established in this trade since the last century. They plied their trade all along the coast of East Africa and especially on the exotic and romantic island of Zanzibar.

At the same time, they were involved in slave trafficking, an activity which they found mixed very well with ivory hunting. When they brought those poor wretches out of the interior, they had them carry the tusks on their sweaty and beaten backs. When they got to the coast everything was sold—human beings and ivory, with double profit for their Arab "caretakers." "White gold" and "black gold," they were called, with a remarkable lack of sentiment.

Of those wily tradesmen, one of the last seekers of ivory and slaves in East Africa was Shundi, a Kavirondo native from the shores of Lake Victoria, who in his youth had been captured and sold to an Arab in the Zanzibar slave market. Shundi was no fool, and soon won the affection of his master by, among other things, becoming a Muslim. The old Arab trader had full confidence in Shundi and sent him into the interior at the head of an armed troop to continue rounding up slaves and ivory. Things went so well that he was able to buy his freedom and to form his own company to hunt people and elephants, concentrating principally on the area to the south of Mount Kilimanjaro where he became the terror of the region for his acts of cruelty and brutality.

In 1884 the Germans established themselves in East Africa through the German East Africa Company headed by Dr. Carl Peters. Lamentably, Dr. Peters brutalized the local population and committed notable atrocities, including the hanging of several thousand natives who didn't want to come under his "protection." At last in 1891, in view of this disaster, the German government dissolved the company and passed everything over to Kaiser Wilhelm I. The colony

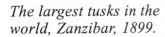

The largest tusks in the world, Zanzibar, 1899.

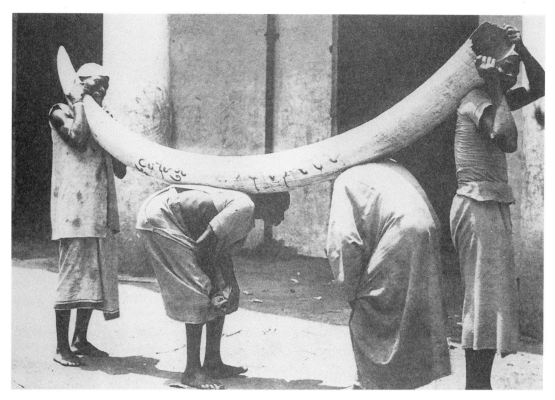

One of the longest tusks on record, Zanzibar, 1899.

then officially became known as German East Africa. Things weren't easy for the new colonizers, and in order to strengthen their presence in the interior, the Germans arranged for the most powerful people of each district to be named political agents.

This was how the bloodthirsty Shundi became nothing less than a representative of the German government. Instead of being paid with money, as were the rest of the agents, Shundi made a deal to monopolize elephant hunting and ivory found in his jurisdiction, which was the area south of Kilimanjaro. With a troop of slaves at his command, armed with old muzzleloaders that used lead bullets and blackpowder, Shundi took advantage of his "legal" position to slaughter any elephant he found. He killed everything, bulls and cows, old and young. In the course of this butchery, they shot the elephant with the largest tusks on record, in 1898, at the base of Kilimanjaro.

In his new "official" capacity, this belligerent man soon became a serious threat to the Germans themselves, who finally forced him to leave the country after several armed skirmishes with his troops. In search of new horizons, he took his reduced corps of thugs and headed north, crossing from south to north all of British East Africa, the area that was to become Kenya in 1922. Eventually he reached the area south of Lake Rudolf in Turkana territory, where there

LAST OF THE FEW

was no authority. At that time, English control ended south of the Turkwell River, leaving everything between this point and the Ethiopian border in the hands of primitive and violent tribes.

Shundi again found magnificent opportunity for his activities and devoted himself to his brutal business. There was no one to give him trouble because the area was almost entirely unexplored. Up to that point, only three Europeans had ever been there: the aristocrat and explorer Teleki, his assistant von Höhnel, and the professional elephant hunter Arthur Neumann. There were large numbers of elephants, and from his main camp, which was later called Loima Hills, Shundi began his raids all over the region, including northwest Uganda where the Karamojans lived. He sold to Ethiopian chiefs slaves and ivory from one end of the frontier to the other. The traditional markets, as well as being far away on the coast, had been abolished by the British and Germans in their battle against slavery.

Shundi continued terrorizing the area for a while, establishing himself as lord and master and taking a hundred local beauties for his harem. What he didn't take into consideration was that the natives weren't as meek and resigned as the people near Kilimanjaro. The Karamojan warriors, sick of his atrocities, prepared an ambush so perfect that, even though they were armed only with spears and clubs, they slaughtered Shundi and his henchmen, chopping them into pieces and leaving the remains for the buzzards and hyenas. With this, they wiped from the face of the earth those to whom destiny had bestowed the unique opportunity to take the most famous elephant in Africa.

The person who killed the record elephant was a slave named Senoussi who met the beast by surprise in a forest at the foot of Kilimanjaro. This account contradicts some reports that I have read that state Senoussi pursued this great elephant for weeks before finally slaying him. No one knew of the existence of this elephant. He must have spent his life with abundant food and water in remote wooded valleys and mountain slopes. Only when he felt he was growing old, with his strength fading, did he descend to easier terrain, which was where he met Senoussi. Fortunately the slave, unsophisticated and primitive though he was, stood amazed by this gigantic tusker and watched him for some time before firing. Thanks to Senoussi, we have some idea of what the king of elephants must have been like. As the slave later recounted in Zanzibar, the elephant was not very large but his shoulders and haunches were well-developed, perhaps because of the weight he carried in his mouth. The tusks reached the ground and the points curved inward until they nearly touched. When he walked, he had to lift his head to avoid tripping over them.

Senoussi, with his muzzleloader, got as close as he could and fired, hitting the elephant in the lungs. The animal took off at a run, but stopped less than 300 yards away, where he stood, trembling, until he collapsed. So ended the great patriarch of Kilimanjaro, slain by a slave, ignorant, poorly fed, and even more poorly armed.

Some huge tusks in the National Museum of Kenya in Nairobi. The biggest two weigh over 170 pounds. each.

When Shundi saw the tusks, he couldn't believe his good fortune. But when he arrived in Zanzibar, he found that the tusks had exceeded his expectations and had caused a sensation among the ivory dealers, who were used to seeing amazing examples every day. There were many offers, but Shundi sold the tusks to an American company in Zanzibar which imported and exported ivory. They paid almost £1,000, or $5,000, which, in those days, was a real fortune.

As they had in East Africa, the enormous pair of tusks made a great impression in Europe and America. The Germans tried to buy them, sending the naturalist-traveler C. G. Schillings (the first to take night photos of lions using a complicated system of wires and flashes) to Zanzibar, but they could not arrive at a price and the tusks went to the United States. After they were exhibited all over, including at the famous jeweler Tiffany in New York, the British company of Landsberger, Humble & Co. imported them and separated them. The British Museum bought the left one in 1901 while the right went to the Sheffield cutlery manufacturing company Joseph Rodgers & Sons, which displayed it in the entrance of their showroom. In 1932, The left tusk was bought by W. B. Wolstenholme, also of Sheffield but he kept it only briefly. Noted London taxidermists Rowland Ward Ltd. mediated its sale to the British Museum, where it was reunited with its right side after thirty-two years.

For many years the tusks were left in the basement and were not exhibited to the public, but could be seen only by private arrangement with the conservator. In 1978, if I remember correctly, they decided to exhibit them in the Kensington Museum, where they were mounted on wooden stands and set on the first floor. They were taken off display again in 1982 and returned to the basement, out of visitors' sight. The argument was that by removing them they were condemning hunting. As an old elephant hunter, the sight of those tusks always fascinated me and I never tired of looking at them during my frequent visits to London. I liked to imagine how Senoussi felt when he had them in his sights. I expect he probably felt as though he would die from sheer excitement.

On arrival in Zanzibar, the "fresh" tusks weighed 235 pounds for the left and 226 for the right, for a total of 461 pounds. They were officially weighed again in 1962 and they had slimmed down to 226 and 214 pounds respectively. The loss of twenty-one pounds is due to the fact that ivory is organic and loses weight with the passage of time.

The left tusk, a little shorter than the right, was the heaviest and measured ten feet, two inches long and was twenty-four inches in diameter at the thickest part. The right was three inches longer and twenty-three inches in diameter, which means that the two were quite symmetric. This indicates that the elephant lived a quiet and sedentary life—because, if he had to travel far, it is likely that he would have snagged the tusks on rocks, stones, or tree stumps, damaging or breaking them.

Nothing gives a better idea of their size than a photograph taken outside the door of the Zanzibar house of E. D. Moore, agent of the U.S. company that bought them. They are as tall as the door and need two people to hold them up. Their value has been calculated several times, but it is impossible to come up with a concrete figure. I suppose that, since they hold the absolute world record and are truly one of a kind, an international auction would bring a very high price, probably over £1,000,000. Years ago, the Rowland Ward Company of London got the authorization from the British Museum to make several pairs of fiberglass replicas. They looked exactly like the originals and were destined for museums and private collectors who wanted copies of these renowned tusks.

It is possible that there at one time existed tusks that were even bigger. I have seen references that larger tusks existed, but I have been unable to verify the stories. In 1872, the explorer Sir Richard Burton spoke of a pair of tusks sent to the King of Portugal from Mozambique that weighed 280 pounds each. Von Höhnel, aide to the aristocratic Teleki, wrote in his memoirs about the exploration of Lake Rudolf that the native guide who led them was a well-known ivory merchant named Jumbe Kimemeta. Kimemeta knew of a tusk that weighed 264 pounds, but the Europeans were never able to see it. At the Grand Exposition of Paris in 1900, supposedly a tusk from Dahomey in West Africa was on display that weighed in at 260 pounds. I've tried to find out more about it, but was never able to run down more than that one simple reference, which is suspicious. Something that large just doesn't disappear.

It's possible that there have been bigger tusks than the great pair from Kilimanjaro, but they are the only ones we are able to verify, and so they hold the record for all time. On Rowland Ward's list, the tusks in the two, three, and four spots weigh as follows:

No. 2—192 and 189 pounds
No. 3—198 and 174 pounds
No. 4—185 and 183 pounds

As you can see, these fine trophies are considerably below the record pair. Sadly, no elephants exist now in Africa that can even come close to these numbers. Every day there are fewer, even in parks and reserves . . . and one day they will only be a memory.

THE BIG ONE-TUSKER OF DEBIO

Many years ago I had a camp in the Debio zone, in the extreme southwestern part of the Sudan near the border with what is now Zaire, beside the road that goes from Yambio to Tambura. The area was woodsy, almost untouched and full of some excellent elephant. Angelo Dacey and I were the only hunters who regularly operated there, and with patience and a little luck it was not difficult to get good trophies. I remember the large number of fine bulls that wandered the area, until an excessive number of hunters, not to mention the poachers, practically wiped them out.

I was with a good friend trying to use up our licenses. The price of ivory kept going up and ivory hunting was still profitable. Following our daily routine, we would get up early, eat a good breakfast, and after dawn we would go to work, full of good spirits and hoping to find a "monster" eating a mango or refreshing himself beside a stream. We never lost hope.

We put the minimum of equipment necessary for hunting into the car, usually taking some canvas water bags, some fruit juice and a packet of dried fruit, which weighs little but give quick boosts of energy. As is my custom, I gave the first chance to my buddy who loaded his .375 magnum with solids while I loaded my inseparable .416 Rigby with four solids of 410 grains.

We left the small camp and headed toward Tambura. After ten miles we left the main road, headed west and entered the forest on a path we had opened and that allowed us to drive a car about five miles farther into the interior of the zone. We then took off on foot, walking many hours and lots and lots of miles. Elephant hunting is like that, and in all my years of doing it I've never found any other way but to walk . . . and walk . . . and walk.

Slowly we drove the five miles along the trail until we reached a clearing where we left the car in the shade of a tree, watched by a native. We planned to take a look at the area, starting with the hills we could see rising out of the tropical forest. We knew that elephants would seek refuge in their lush valleys during the day.

Taking the water and other provisions, we began walking with rifles loaded and the safeties on. The car was parked on the high part of one of the valleys so we began descending, this time to the east. The long trail finally lead us into a thick and beautiful forest, made up of great trees that formed a kind of dome. We called it "the cathedral." It was the perfect name for this lost paradise of nature. We moved farther into the forest, following the path beaten by the elephants, silently and in single file. At one point a large group of colobus monkeys observed us from the branches, grooming their black and white fur.

We had advanced more than a mile when the tracker stopped all of a sudden, gesturing at us to stay quiet and at the same time he pointed at some bushes ahead of us, where we saw the rump of an elephant, his tail slowly swaying. The first thing I did was check the direction of the wind, which was to our advantage. Besides being asleep, the elephant wouldn't be able to smell us. All we could see of the animal was his behind. From it, we could tell that the elephant was old and corpulent. The clue was his tail, which only had a few hairs left—a sure sign of old age.

From our position, it was impossible to see anything more of the elephant. Because I had more experience with this kind of hunting, we decided that I should try to situate myself where I could see the tusks so that we could then decide what to do. As we had already agreed, he would get the first shot.

Taking my .416 Rigby and leaving the others behind some thick trees, I started forward. I moved slowly until I was about ten yards from that rump, but I still couldn't see anything. I knelt down, hoping to see something between the under-

A big one-tusker of over 100 pounds.

brush and the elephant's feet. I was able to see the animal's trunk, smooth and light colored, which began moving slowly from left to right. My heart gave a jump when I saw, right in front of me, an enormous tusk with the point buried in the ground. My eyes popped at the sight and I strained to see the other tusk, but try as I could, I saw nothing. Fortunately, the elephant at that moment had an attack of politeness and shuffled three steps to one side. Now I could see through the vegetation that he only had one tusk, which was the one on the left. I was disappointed, but once I got a good look at that single tusk I could see that it weighed about 100 pounds, which was nothing to sneeze at.

The elephant remained quietly napping throughout all this and didn't stir when I slipped quietly back to the others. I explained what I saw and my friend said that he was not interested in a single tusk, no matter how big. I told him that it was really big but he insisted that he didn't want it. I asked him if he'd mind if I jumped ahead in hunting order and took it myself. "Be my guest," he said.

With all this resolved, I moved again toward the elephant and situated myself a few yards away. The animal had changed position and now had his side facing to the right with the vulnerable head and shoulder points covered by vegetation. I crept as far right as I could until I was near the point where I imagined the ear and brain to be. Slowly, I raised my rifle and aimed the sight of the .416 at where I expected the brain to be. From the other side of a barrier of leaves, I pulled the trigger. At the sound of the shot, the elephant fell like a rock, remaining on his side. I moved quickly toward him to see if I needed to get off another shot, only to find myself face to face with another elephant, ears wide in the listening position.

He was the young "askari" of the old fellow, which I had not seen or heard. I remained as still as a shadow about ten yards from the second elephant and only a few from the fallen one. Snorting, the animal moved away to my right and I sighed with relief. His tusks could not have weighed more than twenty-five pounds each and I would not have liked to kill him in self defense. I heard a noise almost at my feet and at the same time, something touched my leg. Instinctively, I jumped back, freeing myself from the fallen, but still living elephant, which was trying to get me by the ankle with his trunk. I fell backward hard, but before I could even say "ouch" the trunk tried to snag me again. I dragged myself away from the insistent tentacle and shot him again, to no effect. I quickly fired again and this time he was dead. I looked toward the askari, but I saw him escaping, thank God, and in a few moments he was out of sight.

The others arrived at that instant, scared to death. They'd seen everything and had feared for the worst. They had seen the elephant try to grab my leg, and they feared the "askari" might charge just as I was trying to extricate myself from the trunk of the "dead" elephant. Luckily, that did not happen.

After that scare, everything ended perfectly. The single tusk weighed 110 pounds and was of the best ivory, seven feet long, perfect and beautiful. When we removed it and my buddy got a look, he said that if only he'd known how big it was, he would have taken the first shot. I reminded him that I had told him several times and that he still hadn't wanted to go first. He replied that he hadn't believed me because in hunting nobody gets anything for free—in fact, it's the opposite!

ELEPHANTS WE WON'T FORGET

I've always been determined not to make my stories too sensational, and I have tried to stay away from the thrills and chills offered by some authors. This has always gone against my sense of what's right; however, there are times when something unexpected happens that results in a thrilling experience, such as the following tale of misfortune. I had been elephant hunting for many years when the following occurred.

The least expected thing can always happen, and no matter how much experience you have, you learn something every day. I was on safari in Loliondo in northern Tanzania in a piece of Masai territory that lies between the Serengeti National Park and the southern border of Kenya, a beautiful area with an altitude of about 6,500 feet. Here was a great natural reserve with an incredible number of animals. I took out eleven clients in three months, and I saw sixty-

The fruits of the hunt, 1966.

On the banks of the Galana River, Kenya, 1967.

Author with his .416 Rigby rifle and three pairs of tusks.

three lions during that period. I took eleven of them, all of which had luxurious manes.

There were also innumerable buffalo, every kind of antelope, and elephant. The situation for elephants was not so good, due to the fact that poachers were as active there as they were in the rest of Africa, killing as many as they could. In response, the elephants there had become the most aggressive we had ever seen. They had taken to heart the old saying, "If you want peace, prepare for war." The least demonstration of this aggressive behavior, frightening charges, was frequent as I was later to find out for myself.

I was on safari with two clients. We had already taken two lions and now wanted to concentrate on elephants. We'd already seen a number of them and had passed by inferior bulls, hoping to find better ones later. We left camp after breakfast. It had rained all night and the weather was cold and wet enough for me to put on long pants and an anorak. We made a few rounds in the Toyota to see if elephants had visited certain spots in the early morning, which they hadn't. We then headed for a valley a few miles away to see what we could find. We traveled away from the Grumeti River, and, after crossing a few canyons, we arrived at a narrow pass, which overlooked the entire valley.

Right away we saw a group of about forty elephants ambling to the right about a mile away. At that distance, we could only see that they were elephants, not whether there were any good bulls among them. We left the car in the care of Ali, the driver/mechanic, took our rifles, and started down the slope toward the elephants, after checking the direction of the wind. Our group was made up of the two clients, armed with a .458 and a .375 magnum respectively; me with my old .416 Rigby; and two gunbearers, Charles and Kiribai, the latter of whom had been with me for many years.

We moved within 150 yards of them in completely open territory, so we could see that there wasn't a single interesting trophy among them. We decided to go back and continue on to look for more. At the exact moment I gave my rifle to Kiribai, after unloading the chamber, the wind changed, carrying our scent directly to the elephants. They stopped in their tracks, trunks in the air and suddenly, as if they had been shot from cannons, they charged toward us at full speed. Normally when animals smell the hunters' scents, they simulate a charge but stop after a few yards, turn around, and run away like mad.

But this didn't happen. Two elephants, like so many locomotives, continued at full speed in our direction, trumpeting like crazy. I gave the order to run out of the direction of the wind and to hide in the scant underbrush, thinking,

Exceptional double of elephant and lion, Zambia, 1967. I shot these two animals with a .465 Nitro Express.

*Typical elephant of
Selous, Tanzania,
small body and
long tusks, 1984.*

*Zambia, 104 and
107 pounds,
Luangwa Valley, 1968.*

Author with an elephant from Zambia, 1971.

A perfect shot to the brain, the Sudan, 1983.

of course, that the elephants were about to stop. I was wrong about this and the violence of the attack increased every second, if such a thing is possible. My order to retreat arrived a little late as one of the clients, followed by Charles, made a straight line for the Toyota, breaking all records for that distance and never once even glancing back, they later put it.

Only the other client, Kiribai, and I remained in the line of fire, and we were losing more ground every second to those wretched animals. This desperate race lasted more than 300 yards, until I realized that the elephants were not going to stop and were getting closer every second. With this realization, I reached toward Kiribai for my .416 Rigby. As he passed it to me—we were both still racing at full Olympic-record speed—he loaded it. I took it and suddenly saw the chance to get out of the direction of the wind, which had again changed, so I hid behind the remains of a dry tree.

The elephants focused their attention on the client, who was nearly out of breath and barely thirty yards ahead of them. Although they could no longer smell him, he was close enough for even their myopic eyes to see him. I saw that I would have to go on the offensive or they would soon trample him into mush. At that moment the elephants were running toward me, the first at twenty yards and the second at twenty-five yards. I jumped out from my hiding place and gave forth a mighty yell to distract them, hoping to give the client a chance to escape. At the instant I shouted at them, they turned toward me without missing a beat, and there I was with two furious animals only a few steps away.

It was no laughing matter, faced with two enormous elephants whose sole mission at that moment was to crush me . . . and from my vantage point it looked as though they might be getting their wish soon. Putting the .416 Rigby to my shoulder, I aimed between the eyes of the first elephant, scarcely fifteen yards away—an elephant with ears up and head down, ready to trample me. When I pulled the trigger, instead of the desired detonation all I heard was a feeble "click." Meanwhile the bulk of the creature coming at me became greater and greater until it looked bigger than the Cathedral of Notre Dame in Paris.

Thanks to my years of experience in the field and the nerves God gave me (or better to say, didn't give me), I reacted at once, reloading as fast as I could, pushing another cartridge into the .416 and pulling the trigger at the same time. My nightmare collapsed seven yards away at the moment of impact from my bullet. As the first one fell, the second continued, without hesitation, toward me like a locomotive at full steam. With no chance to catch my breath or lower the rifle, I reloaded and fired another shot between the second elephant's eyes. It also fell like a ton of bricks.

I stood there for an instant, breathless. I had stopped those furies at seven and twelve yards even with the rifle jamming on the first shot—or so I thought at the time. After thanking God for saving me from a very difficult situation, I went over what had happened to cause the rifle to fail. The rifle had always been completely reliable, so what had happened? As it turned out, when Kiribai loaded it while running and under the pressure of the moment, he hadn't completely pulled back the magnum Mauser bolt of my .416, so it didn't grab the cartridge. It is a miracle that I lived to write about this happening, an event I can only describe as chilling. I didn't fail to get the moral offered by this chilling turn of events, or the fact that one of the most frightening moments in my life as a hunter came after many years in the field.

What made those elephants react so violently to our presence? The only explanation is that they had been so hunted and harassed by poachers who kill everything—male, female, small, large—they had decided to retaliate and to destroy their hated enemies. It was simply bad luck that we had encountered such a group. The more I thought about it, the more I realized the kind of danger we were in, including facing a double charge with a rifle that gave only a sickening "click." There is no doubt that divine intervention saved me. That is all it could have been, and I believe it with all may heart.

Of course I had to explain what happened to the game department in the town of Loliondo and justify it. You can't just go around killing whatever you please. An official of the department came and did a reckoning of what happened, taking measurements, distances, and positions, and collecting the elephants' tusks, which became government property. The next day when I saw the director of the game department in his office, he said that after all that happened he had only one rebuke for me and that was that I'd waited too long to shoot. Next time, he told me, "You really should do it a lot earlier!"

THE DEVIL OF DEBIO

Usually hunting stories are about the bagging of impressive specimens or fantastic trophies. This story is the opposite because the "guest of honor" is an old elephant without any tusks. The only thing distinguished about him was his reputation as a killer and the longing of the victimized population to get him out of the district or eliminate him—desires shared by the game department, which found in this elephant a fount of endless problems.

I had my camp beside the road from Yambio and Tambura in southwestern Sudan, near the Zairian border. The place was called Debio and offered magnificent opportunities for hunting elephant and bongo. Located in a tropical area, the terrain alternated between clearings and thick forest, which made hunting difficult. Heavy rains every afternoon in those late-March days added to the difficulty.

I was in Debio with my friend Pablo Galvez, seeking elephant and bongo. Pablo not only had experience in Africa but he also has exceptional instincts. On top of that, he is good company, and everything was sailing along nicely. A few days before, he had shot a record male bongo, so there were smiling faces all around. We were after the almost mythical "great elephant," but most of those we had seen were inferior bulls with tusks smaller than the minimum allowed. Then, one day we had a colossus right in front of us, with tusks weighing at least 110 pounds each. At the very instant that Pablo raised his .375 magnum, we were attacked by furious bees. They almost stung us to death, and we only escaped by running like lunatics and slapping at them. The elephant took the opportunity to head in the opposite direction.

In Debio I'd heard the natives speak many times about an elephant they hated and called "the Devil." It was an old solitary bull without tusks, and it was extraordinarily aggressive, trampling farms and attacking the native population. It had already left three dead. It was strange that I'd never seen him, considering how much I traveled the area. Destiny, however, planned for us to meet when I least expected it, on an afternoon when we decided to stay in camp to rest from our many wanderings and to allow Pablo to catch up with his journal, where he recorded the events of each day exactly as they had happened.

We got up after a pleasant siesta and put folding chairs under a shady tree. Pablo wrote, asking me occasional questions, while I leafed through some stamp collecting magazines. Our quiet afternoon was interrupted by the sound of the excited voices of natives. Looking up, we saw them coming, accompanied by an out-of-breath local man on a bicycle. I don't speak Zande, the language of that area, but by using English, Arabic, and Swahili we managed to ascertain that the cyclist had come almost nose to nose with an enormous lone elephant on the road only a mile from camp. The elephant was eating mangoes, which they love and which come from big shade trees planted along the roads by the colonial administration.

This wouldn't be the first time we'd taken fine trophies along the same highway, so this was great news. We threw on some clothes (we'd been wearing bathing suits), and I grabbed my .416 Rigby while Pablo grabbed his .375 magnum. We took off running. With the animal so close and on the same highway, according to the man who had sighted him, we wanted to avoid making too much noise, so we left the car behind and went on foot, walking and keeping an eye out until we reached the place where the elephant had been seen. He wasn't there, but heaps of leaves, branches, and half-eaten mangoes indicated that he wasn't far away.

A few moments later we heard him moving behind a thick stand of trees, breaking branches with his bulk. Tracks in the soft earth showed they belonged to a very large, old animal, which raised our hopes of getting a good trophy. Feeling hopeful, we approached the place the noise was coming from, being careful to stay in the face of the wind and with the animal toward us to make sure he didn't catch our smell and run. In the group were my chief tracker, Yuma, a representative of the game department named Edward, the man who had seen the elephant, and two or three more who tagged along hoping to get some meat if we got lucky. Elephant meat is much coveted in that area.

The elephant had had enough to eat and was now slowly moving into the forest. Being careful of the wind, we were able to get close enough to see him traveling very slowly to the right. The first thing we recognized was his enor-

The Devil of Debio.

mous bulk and the second was that he did not have even the tiniest vestige of tusks. Without saying a word we began to withdraw when Edward and the local man excitedly told me that this was the marauding elephant and that I should kill it as had already been okayed by the game department. The truth is that I didn't have the least interest in plugging the poor thing with its harmless face. Worse than their insistence was the threat that Edward would shoot him with his dirty, mistreated .458 rifle with its worn-out barrel, so I reluctantly accepted the role of executioner.

I left them waiting by some trees and approached the elephant to impose the sentence already passed. The animal continued shuffling along, and I was filled with doubts. What if, instead of killing a murderer, I was about to dispatch an honest senior citizen? With these doubts in my head I crept within a dozen yards of the elephant. While I was waiting for him to put himself into profile for a better shot, he suddenly perceived something—I was very close—and without the slightest pause he hurled himself at me, snorting furiously.

In a second that implacable bulk had been transformed into a blitzkrieging jungle tank, eyes gleaming with fury, and with the unhealthy intention of trampling me. The attack was so fast, furious, and unexpected that I barely had enough time to raise the .416 to my shoulder and put a bullet into that wrinkled forehead that was almost on top of me. The animal stopped at the shot, turning his right knee. But he recovered in a second and with an agility surprising for his size, twisted his body through the dense vegetation to his right and vanished before I could do more than get off another bad shot. I ran after him but I could no longer see him. I could hear the noise as he crashed ahead, breaking everything in his path in his crazy flight.

I was very annoyed and returned to the group. Pablo had measured the distance between the elephant and me, at the time I had fired, at a mere six yards. After cursing the elephant, myself, and every wretched living thing, I quickly went after the beast along the open trail. There were some splatters of blood along the way, which showed that my bullet had hit too high and missed the brain. The day was waning and the sun starting to disappear behind the horizon, which only served to increase my concern. To leave that wounded elephant in a populated area was one of the last things I wanted. When the animal crossed the main road at last, there was hardly any light. We were forced to give up the search, but marked the trail so we could take up the chase the next day. We went back to camp in really bad humor. To make things worse, it rained for several hours overnight. I worried that the rain had wiped out the elephant's tracks, making it impossible to follow the trail the next day.

As I had feared, the tracks were nearly erased. Yuma, though, was an outstanding tracker and bit by bit we followed the track, finding it, losing it, making our agonizing way along. It grew hotter and hotter as the day passed; stickier and stickier we became until we were sweating as if we were in a sauna. We saw bongo tracks fresh that same morning and from the trees a family of colobus monkeys with their beautiful white fur watched us, their faces curious as they seemed to wonder what kind of insects we were looking for in our slow progression as we peeked under leaves and shrubs, touching and looking at everything.

At exactly noon, after nearly seven hours of tramping through the steaming bush and thanks to Yuma's skill (at only five feet, two inches he is a true forest gnome), we saw the elephant under a tree at the far end of a clearing. We held our breaths for fear that the slightest sound would spook him and he would escape, which would be much more serious this time. With the .416 Rigby I tried to approach the elephant while the others remained quietly watching the show from the stands. There was nothing between the elephant and us. I moved closer step by step, completely cautious. But when I had gone only a short distance, the elephant turned and strolled to my end of the clearing, passing only about ten yards in front of me. Saint Hubert must have wanted to compensate me for the worry and distress that elephant had caused because he positioned the old fellow before me like a target at the fair, an opportunity I was more than happy to take advantage of. The moment the shot sounded he fell like a rock. The solid bullet entered the right ear and exited through the left, passing completely through the brain. As he fell, I heard cheers behind me followed by slaps on the back from the smiling Pablo. I gave a sigh of relief equal to the elephant's huge snort when he had attacked me the afternoon before. We saw that my first bullet had struck the animal high on the forehead. His charge had been so unexpected that all I had the chance to do was get off one shot at his head to try to stop him. I was able to get that one shot in thanks to the magnificent handling qualities of the .416 Rigby. Without such a gun, the elephant would surely have squashed me. The projectile passed considerably above the brain and only caused him to pause for a second when his right knee turned, but it stopped his charge and that was what mattered.

The elephant was very old and the atrophied sockets showed that he had never had tusks. On one side he had scars from an old injury, and we retrieved a lead bullet of the kind used in old muzzleloaders. I didn't want to know more about a stupid poacher who would deliberately shoot at an elephant with no tusks. Perhaps this was the cause of the elephant's aggressive character. Often the sloppy practices of inexpert or stupid poachers—or even those who know better—force animals into behaviors they've never shown before by abandoning them wounded and not bothering to finish them off.

At least this was a happy ending. We gave the meat to the locals, and Pablo went on to get his elephant within a few days, which had large and perfect tusks. The "Devil of Debio" had an unheroic end, ending up in the stomachs of his former victims, leaving as the only sign of his passage through this world some bracelets made from the hairs of his tail.

THE MARAUDING ELEPHANTS OF SALE

In August of 1982 I was on safari in northern Tanzania with my friend and countryman Vicente Muñoz-Pomer, companion of many travels under tropical skies and a great sporting hunter. Everything was going well. Among other things, the first day of safari Vicente got a magnificent lion, which was terrific because he has a weakness for lions. Things couldn't be going better and we passed the days hunting, filming, enjoying the landscape, and chatting. Like all good Valencians, we never run out of conversation.

One day at lunchtime, the chief of the game department, Abdallah Kilo, came to camp and asked for a hand in resolving a problem. He had received an urgent request for help from the area of Sale, seventy miles south of my camp and forty miles from the administrative center of Loliondo. Elephants were attacking farms and destroying everything, forcing the inhabitants to watch the destruction of months of hard work in only a few days. The game department was full of good intentions but unfortunately lacked the necessities to offer much help, being short of proper vehicles, guns, and ammunition. Abdallah Kilo explained the situation to see if I could help. The area had become something of a battle zone, and a day didn't pass without requests for help from Sale.

I wanted to help them in any way I could, as I had done many times before during my years of hunting in Africa. It also gave Vicente the opportunity to participate in elephant control, an offer he was delighted to accept. I told

Abdallah Kilo that we'd be happy to help but that Vicente should be given the first shot. I've reached a point in my life that I've hunted so much that now I prefer helping others to do it. I enjoy their enthusiasm as much as I enjoy advising them on how to do things without me pulling a trigger. Abdallah agreed, and we decided to give the area the once-over in order to properly arrange things.

According to the agreement, we left two days later for Sale, stopping in Loliondo to pick up Abdallah. The trip took us along a bad road for seventy miles, so it took at least four hours in the Toyota. Besides Vicente and I were my two gunbearers Kiribai and Ali, a Masai. In Loliondo we picked up Abdallah and some game scouts and, without wasting time, headed for Sale, which is located amidst some mountains in a low, hot area where the Sonyo tribe lives.

The plan was to look around the areas where the elephants were getting into mischief, check out the lay of the land, and come back with enough food and equipment to last three or four days. We brought a box of bottled water, sandwiches, beer, and cans of fruit enough for the day, planning to return to camp in the afternoon to organize the expedition to Sale with everything we needed.

We brought our rifles just in case: Vicente brought his .416 made by Dumoulin in Belgium and I brought my old Rigby .416. As a backup, I brought my .375 magnum.

We arrived at the main village about nine a.m., dusty and curious to check out the situation. Before we had even stopped the Toyota, we were surrounded by dozens of vociferous people, each one claiming to know where to find the hated animals. I was translating the Swahili for Vicente, which was pretty funny. According to some of these poor people, there were at least 200,000 elephants and the tusks of the smallest one weighed at least 120 pounds each. I had to demand silence to put a stop to such tales and begin a conversation with an old man with a face like a saint, someone who I hoped would be less likely to have such flights of fantasy. He told us that it was a rare night when the elephants did not raid some of the farms. By day they hid in the incredibly dense forest that extended beyond the farmland—so dense that it was hard to get through, due to the thorny shrubs that covered everything.

They showed us tracks fresh from that morning, which had been made by a group of six elephants crossing one of many farms and doing a lot of damage in the process. They had destroyed more than they ate. They had returned to the dense forest to wait out the hottest time of day so that they could get back to grazing later in the afternoon. We decided to wait for them to see if we could get a look and perhaps a few shots at them. After a long walk in semicircular pattern, we sat in the shade of a tree, took out our provisions, and had lunch, waiting for the elephants to give signs of life. It was midday and very hot, so we decided to take things easy.

We had rejected the offers of more than fifty people to serve as guides, only accepting four Sonyo warriors who seemed better bets because of their knowledge of the area and elephants. While we were waiting, I sent the Sonyos

*Vicente Muñoz-Pomer with the author and the marauding elephants of Sale,
Tanzania, 1982.*

to check around to see if they could find any trace of the elephants, thus speeding things along a little so we wouldn't have to wait until four or five o'clock
when the elephants again began their wanderings.

At two o'clock on the dot two of them came back and said they'd found the
elephants napping not far away. This was unexpectedly good news. We quickly
grabbed our rifles, loaded them, put on the safeties, and silently followed the
guides in single file. After a short walk, we found the other two Sonyos who
signaled with their spears toward a certain spot. We could hear the unmistakable sound of an elephant chomping on a branch. Slowly, and after checking
the direction of the wind, we crept forward until we could see the elephants
through the bushes.

Vicente had his .416 ready and as a simple precaution, I took mine from
Kiribai. Abdallah tightly gripped his .375 magnum and asked me for more
solids—he seemed to think this was going to turn into some kind of Normandy
Invasion. I told him to calm down and, as a matter of precaution, I put him first
in line so he wouldn't shoot anybody by mistake. We cautiously approached
the animals, which were quite relaxed, but when we were twenty yards from
them they seemed to receive some marching orders, so off they walked, passing

us from left to right. I signaled Vicente and he fired at the closest bull, hitting him in the shoulder and knocking him down. At the first shot the elephants broke formation and spaced out in the tall bush, looking in our direction and making a ruckus with their bellows. Again, I pointed a bull out to Vicente and he shot him cleanly through the head. I shot the first elephant again as he was trying to get up. With all the noise and the Sonyos running back and forth, the elephants did a half turn and stampeded away. They were out of sight within seconds, leaving the two dead elephants and a sudden and complete silence.

Vicente was so happy he was grinning from ear to ear and so was the rest of the expedition. Everything had come out perfectly, and after taking some photos and the tusks, we began the long trek back to camp. We arrived well after dark, exhausted after having been up for nearly twenty hours. After dinner we decided to rest the next day and hunt only near the camp. We would return to Sale the day after to finish off the job.

After a repetition of the activities of the first day, we arrived at Sale where they were again waiting for us as if we represented the Marshall Plan. Everyone had seen thousands of elephants, enormous, huge and all that. We chose to leave with the same four Sonyos who had accompanied us before. After seeing tracks and studying the elephants' movements, we deduced that this new group of habitual sackers of farms were hidden in a place thick with thorny underbrush. We stuck our heads into this without thinking twice. Almost immediately our clothes were so snagged by thorns that we looked like a new brand of Swiss cheese.

We slowly followed the tracks and two hours passed before we heard them at last. We were very cautious of our movements and constantly used matches to check the direction of the wind. The little cloud of smoke left when you put matches out with your fingers will indicate the softest breeze. This is very important in this kind of hunting. Step by step we approached until we could see the gray bulk of the elephants, half hidden in the woods.

This time the terrain presented a different problem, and I explained to Vicente in a low voice that it was unlikely that he could get a shot at more than one. As soon as they moved, they would be out of sight because there were so many trees and big bushes. This time there were seven elephants with the two largest to our right. We were in the middle of the trail the animals normally used, so I indicated to Vicente to move a few steps to the right where he could get a better view of the first bull. I would stay in the path in case they tried to escape in that direction.

At my signal, he fired at the bull, which crashed to the ground with the sound of tearing branches, a .416 bullet in the brain. The rest of the band raced away at full speed and vanished into the jungle, but the only rule in big-game hunting is that there are no rules, and the other big bull turned around and came at us like a locomotive, right down the path where I was standing, his ears up and a nasty look on his face. I had my .416 Rigby ready to fire but wanted to give Vicente the chance to shoot. With no need now to be quiet, I shouted at him to fire immediately, which he did, stopping the charge ten yards away, as we later measured. On impact, the animal turned to our right which permitted a second shot. He fell close to his companion.

Thank God, everything ended well and it was an unforgettable experience for Vicente—there are very few chances like that possible in Africa today. To shoot four elephants in two hunting sessions is serious business, and it made me remember those days when elephants were a plague in many areas and they were hunted by the dozens. Vicente was able to relive for two days what had been our way of life years ago, so now he could understand why we followed the "elephant trail" with so much enthusiasm.

THE DOMESTICATION OF THE AFRICAN ELEPHANT

I have read that the African elephant was never domesticated again after the Carthaginians trained them for war and Hannibal used them to cross the Alps in his conquest of Rome. It is said that the art was lost in North Africa centuries ago. I fear that those who believe that are badly informed. In modern times African elephants are being domesticated again in a positive and satisfactory way, with attempts dating back to 1879.

King Leopold II of Belgium was the founder of the International Association for the Exploration and Civilization of Central Africa in 1876. It was renamed the Committee for the Study of the Upper Congo in 1879, and after the Berlin Conference in 1885 it was again renamed the Congo Free State. Leopold believed that trained elephants could be valuable in opening up the huge territory in Central Africa, traveling through the forests without roads or highways. They were the only creatures capable of crossing those natural obstacles and of carrying cargo and merchandise.

Considering the former domestication of the African elephant precedent enough to put their plan into action, Leopold brought four elephants from India in 1879, accompanied by thirteen specialists in their capture and training. They arrived from Bombay, together with an Englishman named Carter, who had been consul in Baghdad. They disembarked in Masani, to the south of what is now Dar es Salaam, Tanzania. The objective was to reach Karema, one of the first European establishments on the shores of Lake Tanganyika, which was to be the center of the capture and training of African elephants, using the methods and experience of the Indians.

Three Belgians, Dr. van den Heuvel, Mr. Dutalis, and Mr. Popelin, were added to the expedition. Along with an Englishman named Stokes, they arrived at Karema on 14 December 1879, accompanied by only two elephants—the other two had died on the way. A little later a third one died, which made the plan impossible, so Carter decided to head back to the coast with the last remaining elephant, the Indian trainers, and the porters.

The long string of porters was slowly heading toward the coast when they were attacked by 3,000 Rugaruga warriors at Pimboni, warriors sent by the Arab chiefs

Elephant domestication school in Gangala-na-Bodio, Zaire. This is the only place in Africa where the elephant has been domesticated.

Two captured young elephants, to be trained at Gangala-na-Bodio in the Zaire.

Mirambo and Simba who were in the business of annihilating everyone. The guards contracted in Zanzibar to protect the expedition abandoned it, fleeing without doing battle. Carter died along with his men, bringing Leopold II's first try to a dramatic end. No one else tried to domesticate African elephants for many years.

In 1900 King Leopold decided to try again, this time in the Api area of northern Congo where there were lots of elephants. He put Commandant Laplume in charge, who founded the Elephant Domestication School in Api.

To start with, they tried various systems to catch young elephants. Without the necessary experience, the first thing they tried was catching them in pits. They only caught two, and these two died before reaching Api. After several more disasters, Laplume and his team tried one of the methods used in India, Siam, and Burma. This method is called *keddah*, and is based on the premise of luring elephants into a large corral. Only the desired animals are kept and the rest released. Trained animals helped drive the elephants into the corral but poor Laplume didn't have any of these, so the job was tremendous. Finally they caught a cow and her calf. With no way to get elephants in the traditional Indian fashion, they decided on a system that was more cruel but ultimately effective—they killed the cow and kept the calf. By 1910 they had thirty-five trained elephants at the Api school.

Following the death of King Leopold on 17 December 1909, King Albert enthusiastically continued the work of domesticating Congo elephants. (The country ceased to be the Congo Free State and became a Belgian colony on 17 November 1908, when it became known as the Belgian Congo.) During World War I, King Albert supported the school out of his own pocket while Laplume went to Europe as part of the Congo Volunteer Corps. Laplume was taken prisoner by the Germans and was not able to return to Api until 1918.

Because he hadn't gotten the anticipated results with his domestication practices, Laplume brought four Indian experts to teach their successful methods to the Congolese. But one problem followed another, and the results were not encouraging, so the mahouts returned home.

Laplume kept at it with great patience and dedication until finally, in 1925, his crowning achievement consisted of twenty perfectly trained elephants carrying cargo and pulling carts as they did 2,000 years ago in what are now Libya and Tunisia. But now there were new problems. Foremost was a shortage of elephants. After twenty-five years of chasing them, hunting them, and capturing them, there were very few left near Api, so Laplume decided to seek new territory and sent his assistant, Lieutenant Offerman, on an exploratory trip. After some hard prospecting, Offerman found the ideal place some 350 miles to the east, toward the border of what was then the Anglo-Egyptian Sudan, in a place called Gangala-na-Bodio on the banks of the Dungu River where the school remains to this day.

Once the new Station for the Capture and Domestication of Elephants was established at Gangala-na-Bodio, things got better fast. Offerman was in charge and over time became one of the leading authorities on the African elephant, discovering many formerly unknown elements of the lives of these giant animals. These studies interested me greatly, and I was fortunate to be able to visit the station in Gangala-na-Bodio several times over the years.

Contrary to the dreams of King Leopold II, the domesticated animals in the Congo became a mere tourist attraction with the invention of tractors and all-terrain vehicles. But at least the experiments showed that they could be trained and put into the service of man, just as they had been in ancient Carthage. Time, money, and effort had paid off.

The negative side was that the hand of man nearly destroyed this titanic effort. Everything was fine until 1962, but after the so-called rebellion in 1963, Gangala-na-Bodio was sacked by mobs of rioters. Many elephants died and the operation nearly brought to the point of ruin. Luckily, some of the trainers escaped with their elephants and hid in the woods for months until the coast was clear. But when they returned to Gangala-na-Bodio, they found it in a terrible state.

They tried to reorganize the Station for Capture and Domestication but a lack of funds impeded progress and even with the best intentions in the world, the station began slowly disintegrating. In January 1989 I had the honor to be the guest of president Mobutu of Zaire and among the places I visited was Gangala-na-Bodio, where there were only four trained elephants and another two calves in the process of being trained.

The use for these animals has been limited to transporting people to the least accessible parts of the Garamba National Park, where there are no roads and plenty of marshy areas. I recently did a study and made some recommendations on the exotic method of transportation, which I felt to be of interest.

My study saw the possibilities of increasing the number of trained elephants in the "flotilla" as quickly as possible. The elephants were to be used by tourists who come to visit the park in Garamba, the last place in Africa where the rare northern white rhino (*Ceratotherium simun cottoni*) can be seen. There are many other attractions as you leave the park's administrative center at Nagero, especially its remoteness.

The last time I went to Gangala-na-Bodio, less than an hour from Nagero, I met an old man who had been in charge of the bar and rest-house for fifty years. He remembered me right away and offered me the fresh lemonade he recalled that I always drank. He asked if I still hunted elephants, which showed how great was his memory that allowed him to place me as soon as he saw me, as if many years had not passed.

•••

CHAPTER V

The Bongo,
Phantom of the Forest

The bongo is the trophy every serious hunter who goes on an African safari longs for and dreams about. Very few, comparatively, get one due to the difficulties in hunting it. It is completely adapted to its environment, and is born, lives, and dies in the dense equatorial and tropical forests where it is almost impossible to spot. Even though numerically there may be more than many experts say, it has evolved into a phantom species, surrounded by mystery and legend which have helped make it one of the most desired trophies in the hunting world. I've always been fascinated by this beautiful and little-known animal and have dedicated a good part of my life to its study.

The bongo belongs to the *Tragelaphini* tribe, which is to say it has spiral horns twisted around themselves, the two horns curving to look somewhat like a lyre. Two well-known subspecies exist. The first, scientifically known as *Tragelaphus euryceros euryceros*, lives in an area extending through West and Central Africa, from Sierra Leone to northwest Zaire and southwest Sudan. The second, *Tragelaphus euryceros isaaci* is found in mountainous parts of Kenya.

Some scientists believe there are two other subspecies, both in the old Belgian Congo (now Zaire). *Tragelaphus euryceros cooperi* lives in the great Ituri forest and has stronger, thicker horns than the *Tragelaphus euryceros katanganus*, which is lighter in color and with more dense stripes, which trace the sides from top to bottom. I must confess that I've never been able to consistently note these differences, and Rowland Ward only refers to the Kenyan variety and the one found in West and Central Africa.

The bongo was discovered in western equatorial Africa during the first part of the nineteenth century. It was first described by Ogilvy in 1836 following his study of horns and a complete skull from Gabon. The species from British East Africa was not recorded until the twentieth century, when Mr. F. W. Isaac

Bongo killed in Bengangai, the Sudan, 1974.

took one in Eldoma Ravine in April 1902. Thomas analyzed it that same year and named the species *Tragelaphus euryceros isaaci* in the hunter's honor. Until the middle of 1910 only four of these bongos had been taken by Europeans. One, a female, was shot by Kermit Roosevelt at the Mau Escarpment on safari with his father, former U.S. president Theodore Roosevelt.

The bongo is a robust animal, the largest of all forest antelopes with a height between 47 and 55 inches at the withers, and a weight of about 500 pounds. Those measurements are for adult males, while females are about twenty-five percent smaller. The legs of the bongo are strong and short, perfectly adapted for carrying it across the difficult terrain where it lives.

The males are a bright chestnut color, which gets darker as they age. The females are redder in color, which helps to differentiate between males and females in the herd. This can be a great help to the hunter trying to select a trophy while peering through a veil of foliage.

A short mane runs down the bongo's neck and back, and it has vertical white stripes that shoot down the sides. There are usually between eight and fourteen of these, but the number of stripes differs from one side to another, often noticeably. The face is darker than the rest of the body with a white half moon between the eyes and two white spots on the cheeks—altogether a beautiful animal. Perhaps because of their mountain habitat and diet, the Kenyan *Tragelaphus euryceros isaaci* is heavier, the males are darker and the horns are potentially longer.

Because both males and females have horns, the hunter needs to check carefully before pulling the trigger. The thickness of the horn is one way, but size is always a clue since the males are much larger than the females. It is easy to pick out the males because, besides their size, the horns are sturdier all the way along the horn, and the tips are parallel or point outward. The females have more delicate horns, stretching back with the tips nearly touching. The tips of the horns are an amber color, which adds to the beauty of the prize. I have taken examples where this coloration extends four inches or more.

The record-length horn for the subspecies found in West and Central Africa is thirty-six inches, following the curve from base to tip. To be listed in Rowland Ward's record class, the minimum is twenty-six inches. The Kenyan bongo record is forty inches, with twenty-six also the minimum.

Officially, bongos can be found in eleven countries in West and Central Africa, but quantities vary greatly from one country to another. I've had the opportunity to visit all the countries where they live and this is the situation in 1994:

SIERRA LEONE: Because of the population explosion and the resulting decrease in habitat, the bongo has become increasingly rare in this country. A very few can be found in the southeast in the areas of Pendembu, Joru, Potoru, Pujehum, and Fairo. There has been no news of any being taken there in the last few years, and personally, I've only seen the track of one male, and that was a long time ago in 1962.

LIBERIA: The civil war is having a very negative effect on the population and distribution of bongo because they are being killed for food. Before the hostilities, there were good numbers of them, with many excellent trophies. Most were to be found in the eastern part of the territory near the border with the Ivory Coast, from the Tchien district in the north to Webo, Peluke, and Juarzon in the south along the Duabe River. Because of the political situation, it is now impossible to hunt in Liberia and to get reliable information about the status of the bongo today.

IVORY COAST: Bongo are more or less distributed throughout the southwestern part of the country in the areas of Tulepleu, Guiglo, Subre, Tai, Grabo and along the Hana and San Pedro Rivers. Because there has been a total ban on hunting in effect for many years in the Ivory Coast, there are still bongo; in fact, it is said that the bongo population is increasing.

GHANA: Due to the loss of their natural habitat, the number of bongos has fallen greatly to the point where they are very rare. A few still live in the Kakum forest in the southwest, and there are a few head south of Kumasi and along the Bia and Tano Rivers where they are protected. Many years ago I had

*A magnificent
Sudanese bongo, with
33 inch horns shot by
the author near Debio,
the Sudan, 1976.*

*Bongo shot in the area
of the Shanga River,
Cameroon, 1992.*

the rare opportunity to see two females and a baby drying themselves in the sun after a rainy night, but I never saw a male.

TOGO: Years ago a few were seen in two places: the mountain forests of Klute, south of Sokode, and the Lokulu forest. The most recent information is negative, and it is possible that the bongo is now extinct in Togo.

CAMEROON: Bongo are widely distributed in the southern part of the country, with most of these found in the southeast, in the area between the Yokaduma/Molundu road and the Sangha River to the east. In this area there are bongos everywhere, giving the hunter ample opportunity to take one. This is one of the best natural reserves for these animals in all Africa. I know this area well and have shot many bongos there with my safari clients. In five weeks between April and May 1992, I saw fifty-three bongos, a truly surprising number. This was in the extreme southeastern point of Cameroon between the Ngoko and Sangha Rivers. I took a bongo there with a thirty-three-inch head.

CONGO (Brazzaville): Bongos are found anywhere in the northern part where there are no marshy forest, for example, between Ouesso and Bomassa along the left bank of the Sangha River where I've seen a density similar to those in Cameroon. They are to be found on both sides of the road between Ouesso and Bellevue, via Ketta, Sembe, Elogo, and Suanke, in the northern part of Mandzala, and west of Liuesso. They are also to be found in the far north along the Motaba, Ibanga, Lola, Dzanga, Tokele, Ndoli, and Lokumbe Rivers that pass through little-explored areas. I have always found a high number of bongos in these areas, which is, without a doubt, the finest habitat in Africa for them.

GABON: Bongos are found in the little inhabited forest zones of the interior, such as the entire area between Minvul to the north and Makoku to the south, east of Booue, north and south of Mekambo, north of Lasturville, and north of Okandja. In these areas there are a good number of bongos, but they are hard to get because of the nature of the country.

CENTRAL AFRICAN REPUBLIC: Bongos can be found in two very different areas of this country:

A. The forest area located in the southwest border with Cameroon and the Congo, and in the areas of Bambio, Nola, Bayanga and Lidjomo.

B. Another important population is east of Bangassu, where they live in forests along the rivers stretching from the Sudan border through all the Upper Mbomu. There are excellent chances of hunting bongos in the Central African Republic, especially in the forest that covers the southwestern part, toward the Congo and Cameroon.

SUDAN: Bongos are only to be found in the southwestern part between Yambio and Tambura, along the border with Zaire. The area is quite small, but they are plentiful in the tropical forests that cover James Diko, Bengangai, Sakure, Biki, Ringasi and Debio. During the many years I hunted in Sudan (1959 to 1984) I saw many and took quite a few with my friends and clients.

Because the terrain is more open and offers better visibility, this is one of the easiest places in Africa to hunt bongo. There has been no hunting in the Sudan since the civil war began in 1984, and their present status is unknown.

ZAIRE: In the old Belgian Congo, bongos are found over a large area:

A. In the north: Gemena, Lisala, Buta, Ango, Gwane, Doruma and Opienge.

B. In the center between Opala y Katako-Kombe along the Lomela, Tshuapa, and Lomami Rivers.

C. In the east: In the Maniema district along the Luama River.

D. In the Ituri forest, the areas of Nia Nia, Epulu, Mambasa, Angumu, Panga, and along the Ituri, Lindi, Epulu, and Aruwimi Rivers. I've been able to see and hunt bongos in Zaire since it was still the Belgian Congo and especially recommend the areas in the northeast because of the terrain and the large number of animals.

With the discussion of Zaire, we finish with the enormous territory where the common bongo species *Tragelaphus euryceros euryceros* is found. We move on to East Africa where the *Tragelaphus euryceros isaaci* exist only in Kenya.

KENYA: In this country bongos are only found in high, mountainous areas. They've been found up to 10,000 feet on Mount Kenya, where there is

Two giant forest hogs shot in southern Cameroon, 1990.

an important group of them. It extends through the Cherangani Hills on Isanga Ridge to the Mau slope of the Aberdare Mountains. Because the mountains are covered with dense, damp forests that are difficult to get through and because there has been a complete ban on hunting since 1977, the bongo population is large and on the increase according to the latest news.

•••

I find a note appearing in the book *A Field Guide to the Mammals of Africa* by Theodor Haltenorth and Helmut Diller completely strange. Here is what the authors have to say about the bongo and its distribution: "In southern Ethiopia many have been seen and hunted but as of today, none exist in scientific collections. . . ." I might add to this that none ever will be found in scientific collections because the bongo has never lived in Ethiopia; consequently, that any have been seen or hunted is an hallucination. I fear that the appearance of that note must be a joke or the work of a nutcase.

The best areas for hunting bongos today are southeastern Cameroon, northern and northwestern Congo (Brazzaville) and southwestern Central African Republic. The successful bongo hunt needs humidity to promise a certain degree of success. It is impossible to get near them during the dry season when crackling fallen leaves warn the animals of the hunter's approach and give them time to escape. In these unfavorable conditions, an animal can be bagged only by pure luck. Don't plan a trip during this season if you want to avoid being disappointed and frustrated.

The best time to hunt bongos is at the beginning of the rainy season when the forest floor becomes a moist, silent carpet of vegetation and the murmur of the raindrops falling from one leaf to another may camouflage the noise a hunter may make. It is also easier to follow tracks in soft earth. It does not rain continually at the beginning of the rainy season but downpours and storms every two or three days, which maintains the humidity necessary to hunt without impediment. Later, the areas are almost totally blocked off when the rains become continual torrents and swollen streams become impassable.

The best months for hunting bongo are April, May, and June in the areas of equatorial forest in the three countries just mentioned. With the climatic conditions particular to northern Congo (Brazzaville), bongo can be hunted through the end of September. In the gallery forest of the Central African Republic, it is possible to hunt bongo until July. Later than this it's almost impossible to hunt them because of the height of the grass, which cuts off all visibility. Basically, there are three ways to hunt bongo:

A. Lie in wait for them at a salt lick, after checking the direction of the wind at dawn and at twilight. The results with this system are not terrific, and it is

the one least recommended. I personally feel that it isn't very sporting, either.
B. Follow the old forest roads, if you can find one. After a rainy night, bongos like to stroll along them to dry off. The results can be excellent and this is how most bongos in the Cameroon, Congo, and the Central African Republic are taken.
C. Track after finding a good fresh print. In countries where they live in small forests and are less protected by the environment, they have become nocturnal and return to the depths of the forest at first light, traveling between 5 and 7 A.M. to where they'll spend the day. Once the hottest hours of the day are gone, they travel again between about five and six in the afternoon, usually toward the salt lick, where they like to linger. Salt licks exist in all the areas where they are hunted. Follow the trail slowly and cautiously, and check every scrap of thick bush where they can hide. Keep your gun ready. Bongos can appear at any moment, napping or sprinting away to escape.

Wary, as are most forest animals, the bongo will flee at the first sign of danger, instantly going into a speedy gallop that can be kept up for hundreds of yards. Then the animal will stop to see if he is still being chased, trying to locate suspicious sounds with his big ears that are planted like radar screens on his head. If the animal is still nervous, he will again run and keep up such a constant state of alert that it will be very difficult to find a second chance to take him.

How quickly the bongo can move through labyrinthian forest is amazing. He puts his head up and seems to rest his horns on his back as he slides ahead easily without catching the horns on branches or dense low brush. Perhaps the greatest problem the bongo presents the hunter is to see him and shoot before he escapes.

Bongos are social animals and usually travel in groups of five to ten, although it is not uncommon to see larger herds. The old males leave the herd when their sexual activity wanes or when they are displaced by younger and stronger males. These live a quiet life, getting together occasionally with other retirees. In the equatorial forests where they are rarely hunted and feel safe, bongos travel about in the day, and I have shot several between ten in the morning and one in the afternoon. The bongo's diet consists of tender shoots, leaves, fruit rinds, and roots. The Kenyan bongo loves the bamboo shoots, which are plentiful in his mountain home. Only occasionally do they make nocturnal visits to farms to nibble fruit and bulbs.

The problem in hunting bongos is that they live in a terrain shrouded by so many branches and leaves that high speed, light projectiles, appropriate for an animal of around 220 kilos, cannot be used. To make sure that the bullet doesn't lose its trajectory or disintegrate when it hits a branch, it is necessary that it be of a medium or heavy weight with a moderate speed. The weapon used should also be easy to handle and light enough for the hunter to carry all day without becoming exhausted. Keeping those factors in mind and using a projectile of not less than 270 grains or more than 410 grains, the perfect calibers for hunting bongos are the following:

A fine bongo from the Shanga River area, southeastern Cameroon, 1989.

.338 Winchester with a projectile of 300 grains
9.3x62 Mauser with a TUG projectile of 293 grains
9.3x64 Brenneke with a TUG projectile of 293 grains
9.3x74R with a TUG projectile of 293 grains
.375 H&H Magnum with a projectile of 300 grains
.404 Jeffery with a projectile of 400 grains
.416 Rigby with a projectile of 410 grains
.416 Remington with a projectile of 400 grains

The three 9.3 calibers should only use a TUG projectile which gives magnificent results. It is recommended that the rifle have a telescopic sight to pick the animal out in the shadows of the great forests, where often only a dark form can be seen and where there will be no clues as to whether it is the tail or

A yellow-backed duiker, Cameroon, 1992.

the head in the sight. With a properly focused, variable scope from 1.5-6X, a quick and sure shot can be done. What counts in this kind of hunting is always the first bullet.

Don't forget that the bongo can be surprisingly aggressive when wounded or trapped, as more than one experienced hunter has found out to his detriment. In 1961 we had to hunt a bongo near Yambio in the Sudan. It had killed an old woman returning to her village after fetching water from the river and had injured another the following day. After watching the animal, we saw that it was not wounded and that it had attacked the people deliberately. This was something almost unheard of and something for which I have no explanation.

Here's a curious story. I once encountered a bongo fast asleep and snoring like a buzz saw. I was following the tracks of five bull elephants in Biki, in the southwest Sudan, when my attention was drawn to those snores. My tracker and longtime gunbearer Yuma signaled me to a place behind a termite hill, indicating silence. He then gestured with his hand to describe the bongo. Very slowly we approached and there, stretched out and happy, we saw the animal. He was snoring to beat the band, and after watching him awhile, we left. The bongo had never been so close to two humans with such harmless intentions as ours. As compensation, a couple of hours later I took a magnificent elephant with tusks weighing ninety-six and ninety-seven pounds, thanks to my .416 Rigby.

Luck plays a part in any kind of hunting, as happened to me in southeast Cameroon in 1990 when I took a German doctor on safari whose dream was to hunt a bongo. In traveling back and forth through the forest we had seen many bongo tracks, but it was impossible to get them. It had rained little that year and everything was dry and rustling. This always alerted the animals and all we ever got to see of them was their tails vanishing into the forest. We hiked epic distances but were not discouraged. It is all part of the game.

Time passed slowly and we began to feel a certain apprehension. There were plenty of bongos but not a drop of rain, which made tracking very difficult. The night of the seventh hunting day there came an impressive storm with lightning and sheets of rain that looked like the end of the world. While we ate,

A western sitatunga, southern Cameroon, 1989.

nice and dry in the dining tent, I half-joked with the doctor that the next day we'd get a bongo, now that everything was soaked. The storm would have erased the old tracks and we'd have fresh ones to follow from that night. The pygmy trackers backed up my opinion.

We got up the next morning at 3:30 as usual, ate a hearty breakfast and drove the Toyota along the main forest road toward a salt lick near the Sangha River, about thirty miles from the camp. Everything was a mess from the rain, and we skidded so much that it seemed we were traveling by boat rather than by car. The big bongo we saw crossing the road, lit by our headlights, was an omen. We saw plenty of bongo tracks throughout that difficult drive, arriving late at our appointed destination.

I had barely turned off the motor of the Toyota when the pygmy tracker and gunbearer Vincent signaled that he found a large track, so recent that it was still muddy. This meant that the bongo had passed within moments.

We quickly loaded up, both of us with .375 magnums. The doctor had a variable telescopic sight, which he set at two power. We moved like shadows in single file, Vincent the pygmy going first, followed by the doctor and then by me. Two more pygmies brought up the rear, carrying the photographic equipment and first aid kit I always bring along, which among other things included anti-snakebite serum. I habitually check the time when I leave the car in order to calculate the trip back. Many make the grave mistake of walking as far as they can without thinking that they have to get back. This can lead to trouble and more than once I have had to help exhausted people back to the Toyota.

It was eight in the morning when we began following the bongo's tracks, which were headed down a small path into the forest. We'd only gone 200 yards when a gorilla on our right started creating a ruckus, roaring and making a perfect show of himself. We hurried to get past the furious creature, who was violently tearing branches off a tree, and a little farther along a tight curve in the trail we came face to face with the bongo. He was about twenty yards away, head up, watching us. The pygmy made no movement whatsoever as I touched the doctor's arm, signaling him to shoot. The doctor had already raised his rifle, and he shot at the center of the animal's chest. The bongo jumped as if catapulted backward, but recovered in an instant and fled to our left. We could hear the racket as he went crashing through the thick forest.

I told the doctor to cover the road because bongos often return to it, while Vincent and I followed the trail, which we did by following the blood. We found him only 100 yards into the labyrinth of the forest, propped up against a tree, struggling to stay on his feet. I put him out of his misery, and he fell, an extraordinary specimen at the top of his form. The doctor's bullet had hit at the base of the neck and was fatal.

When they heard the boom of my .375 magnum, the doctor and the other pygmies called to us and when we shouted back that we'd gotten the bongo they began to howl with glee. They were there in a moment and the doctor was so overwhelmed that all he could say was, "Fantastic, fantastic."

Once the initial celebrating was over, we were presented with the problem of getting the bongo to the road, which was 100 meters away. The only way to do it was by brute strength, so we all put our backs to it. When we reached the road, we were covered in mud. Once out of the woods we realized that we had a magnificent trophy with horns just over thirty-one inches long, very high on the list of records.

I brought the Toyota over, managed to load the bongo, and began our triumphant return to camp. I had checked my watch after administering the *coup de grâce* and noticed that only twelve minutes had passed since we left the car. Because of that gorilla, this is what happened: The bongo heard the racket, but instead of fleeing decided to go see what was going on. The tracks in the mud showed what a coincidence it was that we had come face to face on that curve in the road and used the element of surprise to take him. Maybe we would have found him later, maybe not, but the gorilla had served him up to us on a platter, something he probably would rather not have done. Bongo hunting brings three elements together: skill, patience, and luck; for me it is one of the greatest pleasures in hunting. Let me include here some lines I wrote about the bongo many years ago:

"My first contact with the bongo was when I read Commandant Attilio Gatti's book *South of the Sahara* when I was eighteen years old. I can't explain why, but from that moment I was attracted to that beautiful animal, the largest of the African forest antelopes. Many years have passed, and since that first literary encounter, the bongo and I have gotten to know each other well, crossing paths many times in the fascinating forest he calls home. For many, the bongo is merely a fine trophy to hang on the wall. For me, it is more. It represents the spirit of an Africa that still has not been conquered by man and his ways. Hunting it is one of the purest forms of the sport, where the true hunter can enjoy every second, far from the sad farce that many safaris have become today."

• • •

CHAPTER VI

Operation Nile Lechwe

The Nile lechwe—or Mrs. Gray lechwe as it is usually known—is one of the great African trophies and very high on the list of internationally desirable species. It is a beautiful animal only found in a reduced habitat in the Sudan and Ethiopia, in marshy areas that are difficult to reach and that provide its principal protection.

The Nile lechwe, *Kobus megaceros*, is found throughout the marshy parts of the Sudan, from Malakal to the north of Bor, in varying densities along the White Nile. Also in the upper part of Bahr el Ghazal, in the immense, impenetrable swamps of Machar, situated between the east of Malakal and the Ethiopian border. The lechwe can also be found in Tonj, Lake Nyubor, and Pagarau. In Ethiopia, they are found in the far west area of Gambela, in the Akobo and Gilo which are fed by the Machar swamp in the Sudan. The number of lechwe in Ethiopia is variable, and always much fewer than in the Sudan.

This antelope can weigh between 175 and 200 pounds, reaching about thirty-nine inches at the withers. Only the males have horns, which are long and stretch back in the form of a lyre. Lechwes get darker in color with age, going from shades of red to black. Characteristically, they have a white spot in the middle of the back. The females are smaller and reddish in color.

The Nile lechwe is just one of four African lechwe, all similar in size and horn configuration, and all creatures of marshlands surrounded by floodplains. The other three are in the south—the red lechwe of Botswana's Okavango and along rivers north into Angola and Zambia; the longer-horned Kafue lechwe of the Kafue flats southwest of Lusaka; and the black lechwe of Zambia's Lake Bangweulu. The black lechwe is actually a mixture of red and black, with only some of the old males appearing nearly black. All are beautiful trophies, but the Nile lechwe is the most prized of the group

Nile lechwe, Pagarau, the Sudan.

The author, Dinkas and Nile lechwe, 1983.

because it lives in the most remote country and has by far the most strikingly beautiful coloration.

The following story illustrates a normal Nile lechwe hunt, so typical because of the country in which the lechwe inhabit. This is a hunt I took many years ago with some friends in the Sudan. Two old Spanish companions of many African hunts arrived in Juba, in the southern Sudan, on 1 March 1982. Luis Fernandez-Vega and Severino Canteli were accompanied by another friend from Madrid named Jesus Santos, and their objective was to hunt Nile lechwe. After collecting the luggage at the airport under a burning sun, we raced home to change clothes, load the Toyotas, and head immediately for the camp at Pagarau. It's an area I've known for many years, about nine hours by car from Juba, between Yirol and Shambé, and southeast of Lake Nyubor. It was also one of my favorite places in those early days for hunting elephant, in the heart of Dinka territory where Nile lechwe were plentiful in the swamps. After a very rough ride along the Juba/Rokom/Tindalo/Tali/Madbar/Yirol road, we reached camp about eleven that night. Everything had been readied by my assistant Manuel Silva, a veteran hunter from Angola and an all-round good guy.

Three record class Nile lechwes, shot in the Nile swamps of Shambé, 1982.

We ate dinner and soon after went to bed in order to be able to get up at dawn to start hunting. Before going after Nile lechwes, we decided to hunt several other species first, such as white-eared kob, roan, buffalo, and water-buck. It would give us the chance to check out the terrain and test the rifles.

Finally, on 4 March, we decided to go looking for Nile lechwe. Arising at five in the morning, we had breakfast and started for the swamp at first light. We got there half an hour later, crossing streams and mud holes until the vehicle could go no farther. We left the two Toyotas under the watchful eye of the driver to make sure the Dinkas didn't mess with them while we were gone, and we organized the hike. There were five Europeans (Luis, Jesus, Severino, Manuel and I) and ten Sudanese carrying rifles and water. A few feet from the cars was a large pond and we all jumped in, sinking up to our calves in gooey mud and with icy water reaching our waists.

Following the cooling break, we reorganized ourselves, using the Dinkas' spears like walking sticks to help us keep our balance across the shifting marsh. We began slowly but traveled without stopping. We had to cross three miles of marsh to get to the dry area where the Nile lechwes graze, planning to arrive before the sun reached its peak. In the midday heat they would take cover in the grass, where it would be impossible to hunt them. We splashed, slipped, and laughed at ourselves as we moved forward. We were completely covered with mud after a few yards. Severino Canteli, who weighed more than 220 pounds, kept sinking in the semiliquid marsh. The Dinkas loved this and were delighted to pull him out of the mud, which became a big joke between Severino and them.

After about an hour, we arrived at a kind of canal in the marsh, which was more than six feet deep and very long. The tallest formed a bridge for the shorter ones and helping one another, we got over it, holding the guns and ammunition over our heads. Past the canal, the swamp became more passable and finally, disappeared. We rested after setting foot on dry land for the first time in hours—struggling through a swamp is exhausting. Once again on solid ground, we increased our speed and shortly arrived at a Dinka village on a little hill. Fishing is the main industry of the village and they smoke everything they catch, which they sell in the markets in Yirol and Pagarau. They greeted us with pleasure, shaking our hands and asking for cigarettes. These were soaking wet and had to be dried in the sun before they were any good.

A very fine Nile lechwe shot near Shambé, the Sudan.

I asked them about Nile lechwe, and they signaled that many could be seen west of the village, from the very spot we were standing. As far as the eye could see, there were huge concentrations of them, something really incredible. In other areas of the White Nile islands, you would only see females with two or three males, hard to approach and very flighty. I had been to Pagarau many times over the years but never had I seen so many. The Dinkas said that over the past two years, for unknown reasons their number had been steadily growing. This was terrific news. This was the promised land of Nile lechwes, and we went after them with great enthusiasm. We added some local volunteers to our group who signed up in hopes of getting meat.

After checking our rifles and ammunition, we went after the Nile lechwe. Jesus Santos carried his Holland & Holland .300 Magnum with a 4X scope, while Luis, Severino, and I were united by our 9.3x64 Brennekes with Zeiss Diavari 1.5-6X scopes, leaded with the fantastic 293-grain Torpedo bullets (TUG). Instead of a rifle, Manuel Silva carried the tripod we used for firing, necessary in the vast treeless floodplain where there was no place to support a gun.

We crossed a small stream of running water that vanished into the swamps before we moved within 300 yards of the mass of Nile lechwe that nearly blocked out the horizon. At that point we had to assign a shooting order because if we approached them together they would spook and run into the tall grass where they couldn't be seen. Unanimously, we gave the first turn to Jesus Santos, so Jesus, Manuel, and I approached the antelopes while the rest sat in the huge carpet of weeds, trying to stay out of sight.

We shortened the distance between ourselves and the Nile lechwe. The animals showed more curiosity than fear, turning to face us, wondering what kind of pest was approaching them. The females bunched up to one side while the males, their curiosity satisfied, began a stately parade in front of us in single file, muzzles lifted, horns back, the neck horizontal with the back, rump higher than the withers. There were many males, and their coloring, from light chestnut to black, sprinkled the plain with dark points.

We felt like kids in a candy store at the sight of so many good trophies. We looked, and looked again, and as soon as we'd chosen one, we'd see a better one until we were completely confused. Then we saw a magnificent male there on our right. It was up to me to decide, so I indicated this antelope to Jesus, and as soon as Manuel had the tripod in the ground, he took his position and fired at the shoulder. With a violent leap and a brief run, the lechwe fell dead.

We went over to inspect the lechwe, and while we were making the usual comments we heard a shot, followed by two more in rapid succession coming from where we'd left the others. Through the binoculars we saw that Severino had taken another lechwe. Our movements had sent some animals in their direction and one large one had parked himself less than a hundred yards away from the group of Europeans. Unable to resist the temptation, Severino had fired and the bullet had found its mark. We got there to see a magnificent trophy, and after congratulations all around, we turned our attention to Luis, who was able to get his trophy within fifteen minutes.

This story may give the erroneous impression that hunting Nile lechwe is like shooting fish in a barrel. Nothing is further from the truth. Hunting this antelope has always been most difficult, and many, many hunters have arrived empty-handed after days of slogging through the mud and being devoured by mosquitoes. The place we found in Pagarau is exceptional, and I doubt if there is another quite like it in the rest of the Sudan, at least for the number and the quality of trophies.

I simply cannot say what the current status of Nile lechwe might be. No sportsmen has visited war-torn southern Sudan for more than a decade, and in Africa bush warfare means not only local poaching by starving people, but also wholesale slaughter by foraging armies. Bands of Sudanese poachers with long donkey caravans may now be encountered many miles into the Central African Republic, which bodes ill for game in the Sudan. The lechwe, being a herd animal most at home on open floodplains, is a vulnerable creature. As I said, there used to be smaller numbers across the border into Ethiopia, but it has been years since a sportsmen took one there—though several have tried. In any case, Ethiopia is also closed to hunting at this writing, so the Nile lechwe seems part of hunting history now. But just perhaps, in remote corners of the Sudan's great marshes, like the one where this hunt took place, there still remain pockets of Nile lechwe waiting for happier times.

After this exceptional trip, I returned many times, always with great results, and I can only hope that this hidden corner of the world remains so for a long time—with its huge herds of beautiful, serene Nile lechwes presenting a vision of what those lands were like before the arrival of man with his deadly firearms.

•••

CHAPTER VII

The Derby Eland

With its enormous size and impressive horns, the Derby eland joins the bongo as one of the world's most coveted prizes for sport hunters. Although I have never been interested in hunting nondangerous animals, the Derby eland and the bongo were the exceptions. Both are attractive because of the difficulties in taking them, the remote areas they live in, the sport of hunting them, and the exceptional trophies produced after unforgettable hours devoted to the chase.

Most hunters consider the Derby eland and his slightly more drab cousin, the common eland, as part of the spiral horned group, the *Tragelaphinae*. This is a natural grouping, for the eland does indeed have horns that curl around themselves much like the kudu and bongo and others of the spiral horns. However, the eland's horns grow with a prominent keel that starts on the forward, inside edge and curls around the horn for as much as two-thirds of its length. This keel is generally absent with the other spiral horns, which is just one taxonomic reason why the eland have their own separate genus, the *Taurotragus* comprised solely of the several species and subspecies of eland.

It really isn't important whether you personally consider them part of the spiral horns or not; what is important is that you recognize that all eland are among the wariest and most difficult to hunt of all Africa's antelope species. And then that you appreciate that the Derby eland is not only the largest and most beautiful of the eland, but also the most difficult to hunt. This because of the wild, remote parts of Africa it calls home, and also because I have found the Derby eland even more spooky and hard to approach than the common variety—which is saying a lot! There are two geographically separated subspecies.

A. The first known comes from West Africa, where it was discovered in the mid-nineteenth century when a set of horns were sent from Senegambia to Lord Derby, an amateur zoologist, by one of his agents. The man in charge of studying the new species was Dr. J. E. Gray, conservator of the zoology department at the British Museum between 1840 and 1874, who named the antelope *Taurotragus derbianus derbianus*, after the person who facilitated its discovery.
B. The other subspecies was found years later by Martin Theodore von Heuglin during his travels along the White Nile in the Sudan. He described it in 1863 for the first time, naming it *Taurotragus derbianus gigas* in consideration of the differences between the subspecies separated by thousands of kilometers of distance. To hunters the two are virtually indistinguishable, and collectively they are popularly known as Derby eland.

The Derby eland is the largest antelope in Africa and the world, strong and robust, standing five feet, five inches to five feet, eight inches at the withers for adult males with some exceptional animals reaching almost six feet. The average weight runs between 1,450 and 1,600 pounds. Put all together, the Derby eland is an imposing animal, which is probably why there are so many exaggerated stories told about its size. Some give it a stature of over six feet and a weight of a ton, which is far above average and simply not true. The females are about thirty percent smaller and lighter.

The color of the males—we are only interested in males, the females are not hunted—is usually light chestnut, growing darker with age except for the neck, which has a brownish gray mass of hair, the size of which depends on the individual. A short mane runs in a black line from the base of the neck to where the tail begins. Vertical white stripes run down the flanks, usually numbering between ten and fourteen. The forelock is thick and dark and a large flap of skin, the dewlap, hangs down the length of the neck.

A good male's horns is one of the most magnificent trophies that can be imagined, long and thick with divergent points. The first third of the horn curves in a tight spiral with an ample border, and this curve gives them majesty and personality. The females have horns, too, but theirs are straight, delicate and parallel. They are so different from those of the male that there is no chance of confusing them.

According to the measurements established by Rowland Ward to classify record trophies, there are two different standards, depending on whether the animal is from the West or Central African subfamily.

A. West Africa (*Taurotragus derbianus derbianus*). The record is 37½ inches, measured along the curve. The current "around the spiral" measurement is, of course, longer. The minimum to enter the record category is thirty-one inches.
B. Central Africa (*Taurotragus derbianus gigas*). The record is forty-eight inches along the curve; the minimum to enter the book is thirty-seven inches.

An old Derby eland, shot on a rocky hill in the eastern part of the Central African Republic, 1968.

Besides the difference in the size of the horns, which are always larger for the Central African Derby eland, the West African species is a brighter red and has more stripes down the sides, usually about fourteen or fifteen. The western variety no longer exists in huntable numbers anywhere in its range, but, as we shall see, there remain good numbers of the larger Central African variety.

The Derby eland is a social animal and is usually found in large groups; herds of more than twenty are not unusual. An old male is in charge of the herd but when his sexual activity begins to wane because of his age, he leaves the group and becomes one of the specimens most coveted and sought after by hunters. Older animals are easier to approach and being alone, don't present the difficulty level of shooting at one in a herd. It is always more difficult to pick one animal out of a closely mingling herd, especially when each animal is endowed with the excellent senses of sight and smell.

Their diet consists of such plants and leaves as the *Gardenia ternifolia* and the *Tamarindus indica*, but during the dry season, which is the best time to hunt them, they wander seeking *Isoberlinia doka*, leaves of which are their main diet. They also eat the young branches, using their horns to break them off. When the rains begin and the vegetation is thick all around, they travel less and stay in high areas or in the hills where there is less water and mud.

There is only one way to hunt the Derby eland, and that is to track it. Occasionally a hunter can lie in wait for a herd or a lone animal visiting a favorite salt lick, but this is rare. The hunter must be ready for long hikes during the hottest hours of the day. Contrary to the regular customs of other species, they do not doze in the shade but nibble here and there, resting awhile in the dark before beginning their wanderings in the earliest part of the day.

Given that their habitat is the wooded savanna with ample visibility, the hunter must carefully follow the track, all the while keeping a eye out ahead for eland hiding in the weeds before they see him. Despite their size, the Derby eland are hard to spot if they are quiet. Watch for flickering ears or the tail swishing away the flies that always annoy them. This is not an aggressive animal, not even when wounded or trapped, and it presents no danger to man.

They are very wary and at the tiniest sign of danger speedily gallop away, slowing then to a trot they can keep up for a long time. It is very hard to get close once they have scented the hunter. For that reason it is very important to move carefully from the moment tracks are spotted and do things right. Mistakes in hunting the Derby eland can result in physical exhaustion, as I found to my detriment. It is incredible how quickly they can move their big bodies through the bush and be out of the range of the hunter, who travels much more slowly.

Because they may travel more than thirty miles in a day, hunting the Derby eland is done in the toughest and most traditional way—walking from sunup to sundown and putting aside such luxuries as all-terrain vehicles. This magnificent trophy is first killed with the legs and only secondly with a rifle, and anyone not prepared for long marches, thirst, and every kind of inconvenience can forget about the Derby eland.

Because it is a very tough, strong animal, calibers shooting small projectiles are out of the question . . . no matter how fast and how much energy they have on the ballistic tables. More than one frustrated hunter has spent days tracking a wounded eland only to lose it.

Keeping in mind that the animal weighs around three-fourths of a ton, it is definitely necessary to use calibers with sufficient power to knock it down and leave some extra energy for a margin of error. The bullet used should not have a weight of less than 293 grains, and especially recommended for hunting Derby eland are the following:

> 9.3x64 Brenneke with TUG projectile of 293 grains
> .338 Winchester with 300-grain projectile
> .340 Weatherby with 300-grain projectile
> .375 H&H Magnum with 300-grain projectile
> .404 Jeffery with 400-grain projectile
> .416 Rigby with 410-grain projectile
> .416 Remington with .400 grain projectile

All should be fitted with a good scope between 1.5X to 6X, and with a mount that allows it to be quickly detached.

Derby eland taken in the Ndok area, northern Cameroon, March 1992.

The Derby eland's habitat has been shrinking in some areas, and poaching, bovine diseases, and the political instability in recent decades have all taken its toll on this wonderful animal. The following indicates the animal's distribution and status in 1994:

WEST AFRICA: In general, the number of Derby eland is much reduced in this part of Africa for various reasons. Besides the fact that they have never recovered from the attack of bovine disease that decimated their numbers in 1938, the small number that survived have had to face the constant growth of the human population as well as poaching; as we all know, poachers do not bother about such trifles as the sex or the age of the animal when they are out foraging for meat.

The result is that they are nearly extinct in many of their old habitats such as Mali and Ivory Coast. They only can be found in the Niokolo Koba National Park in Senegal, with unconfirmed rumors that a few have been sighted along the border of Senegal and Guinea, east of Samballo. The same is said about a small group in the Faranah area near the border of the Republic of Guinea and Sierra Leone. Given the scarce number of Derby eland in West Africa, it is considered one of the rarest animals in the world. It has been listed in the *Red Data Book* since 1976 as an animal in danger of extinction if proper measures are not taken.

CENTRAL AFRICA: In this part of the continent the Derby eland can be found in the following countries:

CAMEROON: It only lives in the northern part of the country between Ngaundere and Garua along a strip bounded on the north by the ninth parallel and a little farther south than the eighth. The best places to find them are, besides the Benue and Bubandjidah National Parks, Rey-Buba, Uarkla, Tchollire, Bandjuki, Sora Bum, south of Poli, and along the Faro River. In general its number is still high and during March, 1992, I had the chance to see a lot in the Tchollire area and the Faro River and was able to take some excellent trophies.

CHAD: It is distributed more or less evenly across the southern part of the country. Because of the civil war that has been raging for many years, it seems that they are nearly extinct in this country.

CENTRAL AFRICAN REPUBLIC: This is the country where the greatest number of Derby eland are to be found, stretching across the northeast (Ndele, Dongolo, Delimbe, Uanddjia, Uanda Djalle and Mount Mela), the east (Adelaye, Yalinga, and across the huge area between the Mbari River and the Sudanese border), the southeast (Benima, Berrua, Djema, Mboki), and the north of Obo and the northwest of Bambuti. When I went to Uanda Djalle many years ago with my friend Quintard, a famous professional hunter of the period, to open up the area for sport safaris, we found gentle, trusting Derby eland everywhere. The first five records for the species came from the Central African Republic or the former Ubangi-Shari. The record-holder, with horns 48 inches long, was taken by Quintard. According to figures from the game department, thirty to thirty-five Derby eland are taken by hunters every season—a high number that shows the abundance of the species in the country.

SUDAN: Years ago there were many, but those numbers are dwindling. They are still found in remote areas such as Rumbek, Wau, Raga, Tambura, and along the Pongo, Sopo, Wau and Sue Rivers. Hunting is now impossible because of the civil war in the Sudan between the north and the south, which has completely closed off access to visitors since 1984. I remember that still in 1982, we found beautiful Derby eland on the road from Wau to Raga and by the Pongo River, but I fear that they have vanished into history.

ZAIRE: The belief is that there are only a few eland in the north, between the Uere River and the Mbomu River along the border with the Central African Republic. The last time I visited the area was in January 1989, as a guest of President Mobutu, and despite all the methods available, including a small plane, I couldn't find a single Derby eland to prove their existence. They are completely protected in Zaire—at least on paper.

UGANDA: The Derby eland has been extinct for many years in Uganda. There were never many and a few were found only in isolated places in the province of West Nile. I never personally saw any there during my hunting expeditions, even the ones before independence in 1962.

Today Derby eland can only be hunted in northern Cameroon and the eastern part of the Central African Republic, where many fine examples are taken every season. Thirty years ago I was hunting in the Sudan, south of the Darfur Province between the Umbelasha and Adda Rivers, west of Kafia Kingi, almost on the border of the Central African Republic. As usual, I was after elephants and Derby eland. There were plenty in those parts, but I was told that there were even more on the other side of the border, in the Central African Republic. The next year, I did the reverse and was hunting in the Central African Republic, north of Mount Mela, almost to the Sudan, where I again heard the story that there were even more across the border, this time in the Sudan. I suppose that it is human nature to project that the grass is always greener on the other side of the river!

•••

CHAPTER VIII

Buffalo

Hunters have always attached a sort of dark legend to the buffalo, telling and retelling stories about its truculent behavior as if it were the Dracula of the animal kingdom. I'm not going to say that the buffalo is a harmless creature because it certainly isn't, but neither do I want to give into the temptation of describing it like the sensationalists do, by assigning it human characteristics—traits that would embody a traitor, a vengeance-seeker, or someone cruel and bloodthirsty. These are the exaggerations of cheap literature. We must not forget that irrational animals are only following their instincts for self-preservation. The buffalo is no exception. It is my opinion, backed up by many years of buffalo hunting, that their bad reputation stems from three causes:

1. The negative response people have to the animal because of its unfriendly, almost sinister expression, which is very important from a psychological point of view.
2. The sheer numbers of this animal make an encounter more likely. It is the most abundant of all the dangerous game hunted in Africa; consequently, this increases the possibility and number of conflicts.
3. The inexperience of many hunters and the use of an unsuitable rifle and ammunition help shape the negative reputation of the buffalo. Many go off to hunt buffalo without knowing anything about them, and some are so inexperienced that they do not even know where to aim the rifle or which angle for the bullet in order to kill the buffalo. Confrontations arise when a "dead" buffalo gets up and charges. I am amazed at how frequently the arms used are inadequate for the purpose intended and how useless the ammunition is for the given circumstance.

A huge Cape buffalo with 50-inch horns, Angola, 1963.

It is logical, then, that the combination of these three points often results in a higher incidence of accidents and, unfortunately, the occasional death. Keep in mind, though, that considering the amount of irresponsible buffalo hunting that goes on every year across Africa, theoretically there should be many more mishaps than actually occur. It's really surprising that there aren't more fatal accidents.

It could also be that the ones who have promulgated the bad reputation of the buffalo are those peculiar hunters who long for recognition—the ones who always feel the obligation to tell horror stories of miraculous escapes, heroic acts, and risk-taking more appropriate to Hollywood than the wilds of Africa, and who feel the necessity to leave their listeners with their mouths hanging open. This stuff is more appropriate to children's stories than anything else.

The buffalo is an easygoing animal which lives quietly with its fellows, doing everything it can to stay away from people. But it can defend itself remarkably well if it is wounded or trapped, thanks to its extraordinary physical strength as well as strength of character. I have had the opportunity to see thousands of buffalo and to shoot hundreds of them. Some of those hunts were risky, but without being overly dramatic I must say that there's no activity in the world that doesn't have some risk, which you've just got to accept as part of the game.

For the hunter there are basically three varieties of buffalo in Africa with two more clear subspecies, each perfectly differentiated and classified, each one located in a specific geographic area.

A. *Syncerus caffer caffer* or Cape buffalo: This is the largest of the buffalo family and the best known through books and stories. It is a large and heavy animal with a height at the withers of about five feet to five feet, four inches, and adult males weigh between 1,350 and 1,500 pounds. It is black all over with thin hair, and its horns are by far the biggest of all the buffalo species. It is found in the following countries: South Africa, Namibia, Botswana, Zimbabwe, Angola, Zambia, Mozambique, Malawi, southern Zaire, Tanzania, Kenya, southern Uganda, Somalia, Rwanda, and Burundi. It is still abundant in Tanzania, Zambia, Botswana, Zimbabwe, Mozambique, and the Kruger National Park in South Africa. In Somalia and Burundi it is nearly extinct.

B. *Syncerus caffer aequinoxalis* or Nile buffalo: It is a little smaller than its Cape cousin but much like it in appearance. It stands about four or five inches shorter than southern buffalo and weighs more than 1,100 pounds. Although its normal color is black, some females and young males are reddish in color. It is found in the southern Sudan, Ethiopia, northern Uganda, northeastern Zaire, southeastern Chad, and east of the Central African Republic. Due to such political problems as civil wars and severe poaching, its number has been reduced in some areas, but it is still so abundant in others it should be considered a common animal.

C. *Syncerus nanus nanus* or dwarf buffalo: The smallest of the family is found in the great equatorial forests. Measuring about 3½ at the withers and weighing about 500 pounds, it is reddish in color and some males are actually a bright chestnut. The small horns point backward. They can be found in the thick forests of the following countries: Republic of Guinea, Sierra Leone, Ivory Coast, Ghana, Togo, Benin, Nigeria, Cameroon, Gabon, Equatorial Guinea, Congo, the southwestern Central African Republic, Zaire, and northern Angola. Angola is the only country where they can be found in open terrain. The dwarf buffalo is hard to spot because of its habitat, that is, covered terrain. It is found in good numbers in southeast Cameroon, north Congo, west Gabon, and central Zaire.

Apart from the three races just described, there are two sub-races that are also interesting for the hunter and trophy collector and that have their own scientific classification:

A. *Syncerus nanus sylvestris* or forest buffalo: This medium-sized buffalo is found in the area of secondary forests, gallery forests, and savanna near forests. It's taller than the true dwarf buffalo and heavier, in weight up to 650 pounds. Its color varies from red to chestnut. The countries inhabited by the forest buffalo are the same as for the dwarf buffalo, but it is more common in Cameroon, Gabon and Congo.

B. *Syncerus nanus savanensis* or savanna buffalo. This inhabitant of the wooded savannas of West and Central Africa stands a bit over four feet tall and weighs between 650 and 900 pounds. The females have a ruddy color and the males are chestnut, with the intensity of the color depending on age. The horns are in the form of a lyre with the tips straight and folded backward. It is found in the following countries: Senegal, Guinea, southern Mali, Northern Ivory Coast, Burkina Faso, northern Ghana, northern Benin, southeastern Niger, northern Nigeria, northern Cameroon, Chad, the Central African Republic, and northwest and northern Zaire.

Besides these five types of buffalo with notable differences among them, there are a number of local races of no interest to the practical hunter. There are about forty-seven of these and their colorations, the shape of the ears, tail, and fur depends on the imagination of who's describing them.

The sport of hunting buffalo is one of the most challenging, but it can be risky if things are badly done. It is definitely a top attraction for sportsmen on safari. Throughout my career as a hunter I have taken 1,426 buffalo, so I have had my share of brushes with them. Since I'm here to tell the tale, it's because I have never taken stupid liberties and always used a weapon powerful enough to resolve any situation. When a buffalo decides to go at you, I can promise that you can never have too much rifle. From my own experience there were times when a .600 Nitro seemed too small, and I wished that I had an antitank cannon at hand.

I've had the opportunity, on many occasions, to try most medium and large calibers against buffalo, but before getting down to details, I want to elaborate on the type of ammunition to use against buffalo.

A. In calibers of less than .400 and projectiles of less than 400 grains, solids exclusively must be used.
B. In calibers greater than .400 and with a minimum of 400 grains of projectile, an expanding bullet can be used if the first shot is at a clear target, but the following shots should be solids. Should the buffalo not fall and should he attack or flee, a solid is the only bullet capable of stopping him. If shot below the tail, the bullet will travel the length of the body to reach the lungs, heart, or cut the aorta. The smallest caliber for hunting buffalo within the margin of safety is the 9.3mm (366). This is not to say that other smaller calibers are incapable of killing buffalo, but it is one thing to kill them and another altogether to stop a charge. I have taken a number of buffalo with the .300 H&H Magnum and the 8x68S, but I would never say that they are ideal for this activity.
C. With medium calibers, always use solids: The 9.3x64 Brenneke, with a projectile of 285 grains, is terrific for a great penetration. The old 9.3x62 Mauser, also with a 285-grain bullet, kills well in lateral shots but lacks power to stop a charge. The 9.3x74R, only used in double-barreled rifles, offers no guarantee against buffalo. I mention it here to make sure nobody makes that mistake. The .375 magnum, with 300-grain bullet, is excellent and has a posi-

Savanna buffalo from northern Cameroon, 1992.

tive record in this type of hunting. Like the .375 magnum, the 9.3x64 Brenneke can be used against buffalo with no problem, except in thick vegetation with poor visibility where a heavier projectile would be needed to stop the charge of a wounded animal. This is just common sense!

D. Heavy calibers:

1. Repeating rifles: .404 Jeffery with 400-grain projectile; .416 Rigby with 410 grains; .416 Remington with 400 grains; .458 Winchester with 500 grains (the expanding bullet with 510 grains works poorly against buffalo); .460 Weatherby with 500 grains; .500 Jeffery with 535 grains; and the .505 Gibbs with 525 grains.

2. Double-barreled rifles: .450/.400 with 400 grains; .450 with 480 grains; .465 with 480 grains; .470 with 500 grains; .475 No. 2 with 480 grains; .500 3" with 570 grains; and the .577 with 750 grains.

I've never had the least problem hunting buffalo with any of the calibers outlined above, except with the expanding 510 bullet of the .458 Winchester, due to its slight penetration. I've stopped a number of charges, especially with the .416 Rigby, the .500 Jeffery, the .465 Nitro Express, and the .577 Nitro Express in the safest and most satisfactory way. Of course I've had some scrapes with buffalo, but never have I had the scares that I've had with lions.

•••

I was out hunting buffalo in the Luangwa Valley in Zambia with one of those clients who thinks everything he says is the absolute truth—a crashing bore, in other words. On this day, he declared that it was impossible to kill a buffalo with one shot. Apparently he had discussed this with many hunters and they all had agreed. It is impossible to have a discussion with people like that and not even worth the trouble to try. So I shut up and tried to close my ears to such nonsense—to the point where he thought I agreed with his picturesque theory. By the end of the day I thought I was going to lose my temper listening to him hammer this same subject, so that afternoon when I saw an old buffalo grazing about eighty yards away I stopped, took my .416 Rigby loaded with solids, and turned to the client, telling him to hold on a minute. Everyone else stayed put while I, covering myself with the scant vegetation, crept within about twenty-five yards of the animal. I gave a little whistle and when he raised his head, I shot him straight between the eyes and he fell dead without a sound. I returned and asked the client, "What do you think of that theory now?" to which he replied, "That I'm a complete idiot." And so ended the discussion.

Another time, in the early 1970s, I was on safari in the Sudan with an American couple, who were nice people but filled with fears and heaps of prefabricated ideas about the dangers of the hunt. The husband was worst of all, having read all kinds of garbage written by the worst hacks. Above all, the buffalo represented the risk of life and limb to him. Whenever we'd see one, the poor guy would turn white and then green.

Finally, one morning we found a good male all by itself, and the client had no excuse not to try to shoot it, even though he'd come up with a number to avoid it before. With that greenish tinge to his face, we moved within forty yards, where I told him to shoot for the shoulder. The animal was broadside, looking to the right which was perfect for a good shot. I had prepared my .475 No. 2 Nitro Express and awaited the chance to see how this supposed wonder hunter would perform. For buffalo he carried some specially loaded ammunition for the .375 magnum. His wife waited with the trackers a little way behind.

At the sound of the shot, the buffalo sprang up and took off into the tall grass. We approached the spot and saw blood with bubbles in it, which indicated that the bullet had hit a lung. I said that I would have to follow the wounded animal, and, under his wife's enraged looks, he insisted on coming along too.

About 350 yards along the trail, we saw the buffalo facing away from us in some bushes at the far end of a clearing. In the middle of the clearing was a large termite anthill. We crept silently forward, taking shelter behind the large mound. All we could see of the buffalo were the rump and the tail, so I signaled that we would have to get close enough to target a vital point. As we continued our careful advance, the buffalo suddenly turned and charged out of the clearing at us. At the moment I put the rifle to my shoulder I saw out of the corner of my eye the client running in the opposite direction. At fifteen yards I put a 480-grain solid in the middle of the animal's chest. Staggering to its knees, it went down. I closed the short distance and used the second barrel shoot to it again in the neck.

The client was on top of the termite anthill saying that he had climbed up to get a better shot but that I hadn't given him the chance. The wife arrived about this time, eyes shooting sparks while he tried, still green-faced, to come up with a way to justify the unjustifiable. I told him that it had been a good idea to get up on the anthill to get a better aim, but unfortunately, due to the speed of the charge I couldn't wait. I also said that wasn't it a shame that I had to shoot the buffalo. I had to say something to defuse the situation, especially when the wife was purple with rage. The poor guy had no better idea than to ask me which animal had left its excrement near the anthill. I said that it was a hyena. He turned to his wife and said, as if this were truly noteworthy, "Look, those are hyena droppings!" Without missing a beat she answered, "And where did you drop yours, honey?"

BUMMER WITH A BUFFALO

Hunting stories often herald the triumphs of the heroic author, who tells his tales to divulge and teach so that poor mortals may learn and stand amazed before such marvels, expressing proper admiration and envy. Having made this introduction, I have to add that the story I'm about to tell is also intended to be instructional—but in reverse. It reconfirms the truth of the old African saying that a cocky hunter is soon a dead one. To underestimate an adversary is a serious mistake, as I learned for myself the time I nearly lost my skin to an animal that was supposedly nearly dead.

I was on safari in the Khordeleib area of the southern Sudan in 1979 with my friends, Luis and Manolo Fernandez-Vega, and Severino Canteli. We were enjoying ourselves and having a good time. We hunted from sunrise to sunset and at night listened to opera on my little cassette deck, talked and told jokes. I repeat that everything was going wonderfully until that morning when, most unexpectedly, things got complicated to the point of becoming dangerous.

We left early, as always. That day Manolo and Severino came with me while Luis headed the opposite direction with my assistant. We took the path toward Mount Isabel, which was eight miles away. Manolo and Severino were up on the Toyota watching for game while I drove slowly. Mount Isabel dominates the entire northern part of Khordelieb, and it is called that because I was the first to become a regular visitor to the area. I opened it up to safaris and named it after my wife.

We'd been traveling for about half an hour when we saw an old buffalo along to the right of the path. I stopped the Toyota, and we got down and hastily organized a simple but sure plan of action. It was Manolo's turn to shoot first and all we had to do was get the proper distance from the animal and fire. Leaving Severino in the car and the Sudanese personnel watching, Manolo, two trackers, and I began our approach. On this occasion, Manolo was using his 9.3x64 Brenneke, which is a great weapon any way you look at it.

We began the approach with no problems, arrived within forty yards, and Manolo dispatched the buffalo neatly with a single shot to the shoulder, which was partly obscured by tall grass. We started toward the animal when suddenly it got to its feet and took off like the dickens, vanishing from sight in seconds. We returned to the car and drove from the spot where Manolo had shot the buffalo. We found it quickly, on the ground in the middle of a big clearing,

A gigantic buffalo from Selous with 51-inch horns, Tanzania, 1979.

breathing hard and in pain, blood running from its mouth and nose. Manolo's shot had hit it perfectly, and it was dying.

I decided to put the poor suffering animal out of its misery. I stopped the Toyota twenty-five yards away and asked Manolo to hand me a rifle without saying which one I wanted. Instead of giving me the .416 Rigby, he handed me the 9.3x64 he was holding. I took it and approached the buffalo to administer the *coup de grâce*. I got within five yards, totally confident that it was nearly dead, when it got up like a shot and charged. I only had time to raise the rifle and fire off a bad shot at the forehead, which did stop the buffalo for a moment. I reloaded in a second, only to find that the rifle was empty, without more rounds in the magazine. Immediately it was on top of me again. I turned on the balls of my feet, and remembering the saying "better to live a coward than die a hero," I ran for the Toyota, hearing its faltering gasps behind me at the same time I felt its hot, wet breath on my back.

As I ran for the car, I saw expressions of horror on the faces of Manolo and Severino while the Sudanese wailed "*ay, ay, ay*" and covered their eyes so as not to have to watch what was about to happen. At the sight of those expressions, I doubled my speed and reached the Toyota with my boots smoking. My hope was to put the car between myself and the buffalo, which despite supposedly being on the point of death was showing remarkable energy. I almost made it, but the buffalo shoved me with its snout, pushing me against the side of the Toyota—the natives still wailing "*ay, ay!*"—in order to stab me with its left horn. This passed beneath my arm without touching me. The blow of the horn against the car knocked the beast off balance and made it step back and turn its head to the right, which gave me the chance to get around the car. It was a miracle that it didn't smash me with its forehead. At that moment, Severino shot it with his .458 Winchester, which resulted in the buffalo sliding underneath the Toyota.

After a tiny pause, the wretched thing tried to squeeze out from under the vehicle, but because its horns were caught between the wheel and the axle, as we later found, it was only able to shake the car, making a noise like a banshee. It was like a scene out of a black comedy: the wailing Sudanese; Manolo and Severino letting fly their finest wisecracks; me, trying to reload; and the buffalo, agitating the Toyota and rattling the teeth of everybody still on top of it. With the rifle ready (I hadn't let it go throughout all this), I dove under the car and gave the damn thing a bullet to the brain, which thank God, killed it. That buffalo seemed nearly immortal, like the avenging angel of its species.

I was a sticky red mess when I crawled out from underneath the vehicle. The damp heat I had noticed during the race was the buffalo's blood. That snout was only inches from my back, flinging a spray of blood onto my back. Thanks to Severino's shot, things ended happily . . . otherwise, I wouldn't be writing this.

The scare was significant and I have to admit that it was all the fault of my stupid overconfidence. To start with, a buffalo is always a buffalo, and until you've got its head loaded in the car it must be treated with respect and caution. Second, don't grab just any rifle before approaching a wounded animal, no matter how close to death it seems. Use the rifle you're accustomed to. And third, don't be too cocky and get too close to the animal. Leave enough space to fire and fire again in case of an unexpected attack, or you may expose yourself to all the grief I did. Manolo's remark that I had certainly broken all Olympic records was little consolation.

THE CHIBINDI BUFFALO

One afternoon in 1969 I was eating lunch at my camp, "Fort Spain," on the banks of the Luangwa River in Zambia. With me were two Italian clients from Milan, who had been on safari with me before. It was hot and quiet,

The author with Vicente Muñoz-Pomer and a double on Nile buffaloes, Khordeleib, the Sudan.

except for our animated play-by-play retelling of the hunting of a handsome lion that morning.

Suddenly, we saw Didion, my gunbearer, running toward us, accompanied by another African sweating heavily, dragging a bicycle. They excitedly told us that a buffalo had just killed a man near the village of Chibindi and afterward the animal lay down next to the body and would not let anyone near. The man on the bike had ridden nearly fifteen miles to see if we could help. I immediately agreed, and once I explained to the Italians what was happening, they joined the expedition right away. Without finishing our lunch, we grabbed our rifles, they their .375 magnums and I my inseparable .416 Rigby, and we headed for Chibindi, accompanied by my team and the cyclist, whose bike we stashed in the Land Rover.

The road was good, so it only took us a half hour to get there. The whole village was waiting for us by the side of the road with two women wailing and crying and making a terrible noise. It turned out that they were the victim's wives. They told us that the buffalo had surprised the man and another fellow while they were out collecting firewood. The animal charged out of the grass and attacked the two, but the younger was able to climb a tree and escape. He saw his friend gored and thrown down before the animal took its fury out on the injured man, butting him with its head and trampling him until he lay motionless, his intestines spilling from his body.

The buffalo walked around its victim a few times and then lay down about twelve yards away. The terrified witness escaped and ran to tell the village the bad news. A group of men armed with spears and axes went to collect the body, but, as they approached the buffalo, it became clear that there was no way to get closer without provoking another attack. They thought of me and sent the bicycle messenger to my camp.

Filled in with the details, we were led to the place where the dead man and his buffalo guardian lay by. The usual assortment of vultures hovered in the trees, just waiting their chance to swoop down and eat the corpse. All in all, it presented a morbid tableau. Our group consisted of myself, the two Italians, Didion, the survivor, and a couple of volunteers. The rest of the village followed at a prudent distance, completely silent.

The accident couldn't have taken place more than 600 yards from the village. In the middle of the clearing was the body with the buffalo beside it. The animal was in a strange position, lying on one side as if dead. I watched it through the binoculars and saw no sign of movement. Vultures took to the sky as we moved closer, but the buffalo remained in the same position. It was so abnormal that I thought perhaps it was dead.

I told the Italians and Didion to wait where they were as I approached to see what was going on. I had my .416 ready, loaded with four solids, and I got

Congressman Jack Fields with Tony in Zaire with a record Nile buffalo, January 1989. This buffalo was shot with a .375 magnum in the Garamba area.

within twenty-five yards of the buffalo without it showing any signs of life. Looking for a good angle to shoot, I gave a few whistles to see if it would react, but nothing happened. I turned my face to the others and started to say in a normal tone of voice that it must be dead when two shouts of "watch out!" filled the air. I turned to see the buffalo charging, eyes full of blood.

With the animal only fifteen yards away, I aimed for the center of the nose. This particular angle results in a direct shot to the brain because of the position in which buffalo carry their heads when charging. That stopped it short and it crashed to the ground. At the same time I felt bullets whizzing past my right ear, which made me jump to the left. The Italians also wanted to participate and each had fired. The buffalo was dead as a doornail, not even twitching its ears after the first shot.

When I got to its side, I saw the reason for its unprovoked attack. The buffalo had an enormous abscess on its left side, filled with pus, flies, and small worms. It had stretched out on its right side to avoid irritating this abscess, which must have been very painful. When we later opened the creature up, we found a heavy caliber lead bullet that had been fired by one of those old muzzleloaders that use blackpowder. Someone had tried to kill the animal with that old piece of junk but had served only to injure it badly. The pain had only increased along with the infection until the animal had been driven crazy and had attacked the first man who crossed its path.

Once the buffalo was down, everyone ran to us and to my great embarrassment, the two widows threw themselves at my feet and kissed my boots, all the while shouting something I could not understand. Finally Didion explained that the widows wanted the buffalo's testicles so that they could take revenge by eating them. This is the worst offense that can be done to an animal's spirit. I told them that they could have the whole animal, if they liked, to eat whatever they wanted.

The poor dead man—who looked horrible—was wrapped in a cloth and taken to the village. We had the luck to meet a police patrol car from Lundazi on the road, so we were able to report what had happened without traveling 125 miles to the police station. Because the buffalo had that huge dirty wound, not even the widows wanted it. They only ate the testicles. The Italians took the tail as a souvenir of their adventure in the African bush, the buffalo's body was left to the vultures. This tragic episode occurred when a poor man, looking for firewood, died because an irresponsible imbecile inflicted a terrible injury on an animal and then didn't have the courage to follow the animal up and kill it. This imbecile, who never knew what happened on that long-ago morning in 1969, indirectly cut short the life of an innocent villager.

AND BEFORE LUNCH, TOO
The morning of 8 September 1984 was one of the most exceptional in all my years of African hunting. I was at my camp in Loliondo (known as "Klein's

A huge, old buffalo, from Loliondo, Tanzania, 1985.

Tony Sanchez, senior and junior, with an exceptional buffalo, Tanzania, 1986.

Camp") in northern Tanzania with Paco, Fernando, and his wife Matilde, who were old friends and companions from other safaris. We'd been doing very well and only four days into the hunt had taken many antelopes, buffalo, and an enormous lion. Amidst the good company, good hunting, and good camping, we couldn't have asked for anything more. Everyone was happy and in good spirits.

We'd left a buffalo, which Paco had shot the day before, as bait to see if we could attract another lion. Very early in the morning of the next day we returned to the bait at the entrance of the valley, finding a lion feeding on the buffalo. Because Fernando had taken his lion two days before, he stayed with Matilde and my assistant, an old Kenya buddy, to watch while Paco and I started the action.

Paco was armed with a 9.3x74R double, and I carried my .375 magnum. We got within firing range, about eighty yards, and at my signal, Paco let off the first shot. The lion was distracted by its breakfast and offered a perfect shot. On impact, the lion gave off a mighty roar and sprang to the right. Paco quickly fired the second barrel, and the lion went down on the grass. To be sure, I gave it the *coup de grâce*, which really wasn't necessary as the lion was nearly dead. It was a magnificent male with a glorious mane, big enough to enter into Rowland Ward's records. After this incredible stroke of luck there was joy, congratulations, and smiles all around. After taking pictures, we loaded the lion into the Toyota and headed back to camp so that the skin could be removed as quickly as possible. On the way we took a Thomson's gazelle. By nine we were back at Klein's Camp where we received a grand welcome.

We decided to have an extra late breakfast and then take a spin in the car to kill time until lunch. After checking to make sure the lion skin was being properly dealt with, we took off again. Only a mile from camp we stopped by a salt lick popular with buffalo because Paco wanted to take a second specimen.

We had just gotten there when we spied a big buffalo, alone among the bushes in the shade of a tree. I pointed it out to Paco, and armed with his 9.3x74R loaded with solids, he shot it. Fernando was beside him with his .458 Winchester, which he also shot. The animal got up, pierced by a pair of bullets which apparently had no effect on it whatsoever. My second hunter, Giovannino and I (he with his .470 Rigby and I with my .505 Gibbs) did nothing more than watch, while offering some practical advice. At last Fernando managed to put a bullet from the .458 in the shoulder, and the buffalo fell. I decided, after this incident, that the 9.3x74R was inadequate for buffalo. There was more rejoicing, more photos, and our morale skyrocketed. We loaded the head in the Toyota along with the meat and decided to take a little detour on our way back to camp since we had some time left.

I don't know why it occurred to me that since we were parallel to a stream leading to the Grumeti River, we should go there to look for bushbuck. We drove in that direction while commenting on the luck we'd had that morning with a lion, a Thomson's gazelle, and a buffalo. We had only gone a little way

A fine Nile buffalo shot near Torit, the Sudan, 1974.

when a leopard sprang from a tree to a gorge—a surprising move. We were able to see that it was an enormous male. We slammed on the brakes and piled out as silently as we could. The big cat was nearby and of course, we were going to hunt it. I quickly noted where it might be hidden and motioned Fernando to get ready. Matilde and Paco stayed in the Toyota against their will, but there were a lot of us, and there was the risk of spoiling everything with so many people.

I signaled Fernando where to stand, and he was ready with his 8x68. Giovannino was beside him with his old but effective Rigby .470 Nitro. Once they were in place, the trackers and I situated ourselves about forty yards from the gully. With my trackers Hamisi, Tangliani, and Moises, we began clapping and rustling the bushes to flush the leopard toward the others. The leopard was about ten yards ahead of us and began to pick up speed in its flight toward Fernando and Giovannino. We shouted that it was coming, and Fernando followed it with his rifle. It again leapt into the gulch, and at that moment he fired and hit it. When a leopard is moving, it is a very difficult target. This was a magnificent shot, but now we had to deal with a wounded leopard, most definitely in a very bad mood. We had to find it right away.

I went back to the car for my rifle while thinking about a small experiment I wanted to perform. I took Paco's double and loaded the 9.3x74R with two expanding Torpedo (TUG) bullets that are perfect for leopard. We decided upon a simple plan of action—to march around the stream and to surprise the wounded leopard. Fernando, Giovannino, Tagliani, and Moises would move along the left side, while Hamisi and I searched the right. Bit by bit we searched the area where the leopard should have been, but there was no sign of it. It was as if the animal had vanished in a puff of smoke. We retraced our steps to see if it had escaped in the other direction, and we peered under every bush for it. Finally, Hamisi and I saw some movement in the tops of the low bushes ahead of us and told the others, who were behind us to the left, that we'd seen something we needed to check out. At that same moment, about five yards away, we heard a furious groan and the leopard sprang from under the bushes, snorting and roaring. It threw itself at Hamisi who only had time to jump behind me. I fired the right barrel, dropping the leopard, and the furious cat fell. It tried to get up again, but Fernando and Giovannino each fired at it, putting an end to the problem.

It was a beautiful specimen, record class, with a superb skin. Fernando had been hunting with me in the Sudan before and had taken lion, elephant, and buffalo, but from the moment he set foot in Tanzania, he had wanted a leopard. Now his dreams had come true. We were delirious with joy. When we returned to camp, no one could believe that we'd taken a lion, a Thomson's gazelle, a buffalo, and a leopard before lunch. But there they were, four genuine trophies to show that it was real and that Saint Hubert had sheltered us well with his cape that day.

•••

CHAPTER IX

Twenty-five Years in the Sudan

In 1984 I celebrated my Silver Anniversary as a professional hunter in the Sudan. I couldn't believe so much time had passed, a whole lifetime for many people. Sitting quietly in my office/library/trophy room, surrounded by the essence of Africa, I close my eyes and relive those twenty-five years. I can't help the attack of nostalgia that accompanies so many happy memories.

In 1958 I was working as a white hunter, which was what professional hunters were called then. I was in beautiful Tanganyika at the time (it became Tanzania on 29 October 1964) when I received a letter from the Sudanese owner of the Sudan Travel and Tourist Agency in Khartoum. Through someone in Nairobi, he had heard that I liked to hunt in the Sudan and made me a business proposition. He was putting together a safari company to work the southern part of the country and he wanted me to lead these trips for him. The old Anglo-Egyptian Sudan has always had a mythical attraction for hunters, a place that everyone talks about but no one actually knows, so I received this offer with great pleasure. I quickly sent a telegram to clinch the deal and wrote a letter at the same time to set up a time to talk and firm up our plans. As soon as I finished my safaris in Tanganyika, I was off to Khartoum where the Sudanese, Aziz Osman, was waiting. We got on well from the start and discussed plans while seated on the terrace of the Grand Hotel, enjoying afternoon breezes along the banks of the Nile and sipping tall glasses of iced lemonade.

Aziz Osman explained to me the world of commercial safaris in Sudan. Because there were no professional hunters in the country, he was forced to organize a few outings for French and American sportsmen led by game department staff out of Juba, the capital of the southern Sudan. These had been quite successful, so he wanted to go all out, buying proper camping equipment in Nairobi and trying out white hunters to get the same quality of service found in

Angelo Dacey, the author, George Kasagbi "Jorgito," in Juba, the Sudan, 1959.

Kenya. So, in this casual manner, I became the first professional hunter permanently based in the Sudan.

Up until then, the few full safaris that had taken place in the country had been booked out of Nairobi. These safaris were all organized in Kenya—to the point that all the vehicles, equipment, and specialized personnel came from the main office in Kenya. The personnel would drive the vehicles and all the equipment back to Kenya as soon as the safari was over. Our plan was that, if we were successful, we would grow and could contract the extra hunters we needed. It would all be under my control, making me a pioneer or "godfather" of professional hunters in the Sudan. I was very proud of this because this sort of distinction was very rare for a Spaniard in those latitudes. For 1958 it made me a "rare bird." I returned to Spain in search of clients and to visit my current girlfriend, returning to the banks of the Nile full of hopes and plans. Meanwhile, Aziz Osman organized Sudan Safari Tours, opened an office in Juba, and bought the equipment we would need to properly launch us. This included two Land Rovers and a five-ton Bedford truck. After a few days in Khartoum, I hopped on the plane for Juba. In those days, this was a pathetic DC-3 that took more than six hours, stopping in Malakal and sometimes Wau, which would mean limping into Juba eight or nine hours later.

Excited and curious both, I was met at the airport by a little, shortsighted guy who grabbed my hand and introduced himself as George Kasagbi, administrator-manager of Sudan Safari Tours in Juba. I immediately dubbed him "Jorgito" and so he has been known ever since, even though he spent only a few seasons in the safari business.

I got my junk out of the plane, threw it in the Land Rover, and drove to the house Aziz Osman had rented for us, which was behind the now-vanished Barclays Bank and fifty yards from the office. I remember that the house, which was on the first floor of an old colonial building, was incredibly hot because the entire outside gallery was closed off and the windows painted white. Although the painted-over windows cut off all outside vision, they offered a unique view. When I asked Jorgito to open the windows, he gave a mysterious wink and whispered that I should take a peek and not make a sound. I put my eye to the tiny opening and saw the terrace of the home of the director of the Barclays Bank. On that terrace was his very nice-looking and young wife, wearing very little. She imagined that she had found a private place to relax, but Jorgito took advantage of the chance to get the only "erotic" vision in the entire southern Sudan. The show never lost its charms, and we each lined up every day for our peek, just to soothe our tormented spirits.

We went to the game department so that I could meet the chief game warden, a man who remains a good friend to this day. With the sunniest smile and the whitest teeth imaginable, Mahmoud Abu Sineina and I got along splendidly and he offered me the full support of his office. His officials showed me the best places to hunt, and one of them, a young, tall, educated Dinka named Isaiah Kulang, became another very good friend and later director of the same department. The last time I saw him, retired from his post, Isaiah was the same as always except that his hair had turned as thin as mine!

In those days the southern Sudan was a paradise for the hunter with scores of animals everywhere, beginning from the outskirts of Juba. One night the game department snared a leopard in the abandoned garden across from my house. It had been cleaning out all the dogs in the neighborhood. Another night a lion killed a donkey by the airport. Buffalo could be hunted in Rejaf, a twenty-minute drive from downtown Juba. Only an hour by Land Rover, near Mount Lado, to the left of the Juba-Terakeka road, was a place full of elephants, white rhinos, and every sort of antelope.

In view of all this, I was able to get permission to put up a sign at the airport reading "Sudan Safari Tours. Welcome to Juba, the hunter's paradise."

For a while I was lord and master of all hunting that went on in the southern Sudan. Besides a few reserves and national parks, it was all open without concessions, controlled zones, or anything that the modern hunter has come to expect. You could travel 600 miles in whatever direction you wanted, put your camp wherever you liked, and start hunting whenever you felt like it. These were happy times, now gone forever.

Every time I ended a safari and returned to Juba, the accountant for Shell, Angelo Dacey, immediately appeared to admire the trophies. With an English father and a Greek mother, he was fascinated by hunting and always peppered me with all manner of enthusiastic questions. We became inseparable, and in the afternoons when the office closed I would go to his house to enjoy the excellent dishes prepared by his Greek wife, Beba, and the pleasant distractions provided by their two children. We'd hunt together on weekends, and I noticed that Angelo was an excellent hunter as well as a nice person, so I talked to Aziz Osman about him and within a few months he left Shell to join Sudan Safari Tours as a professional hunter. Over time he became, by far, the best hunter in the Sudan, and I'm proud to have given him his first break. We have continued a very happy friendship to this day.

Another area we hunted was Karpeto, south of Juba, toward Uganda near the Nile. Herds of elephants were everywhere. They covered entire hills, which seemed to move with them. I saw herds of more than—no exaggeration—500 head, with some glorious examples among them. The largest set of tusks I took weighed ninety-four and ninety-seven pounds and were gorgeous. The last time I was there was in 1984, and I didn't see a single elephant, only their white bones in the grass as I flew again and again over every corner of the area.

Angelo and I traveled all over the southern Sudan seeking new hunting grounds and exploring places that had never been hunted before. I remember Boma Plateau, near Ethiopia, which had thousands of animals everywhere you looked. The same went for Pibor Post with innumerable white-eared kob. In the Aliab-Dinka, 110 miles north of Juba and on the left bank of the Nile, we could see white rhinos, herds and herds of elephants, lions under shrubs or dozing in the sun, and a plain literally covered with reedbucks, tiangs, and kobs.

A place to find good elephant was Falual, between Yirol and Shambé, a little north of Aliab-Dinka, where in 1961 I had an adventure in the style of Jules Verne. With three Spanish clients, we took an elephant near two Dinka villages. While we were waiting to remove the tusks, people from the villages appeared to ask for the elephant meat. I told them that they were welcome to it as soon as we were finished. Meanwhile I put the four-door Land Rover station wagon out of the infernal sun and in a shady spot about thirty meters away. It was a big vehicle and we had removed the doors so it worked better for hunting.

As the clients and I were replaying the kill, Agustino, my personal gunbearer, came up to say that the tusks were off and to ask if the people could begin carving up the meat. I gave the nod, but only moments later an angry ruckus erupted. It seemed that everyone had jumped on the elephant at once, each intending to take whatever meat he could. The first in line defended their places with fists

The author and his gunbearer, Agustino, and some Dinkas, the Sudan, 1960.

The author in his camp on the banks of the Nile.

An enormous Sudanese elephant taken in the Biki area, 1977.

and sharp elbows while those behind tried to cram in by using their spear tips as knives. Those at the edge of the crowd battled forward with harsh blows.

The first group, squashed and suffocated against the elephant, turned and began to fight the others and before you knew it there was quite a donnybrook. The fight moved away from the elephant as the mob formed itself into two groups, one from each village, and they charged each other like raging bulls, poking one another with the shafts of their spears. Barnaba, my chief skinner, tried to separate them but they drove him away with their screams and spears, wounding him in one hand. The situation disintegrated very quickly and blood began to flow. I ran to the Land Rover, where the others already had taken cover, shouting for a rifle.

I ran back to the "battlefield" and fired once into the air. Immediately everyone froze in place. I took advantage of the break in the action to fire twice more into the air and within seconds not a soul was to be seen and the battlefield quiet. In the blessed silence I treated poor banged-up Barnaba, who screeched as if his throat really had been cut, until a few ex-contenders returned to see what was happening. I climbed onto the elephant with my rifle reloaded and called up the chief of each village. After giving them what-for, I dispatched four men from each village to cut up the elephant and lined the others up to wait their turn for their share.

In the heat the elephant was beginning to take on a most unappetizing smell, but I waited until the meat was properly doled out. I made the chiefs get into the Land Rover and after dropping my friends off at the camp, we all went to the police headquarters in Yirol to explain what had happened—chiefs, witnesses, and I. I went because I didn't want some kind of distorted story to get around about me shooting at natives.

We met at the district commissioner's office, and I explained my part and left the room, leaving the chiefs, Barnaba, and Agustino behind. Within half an hour I was called back in, and the commissioner thanked me profusely for stopping what could have turned into a bloodbath—something which had happened before. There were thanks and smiling handshakes all around, and I returned

A typical Nile buffalo from the southern Sudan.

to camp, leaving the chiefs behind and under arrest. All the way back to camp my knees were still knocking at the thought of the part I'd been forced to play in the fracas that had taken place. I'm pleased to say that I later returned to that area many times over the years without the least problem.

The area in all the Sudan that impressed me most was the zone of tropical forests between Yambio and Tambura in the far southwestern part of the country near the Congo border. The great forest elephant were everywhere as were the rare bongo. Angelo and I dubbed this "our" hunting ground and looked with disdain at tusks weighing less than seventy pounds. At the time, because we were residents, the license cost us the equivalent of a mere $18, allowing us three elephants at $45 dollars each with as much ivory as we could take. Tour-

Tony and his wife Isabel in front of the Norfolk Hotel in Nairobi, 1965. This was the traditional starting place for safaris when Kenya was open to hunting.

ist hunters paid $90 dollars for the license and $180 dollars per elephant. Angelo, with his eternal .375 magnum, and I, with my inseparable .416 Rigby, appreciated this gift from the gods of hunting.

Hunting was closed in 1964 because of the civil war between the north and south. We had to find new hunting areas far from the hostilities, so we chose an area in southern Radoum in the southern part of Darfur Province, between the Umbelasha and Adda Rivers, near the border with the Central African Republic. To reach this area took twelve to fourteen hours in the Land Rover from Nyala, which was connected with Khartoum by biweekly flights. Without a doubt it was one of the most remote areas I have ever seen in my life, in the middle of nothing but with plenty of animals to hunt and with the lure of the unknown.

When peace finally returned to the south, we tried to return to our old hunting areas but found the number of animals depleted. Both the guerrillas and the army had had to live off the land and the wild animals had suffered very badly.

To the new professionals, the hunting seemed abundant, but to Angelo and I, who had known the place when we were practically the lords and masters of paradise, were saddened to see how quickly things had changed. For the first time there were controlled areas and a system of concessions, which limited our movements enormously.

Aziz Osman continued Sudan Safari Tours in a limited fashion, while Angelo and I, along with the Kaitaki brothers, formed the Nile Safaris Company. Poor Osman died in Juba on one of his quick visits there. With him died much of the flavor of the old days when it took twenty-four to twenty-eight hours to get from Juba to Yambio, when we were without radios or any other communication, and when everything was left in the hands of Divine Providence.

Who could imagine that the partnership between a lively Sudanese and a Spanish dreamer would help to open one of the least-known countries in Africa to international big-game hunting? But it did, and it is something that is an honor and gives me endless satisfaction. It would be marvelous to revive those "heroic" bygone days along the Nile, in the company of dear friends—Angelo Dacey, George "Jorgito" Zafiro, Nicholas Ginis, John Kaikati, and others—who, all together, worked for the success of the safari industry in the Sudan. Given the present conditions there, it must for the time being remain an impossible dream.

•••

CHAPTER X

The Lado Enclave: Ivory Paradise

The heyday of professional ivory hunting in the era of smokeless gunpowder took place at the beginning of this century in the part of Central Africa called the Lado Enclave, under the control of King Leopold II of Belgium. I've always had a great interest in the history of this forgotten corner of Africa since I was lucky enough to have lived there for many years and to have traveled it from one end to the other, seeing many of the things described in the old stories.

Living there, it was easy to imagine the adventures of the great elephant hunters, who left indelible marks on the pages of hunting history. I was inspired by these great men who were confronted by a hard, dangerous, and hostile life. The tenacity and valor they displayed deeply influenced my life. The lives of these hunters seem to have sprung out of the kind of adventure novel where fantasy surpasses reality. And day after day the fantasy continued, throughout the seven years that this chaotic and unsurpassed period of elephant hunting lasted. Its conditions were unique and can never be repeated.

Since the Lado Enclave is frequently mentioned in hunting books, I think it would be worthwhile to look at its history. The history helps to explain the greatest elephant-poaching adventure of all time, and it gives the modern-day hunter a glimpse into an Africa and a time that are forever gone. Although I have written about the Lado Enclave in other books, my knowledge of the area keeps growing, so I have included the following as an update. So, let us now look at the story of the Lado Enclave, its turbulent history, and the bizarre elephant hunters who challenged everyone, taking their ivory with blood, sweat, and tears.

The name Lado Enclave was given to the territory by the authorities of the Congo Free State, who named it for Mount Lado, which dominated the northern part of the administrative area. The Jebel Lado, as it is locally known, sits fifteen miles north of Gondokoro (present day Juba), which is the capital of the southern Sudan today. The Enclave extended throughout what is today the province of the West Nile in Uganda and part of the province of Equatoria in the Sudan, from Nimule to the old Belgian site of Kiro in the north, on the western bank of the Nile. It covered a total of 25,000 square miles (over 200 miles from north to south, following the Nile from Kiro to Lake Albert) of the most primitive, savage, and hostile territory in Central Africa. Administered by the old Congo Free State (renamed the Belgian Congo in 1908 when it became a Belgian colony on the death of Leopold II), it was considered the finest country in the whole of Africa for elephants. More elephants were found there than any place else on the continent, with a high proportion of big tuskers among them.

Because of this richness of "white gold," the area became the center of attraction for elephant poachers. Working from the east bank of the Nile in British-controlled Uganda, the poachers would cross the Nile and forage into the Belgian-held territory, thumbing their noses at the Belgian patrols when they made it successfully back into British-held territory with their loot. The possibility for making fortunes in the Lado Enclave was virtually limitless because there were thousands of elephants within its borders.

The history of how Leopold II got this territory, which was located between the Congo Free State and the Nile is an interesting one. King Leopold first became interested in this territory in the 1870s when General Gordon suggested to him the many benefits to be reaped by having a port on the Nile. Gordon, who was the English governor of the Sudanese province of Equatoria (1874-1876) and founder of the Lado Post, had moved his administrative center from the east bank of the Nile to the west bank because the west bank offered better navigating conditions from Khartoum during the dry season.

This access was very important, commercially, to Leopold because the Nile route was much shorter, faster, and cheaper for the products coming from the northeastern corner of the Congo Free State. It was very costly to trek the products from the interior to Boma on the Atlantic and then on to Belgium, which was an incredibly long way around. With a clear vision of what was needed, King Leopold wanted at any cost to get a port on the Nile that would allow shipment of exports from the Uele District, very isolated from the rest of the Congo in those days. King Leopold knew, for example, that the cost of transporting a bale of rubber to Belgium via the Nile was a sixth of the cost of shipping it the long way around via Boma and the Atlantic.

Commercial interests were also intertwined with the political interests and aspirations of the great powers in Europe. Like the rulers of France, England, and Germany at the end of the nineteenth century, King Leopold II of Belgium was determined to colonize and develop his "sphere of influence" in Africa. In 1876, at his personal expense, he founded the *L'Association Internationale pour l'Exploration et la Civilization de l'Afrique Centrale*, which was renamed *Le Comite d'Etudes du Haut Congo* in 1878. Unlike the other rulers involved in the colonization of Africa, Leopold kept the Congo territory under his personal

Tony Sanchez and a view of the old Lado Enclave near Nimule, the Sudan, 1959.

management; in fact, until 1908 the government of the Congo Free State and the government of Belgium were two completely separate entities without any common denominator—except for the fact that they both had the same ruler.

Given both the political and the financial exigencies, Leopold II was determined to make the Congo commercially profitable, which led him to unconscionable extremes. In his zeal, King Leopold ravaged the natural resources of the Congo and virtually enslaved its population in order to make his commercial venture succeed. Consumed with debt, Leopold borrowed millions of francs from the kingdom of Belgium, in return for a promise that Belgium would inherit the Congo, should the debt be unpaid at the time of his death.

In 1885, after the Berlin Conference, all of the territory belonging to Leopold's association, *Le Comite . . . du Haut Congo,* became the Congo Free State, private property of King Leopold, who now became the world's greatest landholder. For Leopold, the Berlin Conference was immensely important because it recognized the major powers' spheres of influence in Africa and it allowed the absolute monarch of the Congo Free State to pursue the economic profits of colonial exploitation in his "defined" area, free from outside intervention. What emerged from this conference was a balancing act by the major European powers in which one power would support the territorial ambitions

The Lado post on the Nile, headquarters for the the Belgians in the Lado Enclave, 1908.

of another to gain the right of sovereignty somewhere else. In effect, the Berlin Conference authenticated the concept of political spheres of influence in Africa. What it also did was establish fluid alliances for strategic solutions, based on rivalry between the great European powers over the spoils of Africa. This in turn embittered international relations and helped prepare the way for the First World War.

Thus it was that King Leopold, constitutional monarch of Belgium and absolute monarch of the Congo Free State, and Queen Victoria of Great Britain signed an accord in Brussels on 12 May 1894 in which Leopold ceded part of Central Africa to Great Britain, but kept the Congo Free State and the Lado Enclave. The British, who had entered into the first agreement in bad faith, forced the king on 9 May 1906 to sign a new accord, which would terminate his rule over the Lado Enclave six months after his death, passing this territory over to the Anglo-Egyptian Sudan.

Because of the 1894 agreement, Leopold controlled the Enclave, which represented a great deal of work because of the nature of the native inhabitants of the area. In 1881, after a successful revolt against the Egyptians, Muhammad Ahmed (al-Mahdi, "the guide") established an independent government in the Anglo-Egyptian Sudan, which lasted until 1898. In his effort to overthrow the Christian, antislavery forces in the Anglo-Egyptian Sudan, al-Mahdi imposed a rule of blood and fire as he and his followers pillaged and plundered their way through the territory in their quest for slaves and ivory. The British and Egyptians abandoned their hold on the area after the death of General Gordon at the battle of Khartoum on 26 January 1885. This left al-Mahdi free to pursue his

Bill Buckley with his best tusks, 145 and 137 pounds, taken in the Enclave, 1905.

territorial and religious ambitions almost unheeded—except for the Belgian presence in the southernmost province of the Sudan. From their base at Rejaf, the Mahdists were free to turn their attentions to the Belgians of the Lado Enclave.

The conquest of al-Mahdi's forces in the Enclave was a tremendous challenge for King Leopold, who sent an army under Commander Chaltin on 17 February 1897 to repress the native rebellion. Chaltin led 700 African soldiers into battle against the Mahdists in Rejaf and forced them to abandon their capital. With this victory, King Leopold's army firmly established his sovereignty over the entire area. The Mahdists were far from ready, however, to give up this area that Leopold had defined as the Lado Enclave.

Rejaf became the main center of the Enclave, and the Mahdists fell back to Bor, 100 miles downstream. There the Mahdists waited in vain for reinforcements from Khartoum. In 1898 Major Hanolet succeeded Chaltin in charge of the Enclave, and in May 1898 the Mahdists, desperate after not hearing from Khartoum for more than a year, decided to attack Rejaf for its weapons and ammunition. During the night of the third and fourth of June 1898, they silently approached the city. Despite the precautions normally taken, Rejaf was taken by surprise and nearly fell into enemy hands. By a miracle, the defenders managed to regroup, and after a terrible battle the Mahdists were put to flight. As a result of the attack, half the African troops in Rejaf were killed or wounded, and, of the fourteen Europeans, two were killed and seven gravely wounded. Afterward, the Belgians realized that Rejaf was in a very vulnerable position, so it was decided to create new posts. This began in July with the arrival of Commander Henry and 600 soldiers at the old administrative center of Lado, which was rebuilt into a fort superior to the one at Rejaf.

Meanwhile, the British were preparing a major offensive against al-Mahdi's successor, Khalifa Abdullahi, to rid the area of the Mahdists once and for all. In November 1898 Major Martyr united the Congo forces with a company of Uganda Rifles to attack Bor and destroy the Mahdists. When they arrived, they found the place abandoned. The Khalifa's troops were nearly eliminated on 2 September 1898 on the plains of Kerreri, near Omdurman, when they met the combined Anglo-Egyptian forces under the command of General Kitchener. The battle began at 6:30 in the morning and by midday the Mahdists' losses surpassed 11,000 dead and 16,000 wounded. The Khalifa and his chiefs fled but were captured and eliminated days later. Their defeat left the Upper Nile in peace for the first time in thirteen years.

Remembering the Belgians' vulnerability in the area, Commander Henry established a new post, which was very important for the next five years, at the far north of the Enclave in Kiro near the end of 1898. He had more than a thousand men, and his cannons covered the entrance to the Lado Enclave from the Nile. In 1899 Hanolet was wounded in an ambush and Henry had to fill in until the arrival of Chaltin, who had been promoted to colonel. Chaltin arrived with five European officials and 1,200 African soldiers.

After they arrived in Kiro near the end of October 1899, they continued traveling the Nile to create and organize administrative posts, mostly in the uninhabited south. Between 1902 and 1906 more Belgian expeditions lead by Hanolet, Royaux, and Lamaire completed the consolidation and administration of the entire territory known as the Lado Enclave, building roads and commercial posts. At the same time, the British were reinforcing their presence on the other side of the Nile, which in turn reinforced their position vis-à-vis the agreement signed on 9 May 1906 that turned over the Lado Enclave to the British six months after the death of Leopold II.

The government of Congo Free State quickly realized—even with the Mahdists vanquished—that control of the Enclave was more theoretical than practical, given the distances, the remoteness of the country, and the lack of communications. During the last period of the Belgian occupation of the Lado Enclave, between 1903 and 1910, that hidden nook of Central Africa became an elephant Mecca for hunters, most of whom were poachers. They organized their raids from the "safe" side of the Nile under British control. The Belgian patrols were few and far between and did almost nothing to prevent elephant hunting. The two main points of entry to the Enclave were through the Koba area and Wadelai, where provisions could be bought and ivory sold, although better prices could be had in Gondokoro (present day Juba) farther north.

The Lado Enclave became known as a "no-man's land" because of the nature of the Belgian administration (or lack thereof). The Belgians made no genuine effort to administer the area and justice was nonexistent. The administrative posts, little more that native huts, were infrequent, and native runners were the only means of communication from one far-flung post to another. The *chef de poste* was typically a rank opportunist, who used his position to make a fortune in ivory and rubber. The *chef de poste* depended on armed native askaris (soldiers) to maintain his power and ill-gotten gains. These soldiers were nothing more than vicious, vile thugs who terrorized the natives and who looted and killed with impunity. The native population in the area, not surprisingly, hated their oppressors and were always happy to help the adventuring elephant hunters loot ivory from the Lado Enclave, which is one very good reason why the "Company of Adventurers" (so named by Theodore Roosevelt) was so successful.

Finally, King Leopold II died on 17 December 1909, making it necessary to adhere to the new agreement, which said that all the agents and administrators from the Congo would have to leave the Lado Enclave within six months. To the surprise of the British, the Belgians cleared out in three weeks, leaving the territory as a true no-man's-land for the rest of the six-month period. This gave elephant poachers an unprecedented opportunity. The Enclave was officially turned over to the British at Yei on 16 June 1910, in the presence of the Belgian officials De Muelenaere, Herremere, and Rinquet, the last commander of the Lado Enclave. The Lado Enclave had officially become part of the Anglo-Egyptian Sudan.

It isn't known how the "ivory mine" of the Lado Enclave was discovered or how the situation began that had no precedent in the history of Africa. Ninety-five percent of the hunters operated illegally. First on the scene was Bill Buckley, who arrived in 1903 to hunt legally with an unlimited license good for five months. That license had been granted by the governor general of the Congo Free State in Boma, at the other extreme of the country. Buckley got tired of waiting in British territory for the license to arrive, which could take months in those days, and decided to try a little escapade on the other side of the Nile, to see what happened. What happened was that he found conditions perfect for the uncontrolled hunting of elephants. Bill Buckley succumbed to temptation and started wholeheartedly poaching elephants from the Belgians, forgetting about the license promised by the authorities. He was quickly followed by others.

Until 1908 there were only about eight or ten hunters operating in the Lado Enclave on a regular basis. The avalanche occurred after the death of Leopold II in 1909. With the possibility of so much ivory within their grasp and in unlimited amounts, a torrent of poachers and pseudo-poachers came to the Enclave to try their luck. Many came from British East Africa and Uganda where they had worked as coffee planters, bureaucrats, military men, and tenant farmers. During the following months, until Sudan took control, chaos reigned and the elephants were the real losers with their herds chased and fired at from all sides.

During the time that the Lado Enclave was under Belgian control, poachers had to work carefully so as to not attract the attention of the patrols. The most dangerous moment came on crossing the Nile. The ivory had to be ferried in local canoes and hidden in strategic spots, but canoes were easily detectable once they reached midstream. Often cargoes that had taken months of hard work to collect were lost at the last second, and many were the canoes that barely managed to arrive on the British side because of the heavy fire from the other side of the Nile by the Congo Free State askaris.

The hunters ran enormous risks in their expeditions. In those days the country was plagued by diseases, many of them still unknown and for which there were no cures. All the poachers suffered from malaria, carried by local mosquitoes. Local tribes were still hostile and the Belgian patrols were likely to be tough on poachers.

The hunters who operated in the Lado Enclave tried to be on good terms with the natives. It was the only way to survive. The hunters depended on them for porters, provisions, and information about the elephants' movements and those of the Belgian patrols. The only exception to this was an Italian named Buchieri from Naples who chased local women and cheated the tribes by not paying for his provisions. Finally, one tribe, the Alurs, lost patience with him and killed him after a bloody episode, chopping up his body and leaving it for the vultures.

Of the hunters who operated in the Enclave before 1908, the best known were Bill Buckley, Pete Pearson, Deaf Banks, Charlie Ross, Billy Pickering, Quentin Grogan, Robert Foran, and the Craven brothers. After 1908 the most active hunters were Selland, John Boyes, Billy Bennett, the Brittlebank brothers, Knowles, and Commander Longden. The famous Karamojo Bell also hunted the Enclave during 1908 but legally, with his license good for five months from the authorities in the Congo Free State.

I had the great honor and enormous satisfaction to be Robert Foran's friend until his death at the age of eighty three. He was one of the hunters who operated illegally in the Enclave before 1908 and he gave me firsthand information about what went on. Foran began hunting elephants in 1904 in the former British East Africa and got his biggest trophy early in his career—a single-tusked elephant that weighed 169 pounds, taken at the foot of Mount Kenya in April 1904.

In total, he took about 400 elephants, most of them in the Enclave and Uganda, always seeking quality in place of quantity. In the southern area of the Enclave, he got, on one expedition, ivory worth £3,000. This included five pairs of tusks that weighed more than 100 pounds each. His best trophies from the Enclave included two pairs of tusks that weighed a phenomenal 159 and 155 pounds and 148 and 146 pounds. Foran began hunting elephants with a double-barreled Holland & Holland of the .500-450 Nitro Express caliber, but as he was not a big man, it proved too heavy. So, he decided on a Mauser in .350 Rigby caliber, firing a bullet of 310 grains, which he used until he stopped hunting elephants in 1916.

Ivory collected by Robert Foran in the Lado Enclave, worth £3,000 in 1908.

Pete Pearson began in the Enclave in 1904, the same time as Deaf Banks. Both used .577 Nitro Express rifles, firing bullets of 750 grains, and between them took hundreds of elephants including one with only one tusk weighing 185 pounds. Deaf Banks—who was indeed nearly deaf—never left the Lado Enclave. He entered in 1904 and stayed through its incorporation with the Sudan and was later in charge of elephant control when it became part of Uganda. In total, he took between 2,700 and 3,000 elephants, mostly with his double .577 Nitro. Banks held the record for having shot thirteen elephants in a row with thirteen shots from that same gun. He was active until 1941 when he returned to London after forty-two years of hunting elephants. He died at the age of seventy-nine on 31 May 1954.

Pete Pearson was also one of the great figures of the Lado Enclave, and except for the one time he joined Bill Buckley for an expedition, he always hunted alone. Born in Australia on 16 January 1877, he had a gloomy character, few friends, and lived a Spartan life. Physically he was very strong, almost six feet two inches tall and able to walk forever. He was one of the most successful hunters in the Enclave and took many large elephants, among them a pair of tusks weighing 153 and 155 pounds, always with his .577 Nitro Express. After the Enclave was incorporated into the Sudan, Pearson went to the Belgian Congo where he hunted elephants on a commercial license for a while, as he did in Ubangi-Shari. After the Great War, he hunted again in Tanganyika. Like Banks, he worked awhile in the elephant control department in Uganda, a job that lasted until he died of cancer in Kampala on 10 September 1929, at the age of fifty-two.

Between stints as an ivory hunter and working in elephant control, he took between 1,800 and 2,000 elephants. Until 1912 he always used his .577 Nitro Express, but as soon as he tried the new Holland & Holland .375 Magnum he became a big supporter of this caliber with a Mauser bolt action. He used this rifle, made especially for him by John Rigby & Co. (London), continually until his death.

Bill Buckley, the pioneer of the Lado Enclave, used two double rifles. The use of the .577 Nitro Express was almost a given among the ivory hunters of his period, but he also used a Holland & Holland in .500 Nitro Express along with a small .303 Lee-Enfield repeating rifle for long shots at the heart. His largest pair of tusks weighed 145 and 137 pounds.

Charlie Ross used a repeating .400-350 Rigby and got very good results considering that it is not a terribly powerful caliber. Its 310-grain bullet had an initial speed of 2,000 feet per second and initial energy of 2,760 foot/pounds. "How did he do this with such a small caliber?" can best be answered by, "The bullet has not been invented that kills without hitting its precise mark."

Quentin Grogan, Robert Foran's good friend, also used the .577 Nitro Express during his travels in the Enclave and took his best pair of tusks with it, weighing 134 and 125 pounds.

Pete Pearson in the Lado Enclave with his .577 double rifle, 1905.

It seems that the largest trophy taken in the Enclave was shot by Billy Pickering and weighed 191 and 193 pounds. Unfortunately, Pickering was killed at the age of 31 by an elephant he couldn't stop with his .577 Nitro Express. The elephant grabbed Pickering by the head and dragged him into the bushes with its trunk. It must have been horrible to be pinned by one of those huge feet while the trunk wrapped around his head, pulling furiously as if to tug the cap off a bottle.

One of the first hunters to arrive in the Lado Enclave after the death of Leopold II was John Boyes, a born adventurer who became king of the Kikuyus in Kenya. He was in Nairobi returning from an expedition when he heard about the Lado Enclave and how, literally overnight, it had turned into a no-man's land. He decided to take full advantage of this absurd situation and left immediately for the Enclave.

After arriving in Butiaba, on Lake Albert, he went to Koba along with a buddy named Selland and fifty native porters. On this first expedition he took 1,200 pounds of ivory, with a pair of tusks weighing 125 and 111 pounds. Coincidentally, his partner, Selland, also took 1,200 pounds of ivory. They surpassed their record on the second expedition, taking 1,500 pounds of ivory, including an exceptional pair of tusks weighing 150 pounds each. It is an indication of the richness of the area when such extraordinary ivory could still be found after fifty years of intensive hunting. In total, John Boyes shot thirty-eight bull elephants in the Enclave and made quite a bit of money at it. His favorite weapon was a .450-400 Nitro Express made by Greener, shooting a bullet of 400 grains.

Bill Bennett was captain of the small boat that connected Butiaba on Lake Albert with Nimule where the Albert Nile became the White Nile as it crossed into the Sudan. Through his work he was in constant contact with the elephant hunters for years until, after listening to their stories and seeing their profits, he decided to follow in their footsteps. In 1908 he abandoned his mail boat to become a hunter even though his experience at that point was limited to two elephants. On his first professional run, he joined my old friend Robert Foran and in three weeks they netted a profit of £800 each, which was a lot of money in those days.

He had the bad fortune to become the target of a vendetta by the Alur chief Jura, who was still angry over the incident with the Italian Buchieri, who had killed fourteen Alurs with his .450 Nitro Express before being stabbed and then quartered. Jura captured Bennett and took his weapons, ivory, and equipment. Only escape saved his life. Once he recovered, the other hunters helped put him back on his feet again, and he was soon off hunting elephants everywhere but Alur territory. John Boyes gave him a .450 Nitro Express and ammunition. After the Enclave was closed to open hunting, Bennett went to the Belgian Congo after the elephants and later Ubangi-Shari, where he died of malaria.

Returning from the Lado Enclave, 1905.

Many years later I went to the areas where I calculated he might have worked, but was never able to get any information about him. Perhaps too much time had already passed. How sad that a hunter of Bennett's stature should have vanished off the face of the earth without leaving the smallest trace of the man once known affectionately as the Admiral of the Nile Fleet.

A long time later, when I lived and hunted in the area that used to be the Lado Enclave, I visited the old Belgian post at Rejaf, which still dominates an entire hill and from which they could keep an eye on a wide area. A few almost unidentifiable ruins are all that is left of it, but thanks to missionaries, the cemetery is well cared for even after all these years.

I have contributed in a modest way to the conservation of this last tangible corner of the Lado Enclave. Whenever I arrived to hunt, I would always visit the cemetery with a few members of my African team to clear the area of weeds, leaving it as nice as possible for the anonymous heroes who gave their lives for the flag they served.

Rejaf is one of those places where I like to walk, to climb to the top of the hill and imagine what it must have been like 90 years ago when the Mahdists and the colonial powers faced each other under nearly unbearable conditions, with only their legs and iron wills to support them in a place that was the opposite of paradise, that was, without a doubt, the most lost and lonely spot in the world.

Robert Foran told me that in the Lado Enclave it was common to see herds of 500 to 1,500 elephants, many with gorgeous tusks. I sadly arrived too late for that, but there was still the chance to see 500 to 600 head covering entire hills. I took some good ones, even if they weren't comparable to their grandfathers who had ambled across the same territory. It grieves me to report that today there is not a single elephant in this area—ivory poachers have left nothing but huge bones bleaching in the sun. All the elephants, in what was the most fabulous elephant area in Africa, have been obliterated. After hunting was halted in the Lado Enclave, the new authorities put such zeal into protecting the elephants that their numbers increased at such a rate that it became necessary to establish an elephant control scheme to keep their numbers down. I am glad to say that European hunters had no hand in the total elimination of the elephant inhabitants of the old Enclave. That was done by Africans exploited by the world ivory Mafia.

It is almost impossible to know exactly how many elephants were shot in the Enclave between 1903 and 1910, but according to the official export registers kept by ivory merchants in Rejaf, Koba, Nimule, Gondokoro, and Wadelai, an estimated minimum of 4,000 head with 400 pair of tusks weighing more than 100 pounds each were recorded.

After years of searching, I found a extraordinary collection of photographs of the old Lado Enclave and its hunters that gives an idea of the lives and careers of those "supermen" of the early part of the century. Because I have also participated in this lifestyle, albeit in a more modest fashion than those hunt-

One of the "official" poachers from the Lado Enclave with his bag of ivory, 1908.

ing heroes, I can't help but think about the "mini-men" of our times who whine if the super-organized, super-comfortable, and super-safe safari runs out of the eight cubes of ice they require for their already ice-cold glasses of Coca Cola. I imagine they'd have a heart attack if they saw Pete Pearson drinking Nile water scooped up with his hands.

The post of the Lado virtually no longer exists. Only a few battered signs note that this was once the great administrative center of the Enclave. Only the mountain north of Juba, the Jebel Lado, continues to carry the name. Gondokoro, Rejaf, Kiro, Wadelai, Dufile, and Koba live only in the memories of the few people interested in the history of the area. Few who pass by know that the greatest era of elephant hunting and poaching, in its fiercest and riskiest form, took place here in the romantic, lost, and forgotten Lado Enclave.

• • •

CHAPTER XI

Crocodiles

I've never professionally hunted crocodiles for their valuable skin, but nonetheless, I figure that throughout my African travels I've taken over 200. I don't have any chilling adventures to relate, and I've never found myself between one's jaws or had to go hand-to-hand in order to save my life—and thank God for it! The crocodile is outside my regular scope for hunting, but I've read, heard, and had to put up with so much foolishness about it that I feel obliged to clear up some points about this living fossil, which seems to enjoy not the slightest human sympathy whatsoever.

Although the name crocodile is applied broadly to any creature that crawls through the rivers and swamps of the tropical world, it is not correct. Among those included are the American alligator and the Indian crocodile. The real crocodile (of the *Crocodylidae* family) lives in Africa, Southeast Asia, Borneo, New Guinea, Australia, and certain places in America. I am not an expert enough herpetologist to rhapsodize on the subject, so what I will do is relay information from a practical point of view. The knowledge I've acquired over the years has been gained through what I've seen through my rifle scope. That's how I learned what I know.

I've been to some of the countries where the crocodile lives outside of Africa, but because I didn't hunt them there I'll concentrate on the Dark Continent, the scene of my direct experiences. There are many kinds of crocodiles, but here I'll deal only with the most popular, the *Crocodylus niloticus*, which is hunted for sport as well by professionals, who have brought the species to near extinction in many places. The name comes from the Greek word, *krokodeilos*, given by the Ionics to recall the lizards common in their lands.

They were also described in the fifth century B.C. by Herodotus, but it wasn't until fifty-eight years before Christ that the first live crocodile arrived in Rome. From the time that Herodotus wrote until the time the first crocodile appeared in Europe, many outlandish stories had developed about the almost mythical creature. Surprisingly, these flights of fancy have not disappeared over time, and a number of tall tales have survived as well. Some of these tall tales are so wild that only small children could possibly believe them.

One of the most popular is that crocodile hide repels bullets. If the hunter is using an air rifle, I would agree that it won't do more than scratch the skin, but with a rifle of any caliber above 6.5mm, the poor crocodile is entirely at the hunter's mercy, and it is quite easy to kill it with a well-aimed bullet. Nor do I fall for stories in which hunters claim to shoot crocodiles with a .22 Long Rifle. Some fool in Zambia made this claim to me, and only my good manners stopped me from throwing him in the Luangwa River, which was full of crocodiles. . . .

I find it astonishing when I hear the exaggerations of certain people—those who speak of feet as if they were inches and those who claim to have hunted nothing but huge crocodiles in Africa. This drivel flows from the mouths of professionals and sportsmen alike, so I make it a policy not to believe anything unless I've seen it with my own eyes. I've heard so much foolishness spoken about the size of the beasts that I'm convinced many people have never set eyes on a crocodile in their lives. Tales of twenty-five-foot specimens are pure hallucinations, and there isn't a herpetologist in the world who would back them up. Official figures put the average of the largest crocodiles between thirteen and sixteen feet long, but today they rarely surpass twelve feet. Like elephants with heavy tusks, the number of very large crocodiles has become quite small.

The Swedish naturalist Guggisberg, who has been established in Kenya for many years, charts crocodile sizes over the years in his interesting book *Crocodiles*, which is the result of many years of study. According to this book, Captain Reddick took the largest crocodile on record in 1916 from Lake Kioga in Uganda. It measured twenty-six feet and is followed on the list by another measuring twenty-five feet, taken by Hans Bresser in 1903 on the Mbaka River in what is now Malawi. Runners-up were a monster stretching $21\frac{1}{2}$ feet and two others at twenty-one feet in length. The first two were hunted on Lake Victoria in what is now Tanzania and the third on the Juba River in Somalia. In the middle of the list are two taken in Tanganyika that were $18\frac{1}{2}$ and eighteen feet long, and a third taken in Mozambique measuring seventeen feet. The most modest on record measure around sixteen feet.

The largest crocodile I ever took was in the Luangwa River in Zambia and measured fourteen feet, followed by another just a bit smaller from the same river, but the majority of the ones I've hunted fell well below these sizes. The largest I have ever seen was in the Central African Republic and measured over fifteen feet, killed by the paddle of a steamship that regularly traveled between

Lake Kariba crocodile, Zimbabwe, 1988.

Bangui and Brazzaville on the Ubangi and Congo Rivers. The length of the beast greatly increased its heft and volume.

The largest one on record at twenty-five feet had a body three feet high and fourteen feet around the thickest part—a truly enormous beast. In regards to weight, the data is probably inexact since nobody had the equipment on hand to weigh the examples. It is reported that a seventeen-foot crocodile weighed between 1,500 and 1,600 pounds when cut up into pieces. This means that the really big ones could actually have weighed tons considering the huge increase in volume according to length.

I've been asked if the great measurements of twenty feet and more could really be true, since the only witness was the person who shot the thing and there was usually not even a paltry photograph to back the claims up. The writings only tell us what the writer wanted us to know; besides, the events happened so long ago that we cannot verify the story. After having traveled practically the entire world and visiting the most famous natural history museums, I can say that I have never seen anything vaguely like those legendary monsters. Even in 1903 those monsters must have been worth their weight in gold. The exceptional never goes out of date.

Every time I hear excited stories of enormity, my fingers itch to grab my tape measure. If I'm allowed near the alleged phenomenon, my trusty tape measure consistently marks much less than I've been told. With my measuring, we return to the real world, with measurements of between ten and twelve feet, maximum. There must be an optical illusion that makes crocodiles flopped on the banks of a river look bigger than they are. Many hunters have been chastised by the illusion. The great hunter/naturalist Stevenson-Hamilton, director of South Africa's Kruger National Park for more than forty years and a person with vast experience, once saw an immense crocodile, which he calculated to be at least eighteen feet while in pursuit of the monster. When he actually measured it, he found to be only fourteen feet.

Now that Safari Club is keeping records on crocodiles, it appears that most everyone else's experience is about the same as mine. The largest crocodile I've heard about recently was a genuine monster approaching twenty feet, taken in Tanzania. Such a dinosaur would weigh perhaps 3,000 pounds, certainly well over a ton.

Like all reptiles, crocodiles continue to grow throughout their lives, although more slowly as age increases. It's impossible to say how long it takes for one to reach such proportions, but certainly many, many years. A twenty-footer has always been a most rare beast, but given today's depleted populations, it's amazing such a creature still existed.

These days a twelve-foot crocodile is big, and anything larger is very big. There have been a few taken in the fifteen-foot class, and such animals should be regarded as great trophies. They've lived long enough to be exceedingly wary—and just accurately assessing the size, should a big one be spotted, is difficult enough. Good places to look would be Botswana's Okavango region, Zambia's Luangwa River, and the Rufiji and its tributaries in Tanzania.

It is necessary not to be overconfident and to be careful around crocodiles. They are dangerous animals, but to approach them does not mean certain death, either. Some authors cite figures about the number of people killed every year by crocodiles in Africa. The professional hunter and writer Murray T. Smith found no fewer than 20,000 victims, which must surely be a great exaggeration. First of all, it is hard to get reliable information. Secondly, because the human race is by nature sensationalist, the imagination plays a major role in suppositions that have no real foundation.

I've traveled the four corners of Africa and I have seldom heard about accidents involving crocodiles. One of those happened in my own camp in the Luangwa Valley in Zambia, when a crocodile grabbed the daughter of one of my gunbearers while she was washing in river water up to her chest. The little eight-year-old had waded farther into the river than usual and the animal seized her by the leg and dragged her into deeper waters, drowning her. This is the crocodile's usual method of disposing of its victims. Because of the arrangement of its teeth, the crocodile, unlike the shark, cannot tear off the limbs of its victims; it is also the arrangement of its teeth that produce such great gashes on the bodies of its victims. The crocodile drags the victim to its underwater lair and leaves it to rot. Only when the body decomposes properly can the crocodile enjoy its meal.

In his book *Man is the Prey*, American author James Clarke compiles data about people killed by animals. In speaking of crocodiles, he quotes 1,000 as the number of people killed each year by the reptiles. I don't know where he gets the information but it seems exaggerated, especially when we consider

Crocodile from the Juba River, Somalia, 1962.

that the crocodile primarily eats fish and not meat, that their numbers have diminished greatly everywhere, and that there are very few big ones left, which are the greatest danger to humans. I feel that people who share their habitat with crocodiles take every precaution when they go near water and are very hard to surprise. I've crossed rivers like the croc-ablock Luangwa and never had a problem. Of course I never tried to take a bath among them. I may be crazy, but I'm not stupid, as the old line goes.

The crocodile is disappearing in many African countries, despite measures to protect it. There are few left in places like Lake Turkana in Kenya, the Baro River in Ethiopia, or the Shari River in Chad where there once were many. The places I've seen the most crocodiles are the Luangwa River and parts of the Zambezi River. The largest concentrations of crocodiles today are to be found in the Nile marshes, the southern Sudan, and the Okavango in Botswana.

The crocodile is getting help from an odd quarter today. Due to the value of skins, crocodile farming has become a popular venture in several African countries, especially Zambia and Zimbabwe. For some years only "farmed" crocodile skins could be imported into several western countries. While nothing really stops poachers so long as there's a black market, the ban coupled with increased availability of farmed skins has taken much pressure off wild crocodiles. They have started to recover in many river systems—but this doesn't do much for immediate trophy prospects since it takes so many years to grow big crocs.

If you think that hunting crocodiles requires nothing more than sneaking up on a pond and plugging one, think again. We are speaking of a wary animal with good sight, good hearing, and a good sense of smell; these reptiles must be stalked with patience. The bullet must hit the cervical vertebrae and shatter them, which will paralyze the crocodile. This is the only way to hunt the crocodile, for without this paralysis the crocodile will slip into the water and be lost to the hunter. It will sink like a rock—to be devoured by its unaffectionate brothers. As I pointed out before, any rifle from 7mm upward, with the correct softnose bullet, will be perfect for hunting crocodile.

Very few of my clients have come to Africa keen on shooting a big croc. A few other very experienced hands have turned to crocodile hunting after they acquired most everything else. The majority ignore the big lizards. This is too bad because crocodile hunting is an interesting sport. First you must find a big one. This can take lots of looking, plus a keen eye for judging game. But finding the one you want is only part of the game—and often the easy part. To

The author and his wife with a croc shot in the Luangwa River, Zambia, 1968.

kill a crocodile is easy, but only if the bullet lands in the exact right spot. To hit the brain or sever the spine requires precise marksmanship at a level demanded in few other types of hunting. Since such a shot is much too chancy at long range, it also requires careful planning in orchestrating a stalk and a most stealthy approach. Even so, hitting a walnut-sized target at as much as 200 yards may be required—truly a game for riflemen. One more problem, almost unlike anything else, is that the shot must be taken only when recovery of the carcass is certain. That means when the beast is resting on a sandbar, preferably a few steps from the water. Crocodiles are habitual and will rest in about the same place each day—but they have the annoying habit of slipping into the water just about the time a stalk is almost completed! Even with a perfect shot, you cannot shoot a crocodile in the water, as it will surely sink. Optimally, you shouldn't even shoot one right at the water's edge. Being reptiles with slow nervous systems, even when perfectly shot their thrashing can go on for some time. Many a hunter has been flattened—or had his dugout swamped—by the tail of a thoroughly "dead" crocodile. That same thrashing will often carry a well-hit crocodile into the water. Wading around waist-deep, muddy water looking for a croc is no joke at all—one can't help but wonder if he's really dead. Or, worse, if his fellows are looking for him! Best to find him asleep a few yards from the water—and then shoot very straight.

•••

CHAPTER XII

Snakes—The Invisible Terror of Africa

Nearly everyone feels a natural aversion for snakes, due, no doubt, to the bad press they get and the way they always play the bad guy in novels and films. Snakes represent far less threat than we give them credit for, and without downplaying the risks they do present, the truth is that they are even more afraid of us than we are of them. They will do anything they can to stay out of our paths which, thankfully, rarely cross.

Poisonous snakes are indeed potentially dangerous and the occasional unfortunate accident does occur, but not as often as many think. In all the years I've spent in Africa I've only had to use snakebite antidote twice, and both occasions ended happily. Curiously, both incidents happened in the Luangwa Valley in Zambia and both for the same reasons—the victims were walking barefoot near the villages at night.

Personally, I find snakes disgusting, but if need be, I can pick them up. Popular belief is that they are soft and slimy to the touch, rather like eels. Actually, they feel dry and rough, like a tree branch.

I often hear people say that if it weren't for the snakes, they'd go on safari. Poisonous snakes present practically no danger whatsoever to hunters on safari, and in fact, if someone would like to hunt snakes, I have no idea where to find them. In all my hunting years, I doubt if I've seen more than 100 and those were always slithering away fast. I'm not afraid of them but on the other hand I don't like them much either. I have to confess that on those rare occasions that I see one—sorry, conservationists—I try to kill it without second thought.

In movies there are always snakes everywhere. A python drops from a branch into the tent where the lovely huntress is relaxing in her skimpy underwear. She lets out a scream and runs into the brawny arms of the white hunter, who, without a shirt, has run to her aid. He presents more danger than the innocent snake because the beautiful girl always ends up in the guy's bed. Boy!

Africa has bad snakes, bad meaning very poisonous, since animals are neither good nor bad by our standards—they just react. Fortunately the "bad" snakes are uncommon creatures, and the worst of them are the least common. Even a serious sportsman could enjoy a lifetime of productive safaris without even seeing a snake. This is because most African hunting is done during the dry season. African snakes seem to be least active and visible during the dry months, especially in southern Africa where it's too cold for them in the dry winter months. However, this also holds true in the hotter country to the north.

They are much more visible during the rains, one theory being the holes and burrows they frequent are flooded then. Whatever the reason, the chances of seeing snakes increases substantially with the onset of the rains. Since this is a great time for some hunting, especially elephant and bongo, these hunts offer some of the best opportunities for snake viewing.

Even then the likelihood is fairly remote. And if a snake is encountered, he'll probably be briefly glimpsed slithering off into the bush. Their aggressiveness is highly exaggerated. Thanks to their built-in radar, they will hear even the softest footfalls of approaching humans. Their most probably reaction is to get out of the way.

While it is always possible to see a snake while wandering in the bush, you rarely do. Partly because there aren't many snakes, and partly because they get out of the way. The most likely encounter, regardless of weather, is to see a snake along a road. Snakes like the dust of a roadway, warm where the sun hits on a cool morning, and cool where it's shady during the heat of the day.

Seeing a snake along a road is harmless enough—generally the best place to observe them as far as I'm concerned. However, you do need to keep your eyes open. The mamba, which we'll describe in detail in a bit, is a long, slender snake able, because of its slim body, to raise up more than a third of its length. Like all snakes, mambas like roadways. One thing you do not want to do is drive over the back half of a resting mamba. You can wind up with a very angry front half in your lap—literally! As bizarre as it sounds, this is the basis for quite a few close encounters with one of Africa's most deadly snakes.

Incidents do happen, but generally if you leave snakes alone they will return the favor. Truly dangerous encounters are actually very rare. Still, if you want drama, there are several unfortunate stories involving snakes. But remember, they took place over a period of nearly 100 years of African hunting. The only tragedy I personally have to relate is the death of my dear friend Luis de Lassaleta, who died when a huge viper from Gabon (*Bitis gabonica*) bit him on the neck and temple. He was handling the creature so some friends could film it with their Super-8 camera. Luis kept a number of snakes for people to look at in his home in Bata, Spanish Guinea, and this "*ceraste*," as they are called there, turned and bit him when he least expected it. The bite was very close to the brain, and no amount of snakebite antidote administered at the hospital in Bata could save him. This sad accident may have been provoked by overconfidence on his part, the same as being in a car accident after having driven safely for years. Most snakebites happen—throughout the world—because people mess with these potentially deadly creatures.

One common tale is that 20,000 people in India die of snakebite every year, which I think is all out of proportion. The truth is probably more in the range of one-tenth that number, despite the fact that nearly 700 million people live there in conditions that are not very safe or healthy.

Python, Kenya, 1987.

There are specific antidotes for each species as well as polyvalents capable of reacting with a specific antigen for all poisonous African snakes. This "general antivenin" is made in Port Elizabeth, South Africa, and the Pasteur Institute in Paris, while the Butantan of Brazil works for American snakes. People have been killed by badly administered antidotes, so a word of warning: They must be very carefully applied. Sometimes the cure is worse than the illness.

Among the most famous poisonous snakes in Africa is the black mamba (*Dendroaspis polylepis*). First of all, it's dark green rather than black and much less aggressive than reputed. It is extremely poisonous. Its poison is neurotoxic and absorbs quickly, paralyzing the nervous system in only a few minutes. Two drops are fatal to humans, but an adult male can inject twenty in a single bite. An exceptional (huge) black mamba will be up to fourteen feet in length but usually they measure no more than nine feet. They live everywhere, in hollow trees, caves, and abandoned anthills, but fortunately there aren't many of them.

The black mamba is the most legendary of Africa's snakes. It is fast and its venom is very, very toxic. The danger is compounded by the mamba's ability to "stand on its tail." They really can't do this, but a big mamba can raise its head above a tall man. This means that bites can be in the thorax or head, speeding the spread of the venom and making normal first aid, such as constriction of a limb, impractical.

Even so, it might surprise you to learn that most people survive even mamba bites, given prompt treatment. Mamba bites are deadly serious and a trip to a good hospital—as quickly as possible—is essential for survival. So is antivenin, which good safari operators keep on hand just in case. But the mamba is not a "two step" snake, if such exists anywhere in the world. Especially with antivenin available relatively soon, there is generally time to get an airplane or helicopter in and get to a hospital. Or at least this has been the case in the majority of the relatively few documented mamba bites—none of which have ever involved a safari client.

There is even evidence, based again on very few case histories, suggesting that mamba venom, however virulent, may be short-lived in its effects. Make no mistake, without treatment anything approaching a full bite is fatal. But given treatment—usually including an iron lung since the venom shuts down the nervous system and makes breathing impossible—several victims have recovered fully in just a few days. This is not true with hemotoxic snakes like the Gabon viper; hemotoxic venom generally causes severe and long-lasting muscle and tissue damage around the bite area.

But first one must survive to reach the hospital, and like all accidents this requires calm and a positive attitude. You can't panic and you can't run, since both responses increase blood flow and spread the venom all the more quickly. You can't give up, either. A colleague of mine in Tanzania had one of his staff bitten by a small mamba. He was given antivenin and a plane was sent for, and

A viper shot inside a tent at a camp in Loliondo, Tanzania, 1984.

he was loaded on it. With that peculiar African fatalism he insisted all the fuss was unnecessary; He was going to die. And he did. But the strange part is that the bite was on his hand. That was a survivable bite—but since the victim didn't believe it, it wasn't.

Many are the mamba stories, and I suppose a few are even true. They are fast, but a fleet human can outrun one. However, this is moot because mambas don't chase humans. If alarmed, one might make a run for its den—and you don't want to be in its way. Never take the same line a mamba is taking, even to get away. If one is coming toward you it's probably because you're in the way of a place it wants to reach. Move at an angle—quickly.

Nor are mambas aggressive by nature. Sometimes, when not alarmed, they seem curious—but the normal reaction is to get away. An exception could be the mating season, usually December. Then mambas will defend their territory—give them a wide berth!

The green mamba (*Dendroaspis angusticeps*) is smaller and thinner than its black cousin. It lives exclusively in trees, and at its longest measures seven feet. It is not aggressive, and its venom is not half as toxic as that of the black mamba. This snake is common in tropical forests.

The spitting cobra *(Naja nigricollis)* is a hideous thing that spits its poison into the eyes of its enemies, causing temporary blindness. It can hit its target at ten feet. In general, the spitting cobra represents no threat to man. It is only six feet long and quite common.

The forest cobra *(Naja melanoleuca)* is very toxic and a potential killer of humans. Luckily, it is not aggressive, and lives off frogs and small animals in wooded areas. It measures up to eight feet long.

The Gabon viper (*Bitis gabonica*) is extremely poisonous and deadly to humans. It lives in tropical forests, is thick, and moves slowly. It has a truly astonishing appearance. In size, it reaches up to five feet long and weighs up to twenty-five pounds, sometimes even larger. Its fangs are about two inches long; therefore, they can inject the poison more deeply and, thus, more dangerously.

There are other poisonous species but these five figure more prominently in African folklore. Perhaps the most common of all is the puff adder, a sluggish, slow-moving snake with a lightning strike. The puff adder is not large—usually less than three feet long but fairly thick. The hemotoxic venom is similar to the American rattlesnake's, meaning the bite is generally not fatal to healthy adults. The bite is painful, with the long-term tissue damage typical of this type of venom. Most bites in Africa come from the puff adder because of its habit of lying on trails and not getting out of the way. I always look out for them, especially when leaving a leopard blind at night. Fortunately I almost never see one!

There is more to be said, but these notes are not intended to serve as a monograph on poisonous snakes, just to soothe the fears of those who are considering a visit to Africa and to convince them that encounters with snakes are rare and present little risk. There are incidents involving them, but there are automobile accidents too, and we use cars every day. Does this mean we don't have to worry about snakes? The answer is simple: You probably can forget about them, as long as you don't lay eyes on any.

●●●

CHAPTER XIII

Man-eaters

Some lions and leopards have earned bad reputations because of their attitudes about humans, whom they regularly eat. Unfortunately, these events aren't pieces of history nor the product of modern tabloid journalism. Even today there are cases of people being devoured by these cats. This is a horrible death in which the victim knows exactly what is happening for several frightening seconds. What makes a lion or leopard turn into a man-eater? There are many theories on the subject, but the facts boil down to these:

1. Advanced age makes it difficult for the animal to hunt its usual prey.
2. An injury or accident makes it physically impossible to hunt as usual.
3. The scarcity of animals that usually constitute its regular fodder.
4. The discovery that man is an easy creature to hunt and can be gotten simply by sitting down and waiting by the side of a path.

These man-eaters are the most dangerous because they are in top physical condition, astute, and unpredictable.

The dubious honor of holding the world record for eating people belongs to the Tigress of Champawat, India, which ate 436 humans over eight years before being killed in 1911 by Jim Corbett, a hunter who specialized in destroying man-eaters. Many other felines have also made meals out of large numbers of human victims. I have only run into man-eaters three times during my many years of hunting in Africa. These were all lions, but I've known other hunters who have had more contact with these killers, and their responses to these situations make me respect them more than ever.

Most people think of the tiger when they hear the word "man-eater," probably because of the number of tigers prominent in this kind of literature. Jim Corbett's

Tigers of Kumaon fits this description, as do the tales of Kenneth Anderson, who also wrote of hunting man-eating tigers in India. But in certain areas of Africa, it is the lion that terrorizes humans and takes an incredible number of victims.

The lions of Tsavo are probably the most famous man-eaters; the fear they spread halted the building of the Mombasa-Kampala railroad for several months at the end of the last century (1898). These lions terrorized the workers trying to complete the bridge over the Tsavo River in what was then British East Africa. The military engineer in charge of the project, Lieutenant Colonel J. H. Patterson immortalized the story in the book *The Man-Eaters of Tsavo*, a true hunting classic.

Because there wasn't enough labor to complete the railroad in Uganda, thousands of coolies were brought from India. They lived in camps along the tracks, and their temporary quarters were moved as the railroad advanced. When the project reached the Tsavo River, the lions sprang onto the scene, sowing terror and death among the workers until Patterson had to stop work in order to go after them. One hunter, Mr. Whitehead, had already tried, but one of the lions severely clawed his back and his gunbearer, Abdullah, was killed and eaten. There were forty victims in all, and the lions proved to be in perfect health with no physical reason for their behavior.

The most notable case of man-eating lions took place in the Njombe area of Tanganyika over a period of fifteen years. There was an added, unusual element to this story: These lions apparently had developed the taste for human flesh and had passed down this developed taste over generations. It was my friend George Rushby who put an end to this curse in 1947. It is still unknown why this family of lions began killing and eating people.

The game department immediately tried to deal with the situation, but had no luck. The lions became more aggressive, killing villagers and demonstrating enormous cunning, which made them impossible to stop. George Rushby, the old elephant hunter, was working for the Tanganyika game department at the time, and he was transferred to Njombe in 1941 as head of the game department there. For part of his tenure in the area he was unable to eliminate any of the lions, which killed an impressive number of people: In 1941 they ate 96 people; 67 in 1942; and 86 more by the time they were finally shot in 1947 by Rushby and his game scouts. What he was unable to do over a period of years he accomplished over a few months thanks to favorable circumstances. Fifteen lions were killed, which equaled two generations of this sinister man-eating dynasty. The total number of people devoured over this period is estimated between 1,000 and 1,500, a frightening statistic. Rushby told me that he used the .375 Magnum Holland & Holland and his game scouts the .404 Jeffery. All of these lions, males and females, were in excellent health, so there was no obvious reason that would stop them from feeding on wild animals found in the district.

The reports of lions killing and eating humans are many, and a tome would be needed to tell about them all. It would be impossible in this brief chapter to do justice to the stories of the killers of Tsavo and Njombe or of the four man-eaters hunted by Vaughn Kirby and Austin Roberts, which killed twenty people on the Ruvuma River near the Tanganyika-Mozambique border. Or to the story about Pete Pearson and the lions in the Ankole district of Uganda that killed 138 people over twenty years. Pearson, then of the Uganda Game Department, destroyed all seventeen members of this family of assassins.

When I was in Garba Tula, Kenya in 1968, a lion ate a local woman. I went after it, and ran into the game scout who had shot it about half an hour before I got there. The animal was very old, with scabby skin and worn teeth, apparently without the strength and agility to seek its normal prey. In 1986, upon arriving at my camp in Kizigo (Tanzania) with two clients and my eldest son, we discovered on landing that a lion had just killed a man half an hour before—the same lion that had recently eaten a man and a woman. The poor man's body was still near the camp and we sent it in one of the cars to the closest police station, about twenty miles away, along with a note and two witnesses to explain what had happened.

I was told that the dead man had had the opportunity to hurl his spear into the lion's chest, which left the animal badly wounded. This story was backed up by its tracks. But the trail became more and more faint until, even though we combed the area repeatedly, we lost it all together. A few days later, returning to camp with a large lion we'd shot, we saw a number of vultures circling a thick patch of vegetation while others sat waiting in the trees. This attracted our attention and we decided to see what was up. My client grabbed his .416 Rigby while I took my .375 magnum, and we slowly approached the scene. The stench of putrefying flesh was overwhelming by the time we saw the rotting body of the lion among the bushes. It was still untouched by the vultures, which was odd as there was nothing to stop them eating it and no other lion nearby to scare them off.

In 1960 while I was still a professional hunter in the Sudan, a lioness killed and ate over ten people during the space of several months. At the time I had a camp in Jabur, near the areas of Achong and Falur, where the animal was active. As much as I tried, I was unable to find this lioness. Officials from the game department in Juba came, sent by my friend Shir, but they found nothing. Finally, as I was eating lunch one very hot day, several excited natives came to my camp saying that the lioness was napping nearby.

I loaded my .416 Rigby with expanding, hollowpoint bullets and carried it myself rather than giving it to my gunbearer Agustino, who was serving as interpreter. After going several hundred yards, the villagers motioned us to be quiet and we crept as quietly as we could, avoiding branches and dry leaves as we moved ahead. Suddenly, the man on my left gripped my shoulder and gestured toward some bushes with his arm, but at first, I didn't see anything. Only when I heard a deafening roar was I able to make out the head of a lioness, watching us from the underbrush. I was only thirty then, without the experience or sense that comes from long practice, and it seemed that the creature was eying me and licking her chops. I shot her in the forehead, killing her instantly and exploding her skull into a thousand pieces. I keep that skin in my home in Valencia as a reminder of my own foolishness as well as a reminder of my first confessed and convicted man-eater.

In 1974 the case of one man-eater struck close to home. My partner and hunting companion Peter Hankin was killed and eaten by a lioness while sleeping in his tent in the Luangwa Valley of Zambia. It was prohibited to carry weapons as the safaris that took place there were only photo safaris. The tracks showed that the lioness had circled the tent until she found her victim, clawed open the canvas, and seized his neck in her jaws, dragging him through the slash in the wall. This happened around 3:15 A.M. In his panic, Peter hung onto the camp bed, hauling it after him. His screams brought no help, as his team of natives, not knowing how many lions there were, escaped by climbing trees. Finally, the lioness broke his neck with a powerful swipe of her paw, killing him and leaving a pool of blood ten yards from the tent.

When help arrived at the camp at dawn, the trees were full of vultures about 100 yards away, and under the trees was the lioness eating Peter. At the sight of humans, the animal left her prize and attacked Adrian Carr, son of Norman Carr. Adrian was my assistant at the time; he, Peter, and I had founded Luangwa Safaris many years before. As the big cat sprang, Adrian fired a solid from his .416 Rigby into her chest, which seemed to have no effect on her. He fired again with the same result, and it was not until the third shot that he was finally able to kill her. The lioness was only a few yards away when Adrian's bullet stopped her.

Peter's corpse was horrible to see. The lioness had completely eaten his body from the waist down with only bones and the right arm remaining. We never found the left arm. The sight was indescribable, and let me say we were unable to eat or sleep for days from the shock. To this day, it remains something I cannot speak of. The lioness was very thin and the right paw was atrophied from a poorly knitted fracture. It would have been nearly impossible for her to hunt. The animal had been crazed by hunger to the point that she overcame her fear of humans and took Peter as her victim. It is ironic that Peter, a great hunter who never had any trouble with animals, died when he stopped hunting with guns and began hunting with a camera.

The leopard is the smallest of the potential man-eaters, but it is by no means the least dangerous. An Indian leopard called the "Leopard of Panar" killed and ate 400 people, almost as many as the Champawat tigress, which claimed 436 victims. Hundreds of people have been injured by leopards in Africa and Asia. It is an aggressive animal if wounded, cornered, or if it has cubs. In those cases even the most modest leopard becomes a clawing machine. I have been present at the deaths of 128 leopards, but I cannot say with any certainty if any of them were man-eaters. Two I killed were accused of devouring villagers, but in all honesty I didn't have the least proof.

The author showing the teeth of a Sudanese lion, 1979.

Because of its smaller size and lighter weight, the leopard often picks children as its victims. A classic example of this behavior was the "Leopard of Rupenda" in Tanganyika, which killed and ate eighteen children between the ages of six months and nine years in 1950. Hunters unsuccessfully tried to hunt it and by luck it was captured in a trap and stabbed to death with spears. The animal was in good enough physical condition to hunt its regular prey. The opposite was true of a leopard in northern Mozambique, which was so weak it could not drag any of its twenty-two human victims away from the place it had killed them. His habit was to tear off a chunk of flesh of his victim to eat in nearby bushes. It was finally shot while devouring its last victim under a bush. In the northeast of the old Belgian Congo many years ago, the Azande people told me of a leopard that raided their villages, taking chickens, dogs, and goats. I wanted to help them get rid of this lousy neighbor, but I was busy hunting elephants and didn't want to waste precious time going after a chicken-snatching leopard, which they caught several months later in a trap, anyway. In my African experience there have been many leopards that prowl the camp at night without causing any trouble.

Only once did an altercation occur—funny for us but very unfunny for the victim. My camp on the Luangwa River in Chibembe, Zambia, was like living in the middle of a park surrounded by animals. There were so many that more than once I took the big five (lion, leopard, elephant, rhinoceros, and buffalo) within two miles of camp. In looking back, I can only think how incredible those times were, which now belong to history. We shot several antelopes and had plenty of meat, which the natives on the team divided up, cut into thin strips, and hung up to dry, saving it to take home after the hunting season to feed their large families. The four kitchen staff had their huts behind the kitchen, separate from the trackers, gunbearers, and porters, forming a sort of camp aristocracy. The huts were grass, not very sturdy but offering enough privacy.

One of the waiters was a man with such a difficult name that I renamed him Paquito, which was okay with him. We had problems with hyenas coming into camp and dragging away everything they could find, so Paquito and the others decided that it would be better to dry the meat on the roofs of the huts, out of the hyenas' reach. Once the strips of meat were all laid out, they went to bed.

About eleven at night I was awakened by screams and roars coming from behind the kitchen. I jumped out of bed, grabbed a lantern and my .416 Rigby, and ran toward the noise with my heart in my mouth. It wouldn't be the first time a man-eater had dragged a sleeping human away from a camp. Everyone shouted from inside their huts, everyone but Paquito, whose hut was half destroyed and who had disappeared. As I tried to figure out what was going on, I spied Paquito behind a tree with a face like a soul in torment.

I got him to come out and tell us what happened, and as he did, the howls changed to chuckles. A marauding leopard had climbed the large tree by the four huts and decided to leap onto Paquito's roof to get at the meat drying there. Of course the roof collapsed under its weight and it fell right on top of Paquito, who was fast asleep. The leopard roared in surprise, as did Paquito. When they heard the leopard's howls and their friend's screeches, the others began their own chorus of shrieks. This alarmed the poor leopard so much that it ran in one direction, and Paquito took off in the opposite direction. When we examined the battlefield afterward, there were three holes in the hut. The one in the roof was caused by the leopard's entrance, one in the side was caused by the leopard's exit, and the one in the other side was caused by Paquito's exit. The only undamaged thing in the hut was the door, which neither man nor beast had stopped to use.

Paquito was lucky that his visitor was not the famous man-eater of Panar, which would tear down the doors of houses to get to their terrified inhabitants. In 1919 the government hired Jim Corbett to kill this nightmare, which had ravaged the northern Indian state of Panar. This time, Corbett didn't have to wait long to deal with the problem. His hunt began in April and was ended by September. Corbett put a live goat near where the leopard had just killed a man, estimating that it would soon return for its prize. He climbed a tree thirty yards away to wait. As he expected, the leopard returned, but instead of going after the tethered goat, it went straight for Corbett's tree and leapt up to get him. Corbett couldn't get a good shot and the leopard ran off, wounded. With the courage characteristic of him, Corbett chased the animal with the help of a lantern, found it badly wounded, and dispatched it.

Incredible as it may seem, between the Leopard of Panar with its 400 victims and the Champawat Tigress with its 436, no fewer than 836 people were killed and eaten. Using his experience and courage, Jim Corbett eliminated them both. He was always very fond of Indian villagers and helped them in any way he could.

Years later another duel began between Jim Corbett and a leopard in Rudraprayag, which devoured 125 people between 1918 and 1926 in the northern Indian province of Uttar Pradesh. This animal alternated between eating humans and wild animals and was extremely cunning and wary. It took Corbett years to kill it. The frightened inhabitants and the pilgrims on their way to the temple at Mount Badrinath believed that the leopard was supernatural and nothing could be done to stop it. Without the help of local people in finding the animal, the task of eliminating it became almost impossible. Besides Corbett, other hunters (shikaris, as they are called in India) tried to take the leopard of Rudraprayag. The government offered a bounty of 10,000 rupees—a fortune in those days—but no one could stop this animal. Finally, on 1 May 1926 Jim Corbett did, using a live goat as bait, exactly as he had done sixteen years before to kill the man-eater of Panar.

In the 1950s Kenneth Anderson killed a leopard known as the "Man-eater of Gummalapur," which had claimed forty-two victims. It turned out that the animal was lame and could not hunt the wild species that made up its usual diet. Anderson also took the "Leopard of Sangam," which was very old and had worn-out teeth. But the Panar and Rudraprayag leopards taken by Corbett were in excellent condition and had no physical impairments.

There are occasional cases of leopards attacking humans that never taste a mouthful of their victims. These leopards kill, apparently, for the pleasure of killing—they enjoy it. One of the most famous of these was the "Leopard of Masaguru" in southern Tanganyika, near the Ruvuma River. This aggressive animal killed twenty-six people, mostly women and children, before being killed by one of George Rushby's game wardens. George told me that the leopard never even bit his victims, although it is possible that it drank their blood.

Three man-eating leopards appeared at the same time in the Indian state of Bihar in 1959 and 1960, claiming a total of 300 victims, although I suspect those numbers were greatly exaggerated. One hundred is more likely, but the way information becomes distorted when passed from mouth to mouth, it is likely that the 100 was attributed to each of the leopards, until it equaled a totally unrealistic number of 300.

At the time I write this, there are a group of man-eating lions in the Songea area of southern Tanzania. They began their activities toward the end of 1986, and by October 1987 they had eaten thirty-five people, among them a member of the game department sent to kill them. By 1988 the number of victims had reached fifty, and, according to the latest news, these lions continue to attack, even though two of the five lions in the group have already been killed. Moving south, on the right bank of the Ruvuma River on the Mozambique border, lions had eaten twenty people by the end of 1988, and leopards had devoured nine. Unprotected villages had to move to safer areas. Between Motoro and Kaobong in northern Uganda, lions ate twelve Karomojong people between the middle of 1988 and the end of 1989. In the southern Sudan there have been various cases of people killed and eaten by a group of three lions recently; these attacks have occurred between Raja and Wau. Because of the civil war, no one has taken action against the animals.

In India there are still cases of tigers eating humans, but I doubt they reach the number of victims as in bygone days. They are rapidly eliminated by the wildlife department. In 1987 a man-eating tiger took five victims in southeastern Sumatra. In 1988 the number rose to twenty, despite police efforts. This animal was too clever to be successfully hunted by people with no experience, no matter how many police there are. In Malaysia (formerly the Malay Peninsula) tigers kill and eat people every year, especially in the Kelantan and Trengganu states, which have thick, primitive jungles.

Tigers regularly eat people in the Sunderbans area of the Ganges Delta in the Bay of Bengal, where the territory is divided between India and Bangladesh. In this combination of solid and liquid land, tigers have a safe habitat. The area can only be crossed in small boats along the thousands of canals that crisscross the dense jungles. Fishermen and woodcutters travel along them in search of their meager sustenance, and along the way about twenty-five of these poor simple folks every year become fodder for the tigers. The tiger is a great swimmer and will attack people in small boats, sneaking up on them from behind and surprising them. Many of these people wear masks on the backs of their heads that looks like a human face with wide eyes, mustache, and beard, to trick the tigers into thinking they are being watched. These people hope this will intimidate the animals and keep them away. I have a photo taken in 1988 of thirty-three women left widows because of the tigers of the Sunderbans. . . .

• • •

CHAPTER XIV

The Rhinoceros

THE LAST OF THE BLACK RHINO

Each article I write about the black rhinoceros is more pessimistic than the last. Statistics indicate that if a miracle doesn't happen—and they generally don't—*Diceros bicornis* will very soon be a thing of the past. Poachers have finished them off in every sense. There are two main markets for rhinoceros horns—the Far East where they are alleged to have aphrodisiac powers (scientifically unfounded) and Yemen, where they are used to make handles of daggers much sought after by the local population. What is certain is that by the year 2000, the rhinoceros will not be found in its natural habitat anywhere except South Africa, which has carefully tended parks, and a few areas of Kenya and Zimbabwe where rhinos captured in other areas have been transported and are guarded 24 hours a day by trained personnel.

In 1970 there were still an estimated 60,000 black rhino in all of Africa. In 1981 there were 12,000 and in 1994 fewer than 2,000. There's a lot of talk and propositions by well-intentioned groups, but few of these work out and every day more rhinos vanish forever. I have an official list of the rhino population in various African countries and where they are, or were, in 1980 and 1986. The decrease in the number of animals during this period is shocking:

COUNTRY	1980	1986
Zimbabwe	1,400	1,737
South Africa	630	510
Namibia	300	440
Tanzania	3,795	400
Kenya	1,500	381
Central African Republic	3,000	None Found
Zambia	2,750	200

COUNTRY	1980	1986
Mozambique	250	None Found
Cameroon	110	70
Sudan	300	None Found
Somalia	300	None Found
Angola	300	None Found
Malawi	40	30
Rwanda	30	20
Botswana	30	None Found
Ethiopia	20	None Found
Chad	25	None Found
Uganda	5	Extinct since 1984
TOTAL	**14,785**	**3,788**

As you can see, in these six years the population increased from 1,400 to 1,737 in Zimbabwe and from 300 to 440 in Namibia while decreasing dramatically in Tanzania, Kenya, the Central African Republic, and Zambia, which had a total in these four countries of 11,045 rhinos in 1980 but only 981 in 1986. Namibian rhinos are found only in the northern part of the country near the Angolan border (Etosha National Park), a poacher-vulnerable area which is thus a serious threat to their medium and long-term survival.

Since then things have gotten worse. In the last few years, the population of rhinos in Zimbabwe has been greatly reduced by poachers from Zambia. Recently, the front pages of all the newspapers carried the news that fourteen rhinoceros had been killed in fourteen days in a little corner of the Zambezi. Pessimistic figures confirm the results of this wave of rhino poaching. In 1994, at most only 400 were left in Zimbabwe.

Rhinoceros poaching is very well organized. Don't imagine it is the work of some poor guy dressed in a loin cloth, armed with a bow and arrows. Involved are international businessmen along with well-known politicians and corrupt high-level officials who hire experienced poachers with a lot of firepower. This came to light in Zimbabwe in 1987 when anti-poaching units killed twenty-three poachers based in Zambia. It is very easy to cross the Zambezi River, hunt, and return with the booty, which is sent on to markets in Yemen, Hong Kong, Singapore, and Taiwan. Rhinoceros horn sells for about $15,000 a kilo and the corrupt officials make it possible for the merchandise to leave the country and arrive at its destination.

Except for South Africa, there is, realistically, no hope in saving the rhino anywhere in Africa. Distances and the lack of economic resources for proper control have left even the most concerned authorities helpless in the face of disaster. There is no human way to stop it. Only in Kenya and Zimbabwe, thanks to the combined efforts of Africans and Europeans, are plans to put the remaining rhinoceros in secure, well-guarded places.

The animals are shot with anesthetic darts and taken to these refuges. In Kenya, the one on Lake Nakuru is perfect for them in all respects. Another refuge, called Ngare-Ndare (Timau), is on the farm of my friend Tony Dyer, who now has fourteen rhinos safe and sound behind electric wire watched by armed guards. He expects the number of animals to double in a few years. I believe there are between eighty to ninety rhinos at Lake Nakuru, which means that the species will not become extinct in Kenya, at least for the moment. In 1900 there were believed to be 100,000 rhinos in Kenya. They were the animals most frequently hunted by colonists and early hunters. I've hunted rhinos in Kenya, and I remember that in the 1950s and 60s they were everywhere. In fact, in some places there were too many for our tastes, and they caused plenty of problems with their belligerent charges.

In Zimbabwe, several years ago the game department began similarly darting rhinos in vulnerable border areas and moving them to much safer government and private reserves in the interior, where constant anti-poaching patrols can be maintained. One of the largest concentrations is in the Save Valley Conservancy in the southeastern lowveldt, where there are now nearly fifty rhinos. Unfortunately these efforts probably started too late, for in just eight years Zimbabwe has lost so many black rhino that the survivors are now too scattered to find and dart.

Fortunately, hunters acting through Game Conservation International in San Antonio, Texas, imported a number of rhinos, which has formed an important group in the United States, to try to perpetuate this African species. Certain parts of Texas offer a habitat much like the one enjoyed by rhinos in Africa. The animals are adapting very well, reproducing and caring for their young just as if they were at home. My old friend and Game Conservation International president Harry Tennison began years ago with an impossible dream that is now a wonderful reality. This repopulation of black rhinos in Texas is due to the work and money donated by hunters/conservationists from all over. The "Greens," enemies of hunting and so-called friends of animals, have yet to give one damn dollar to this fantastic program.

The *Diceros bicornis* has arrived at its irreversible end through man's greed. Its shaky future will see scarce numbers in a few parks in South Africa, reserves in Kenya or Zimbabwe, and as a guest-of-honor in far-off Texas. In the rest of Africa nothing will remain but their skeletons bleaching in the sun . . . to our eternal shame.

THE KILLER OF KARIMUNDA

This story happened in 1970, and, although it has not changed over time, what happened then is, I think, still of interest now. I was on safari in my camp at Chibembe, in the Luangwa Valley of Zambia, hunting with two friends who

Record black rhinoceros taken in 1967, Luangwa Valley, Zambia, by Pedro Camps on safari with author. Front horn measured 31 inches.

Black rhino with three horns taken by Armando Bassi on safari with Tony Sanchez, Zambia, 1971.

unfortunately have since died. In those days there was an incredible amount of game in the area and the safari was going very well. We had each already taken an elephant, lion, and buffalo, and for that reason everyone was in a good mood. One of my friends had a license to hunt rhinoceros and this was the only species he lacked to finish off the hunt.

A short time before this safari with my friends, the local people had told me about an old rhino which would occasionally appear and attack people before vanishing into the thick and prickly *Chasera* forest where it was impossible to find. The hunting guard stationed in Mfuwe had tried to get the creature, but hadn't had any luck, so I had been given the green light to liquidate it if I could. The truth is that I hadn't had much time to spend on this rhino because I had been so busy with one safari after another. From time to time I would get sporadic reports of its appearances. I wasn't very concerned when I received these reports because, besides surprising a few people, the rhino really hadn't done any harm. Now, with my friend who had a license for rhino, I had a real reason to go after this malcontent.

Well, I let things go until one day a perspiring native came to camp to tell me that the rhino had attacked and badly injured a man near the village of Karimunda. I grabbed my big first aid kit, heaved it into the Land Rover, and raced toward the village. There was much weeping and wailing, and, by the time I arrived, the whole village was in hysterics. The wounded man was in his hut, and, although he was covered with blood and looked ghastly, I found that he had really suffered nothing more than a broken rib. I gave him antibiotics, a tranquilizer, and left him feeling much better once he found out he wasn't going to die.

The problem now was the rhinoceros, which had changed its *modus operandi*. It hadn't just scared its victim but had chased him until it caught him, then it had butted and poked the man until his friends had driven the animal away with screams and stones. It was this change in attitude that caught my attention and I realized that I would have to finish it off before it did something worse. I spoke with the chief of Karimunda, whom I had known for years, and asked him to let me know immediately if the rhino turned up. He told me it was a big husky male with a broken back horn but a normal front one.

I got back to camp late and told the others what had happened. Because we got up so early, we went to bed right after dinner. After an ordinary morning we went back to camp at midday to rest, shower, and eat lunch. It was about three o'clock when my gunbearer Didion called me. Excited, he said that the rhino had just killed an old woman near the village and that several men had come to tell me the news. These men were waiting to take me to where it had escaped into the bushes right by the cornfield where the poor woman had worked.

When I told the others what had happened, my friend who had the license to hunt rhino said that he'd like to hunt it himself. I explained that it was no great trophy but he said that the size of the horns didn't matter. An animal with this kind of history was more valuable than one that looked nicer. We agreed and headed quickly for Karimunda, my friend with his .375 magnum and I with my .465 Nitro Express Holland & Holland.

A crowd was waiting for us, and we'd barely gotten out of the Land Rover when they pointed out a place about 300 yards away where the rhino was still hiding. It had been merciless with the dead woman, crushing her against the ground several times and her body was very badly battered. It reminded me of when I was a medical student and we had to do autopsies, which was always the worst of my medical memories.

We cautiously approached the place where we supposed the rhino to be. My friend and I went first, followed about twenty yards behind by the others who certainly didn't want to miss the show. About fifteen yards from the bushes we stopped to see if we could hear or see anything, but we had no luck. We had to get closer. We hadn't taken five or six steps when the rhinoceros appeared and came straight at us, snorting wildly.

We couldn't see it very well through the grass until it was a few yards away, and at that moment my friend fired two shots into its chest with his double .375 magnum. The animal did not falter. I fired the right barrel of my .465 Nitro in great haste, which, thank God, made it swerve to my left but didn't stop the charge. I then shot it from the side with the second barrel, and it galloped on several steps before it stumbled and fell. As it tried to get up, we shot it simul-

"The Karimunda Killer" covered with the dried blood of the woman it had killed that morning, Zambia.

Author with a black rhino from Tanganyika, present Tanzania, 1960.

taneously with the .375 and .465, finally killing it. It was a huge animal with the entire right side of its face covered with the dead woman's dried blood.

Our detailed examination of the rhinoceros revealed a wound in the side caused by a lead bullet from one of those old blackpowder guns. I saved the projectile as a souvenir. The wound was old and had probably caused a lot of pain, increasing the animal's natural aggression. One can only imagine how the pain from the wound had directed the rhino's hatred of humans, whom it probably blamed for its pain—as much as its limited intelligence allowed. It had become overexcited by its encounter with the man the day before, and the old woman in her cornfield had paid the price. As always, the innocent pay for the sinners—the fool who shot that lead bullet never imagined that he would be responsible for the death of an innocent woman.

My friend got the killer of Karimunda as his trophy and all the excitement that is supposed to accompany the hunt. I gave the family of the dead woman some money, which I suspect went to help them forget their sorrows via the local beer, *mazabuka*. So as in fairy tales, they all lived happily ever after— except for the poor old soul who had only been working in her cornfield. . . .

THE WHITE RHINO

This huge animal is the third largest land mammal after the African and Asian elephants. There are two races of white rhinoceros, one found on each side of the equator with some 2,500 miles between them. The most common is

The huge head of a white rhino, Natal, 1980.

the race found in the southern part of Africa called *Ceratotherium simun simun*. The first European to see one of these was the explorer/naturalist Burchell in 1817, who found a number of them at the beginning of the European penetration into the virgin lands of southern Africa. About 1845 the absolute record white rhino was taken near the town of present day Mesina, in the far north of the Republic of South Africa. The famous Scottish hunter/pioneer/naturalist R. Gordon-Cumming reported the amazing length of sixty-two inches for the rhino's front horn and twenty-two for the back one, weighing a total of nearly forty pounds.

The other race comes from north of the equator and was discovered by Captain St. J. Gibbs in 1900 in what was then the Lado Enclave, administered by the Belgians and made into the West Nile province of Uganda on 1 January 1914. The horns of the northern and southern cousins are almost impossible to tell apart. The northern rhino was scientifically dubbed *Ceratotherium simun cottoni* after Lord B. Powell-Cotton who was the first to organize an expedition to study them and find specimens for his private museum, which is one of the most complete and interesting in England. The record for this subspecies is fifty inches for the front horn and, again, twenty-two for the back one.

The name "white rhinoceros" has nothing to do with its real color, which is gray. When the first Boer hunters returned from their expeditions to the far interior, they brought the horns and spoke of a new species of rhinoceros called *wyt*, which means "wide" in Afrikaans. The animal they saw ate only grass and had a very wide mouth for that purpose. The English heard the Afrikaans word *wyt*, which sounds remarkably similar to the English word "white." This mistake resulted in the "wide-mouthed rhino" being called the "white rhino!"

It was a long time ago when I read an article by a Belgian zoologist in which he explained why a "gray" rhinoceros was called a "white" one. According to his exotic and silly theory, certain birds sit on the rhino's back, covering it with droppings which turn white when they dry. These must be very intelligent birds to be able to tell between the two species of African rhinos, the *Diceros bicornis*, or black, and the white, *Ceratotherium simun*, so as to crap only over one and not the other. . . . If this is the conclusion the professor came to after years of study, it's pretty sad.

The weight of these rhinos has been greatly exaggerated and I've read absurd data that stated calculated weights between 7,500 and 11,000 pounds. I have the most accurate information on the subject from the Department of National Parks of Natal (South Africa), which weighed dozens of white rhinos over the years and came up with these figures:

Male rhino—between 4,500 and 5,000 pounds.
Female rhino—between 3,000 and 3,500 pounds.

These figures also apply to white rhinos from north of the equator, which are about the same size. The height at the withers averages about six feet and the length of the rhino is about thirteen feet. It is a big animal.

The white rhino used to be found throughout southern Africa, in Angola, Mozambique, Namibia, Zimbabwe, Botswana, and South Africa, but due to intense persecution only fifteen specimens survived by 1912. These were found in the Umfolozi River area of the Natal where they received the maximum protection. Since then the white rhino's history has been one of the greatest stories of successful recovery in the world. This part of the Natal became the Umfolozi Hunting Reserve, and those fifteen rhinos have become the 4,660 found today in South Africa. They have been moved from Appendix I to Appendix II of CITES, which authorizes the hunting of the animal within strict controls.

It's a disgrace that the rhinos from north of the equator haven't had the same luck and are threatened with extinction. There are only twenty-six left. Following its discovery in 1900 in the Lado Enclave, white rhinos were found throughout Central Africa, the Sudan, Ubangi-Shari (now the Central African Republic), the Belgian Congo (today Zaire), and Uganda. In other words, in these four countries of Central Africa in 1914, when the Lado Enclave became part of Uganda, there were many thousands of rhino.

Later on there were between 7,000 and 8,000 white *cottoni* rhinos in those countries until 1960. In the southern Sudan and the northeastern Belgian Congo (Garamba National Park), there were nearly 6,000 head. When I came to the Sudan in 1959 I saw white rhinos everywhere, especially in Nimule, Shambé, and the Aliab-Dinka area as well as near Mount Lado, only twenty miles from the capital of Juba.

Disaster struck with independence and the exit of many people experienced in the conservation and protection of fauna. The new officials had little knowledge and fewer funds and poaching grew at a rate and with an impunity never seen before. By 1983 the white rhino was nearly extinct except for twenty-one head in northwestern Zaire, in the southern part of the Garamba National Park. This has been the greatest massacre in history committed against an animal species by the hand of man, wiping them out in only twenty-three years.

Fortunately, President Mobutu of Zaire took action before it was too late and thanks to him there are now twenty-six very well protected rhino, as I was able to ascertain when I was President Mobutu's guest in 1989. It offers some hope that the species can recuperate over time if the necessary care and protection against poaching is taken.

Man is the rhino's only natural enemy, who has ceaselessly hunted it since it was first discovered by Westerners in 1817. There are occasional reports of a young rhino being killed by a lion, but these are very rare. There is also one case of a rhino being attacked and killed by an elephant that had found the interloper in a water hole where the elephant liked to bathe and drink.

The white rhino is a more easygoing animal than its black cousin and much less aggressive, but it is not the dull-witted creature that some imagine. I remember that in 1960 the game department in Juba, the Sudan, received orders to send some young rhinos to the zoo in Khartoum. The department was to organize the capture of the animals, and it focused the chase on the area around Shambé. The tactic was to separate the adults and babies and immobilize them using lassos and ropes to get them into enclosures prepared for this purpose.

By good luck, I was in Shambé at the time hunting elephants. I took a mini-vacation and joined the expedition, which turned out to be very interesting. Rhinos are not to be messed with and don't believe for an instant that you can play with them as if they were cows or you'll be in for a big surprise. We suffered constant rhino attacks during this expedition—to the point that we ended up killing one in self defense.

Their hearing and smell are excellent and are its principal defense. Its vision is poor beyond thirty to forty yards, but I have noticed that the white rhino sees better than the black, and can easily note a person's movement in the bush. In 1990 I took a specimen that made us sweat blood, dodging, escaping, returning, taking us hours to get it. Keep in mind that the white rhino can run twenty-

Large white rhino, Transvaal, 1990.

five miles an hour if it has to, and its charge can be much faster than you can imagine, given its great size.

Rhinos have ingrained habits and travel along paths well-trampled by their frequent passage. This makes the poacher's job easy, and besides, rhinos are very territorial. They live alone or in small family groups consisting of a male, females, and babies, leading quiet lives looking for food and napping away the daylight hours. White rhinos eat only grasses, which they chomp with their wide mouths, whiling away siesta time in the dense forests where they feel safe.

Their love lives are spirited, and when a male white rhino discovers a female, he'll do anything to woo her. After seducing the lady, the male mounts her, using his back legs to support him during the long love act, which can take up to an hour. After 480 to 490 days of gestation, the baby rhino is born and will spend two years with the mother before breaking away to hang out with other young adults. The white rhino can live forty years and give birth to new calves every two or three years. Sexual maturity arrives when the rhino is somewhere between four and five years old. The female does not have a season, unlike many other species, but can breed all year. A female can produce ten babies during her lifetime.

Because the white rhino is such a large and resistant animal, it can only be hunted with solids. I've hunted them with a .375 H&H Magnum, .416 Rigby, .475 No. 2 Nitro Express, and .500 Jeffery. Even though the .375 magnum doesn't have the stopping power of the other calibers mentioned with only a 300-grain bullet, its penetration is so magnificent that, with a well-placed shot, the results can be as good as those from a heavier rifle.

I get goose bumps when I remember a particular event that concerned a well-known handgun hunter who went after a white rhino with a special pistol that had a telescopic sight. No one knew how, but he managed to get this hunt transmitted live on TV. I suppose he wanted to show the stupefied audience how brave he was and how well he shot with his pistol. The moment of truth arrived, and to everyone's (and no one's) surprise, the rhino was not killed by any of the bullets. The hunter became demoralized and shot more and more carelessly until the rhino was bleeding like a stuck pig. Of course, the fiasco looked like a massacre and gave plenty of fuel to the Greens to try to stop hunting altogether. On that occasion, they were right. Finally, the rhino had to be finished off with a rifle, and the whole thing ended badly.

The survival of the white rhino is now assured, thanks to the strict measures imposed by the South African authorities. The sacrifice of those few shot each season protects thousands of others since the hunting fees go to create more reserves and sanctuaries and to help reintroduce them into new areas.

•••

CHAPTER XV

The Lion

LIONS IN THE 1990s

Up to the moment that I write these notes, I have shot 153 lions and helped my clients take another 162, for a total of 315. While I don't pretend to be an expert on lions, I feel that these figures give me direct experience with these animals and reasonable background for what I'm about to say.

Unlike his Asian cousin the tiger, at home in the thick jungles of Malaysia, India, or Burma, the lion prefers open spaces and lives in areas of savannas, where the animals that make up his diet also live.

It is very difficult to calculate how many lions there are today in Africa, but it is certain that there are many fewer than there were thirty years ago. Basing their opinions on the testimony and information from hunters, zoologists, and game wardens, some specialists have loosely estimated that there are between 60,000 and 80,000 lions, mostly in eastern and southern Africa. There is no way to prove or disprove this figure, but at least it gives us an idea of what the situation might be today.

Until the middle of the last century, lions were found in large numbers every- where, from the Mediterranean in the north to the far south of Africa. With a growth in population and the consequent tilling of land for cultivation as well as the introduction of progress and civilization to many areas, the lion population was impacted very negatively. Not only were their numbers reduced, but in some areas, such as northern Africa, the lion has completely disappeared. In Libya and Egypt they were considered extinct by 1770. In Tunisia lions were abundant until 1850, but the last one was taken in 1891 in Babouch, near Tabarka. In Algeria they were finished by 1893. Lions managed to survive for more years in Morocco due to the rough terrain, and in 1911 some were still left in the zones of Zaian, Beni Mgild, and in the Atlas mountain range. This rough terrain saved them from extinction until 1922, when the last recorded, a lioness, died.

At the opposite end of the continent, in what today is South Africa, things also went badly for lions. In 1715 they were at the very gates of the city of Cape Town, but the last one in the Cape Province was killed in 1850 with a trap. In Natal, they were extinct in 1865 and in the Orange Free State in 1899. Only in eastern Transvaal did they manage to survive, in the lowveldt area near Mozambique. That area later on became part of the Kruger National Park, which today has a large number of lions. One was taken outside Johannesburg in 1898, which caused quite a stir because lions had not been seen around there for quite a long time.

The lion population in West Africa has declined dramatically, and except in some areas their numbers are few and becoming fewer. The Niokole-Koba National Park in Senegal; and the "W" National Park, which stretches through the three countries of Niger, Benin, and Burkina Faso, from the right bank of the Niger River to the Mekrou River, have good lion populations. Outside these two parks, the only places lions are to be found are in the southeast of Burkina Faso (areas of Fada-N'Gourma, Pama, Arly, Yobiri, and Diapaga); in northern Benin (Batia, Kerou, Banikouar, and along the Mekrou and Alibori Rivers); and in northern Ghana (districts of Lawra, Wa, Yagaba, Tumu, Chuchiliga, Zuarungu, Bawku, and Sakogu). Until 1960 there were still lions in the northern part of the old French Guinea near the borders with Senegal and Mali, but if any at all exist today, they must be extremely rare. The same is true of the group that inhabited the northwest of Bamako in Mali, in the zones of Leko, Dindinko, Sjema, and Birou.

The hunter can eliminate West Africa as a land of lions. The occasional taking of one doesn't justify the expense of time, effort, and money—apart from the fact that they are so scarce in general they must be protected at all costs and not one of them eliminated.

Moving on to the next geographic area known as Central Africa, we begin with Cameroon, where lions are found scattered throughout the north. Lions are not numerous anywhere in the northern part of the Cameroon, and in general they are difficult to hunt. The greatest number of them is found in the Waza Reserve, which is logical because they are protected there. In 1964, in an area known as Rei Bouba, I took a lion with a big mane as well as an old, sick lioness I had to kill to save her from the agony of a slow death. In 1992 I saw a pair of lions near the Faro River and occasionally I hear their roars at night around Ndok. Actually very few are shot during the hunting season in Cameroon.

Sometimes lions are seen or hunted in the southern part of the country covered by equatorial forests. Undoubtedly they come from the north, and only God knows for what reason they decided to come south to an area completely different from their usual habitat of open plains. It really is a mystery why they migrated to these forests, where, in addition, food is extremely difficult for them to find. These traveling lions sometimes even make their way to the forests of old Spanish Guinea, where in 1947 a native hunter

A huge Tanzanian lion, shot near Loliondo in 1985. Compare it with the author who is six feet, four inches.

killed a male near the southern post of Kogo with three shots from his 12-gauge shotgun loaded with slugs.

Years ago in the Republic of Congo (Brazzaville), there was a nucleus of lions on the lush plains between Brazzaville and Abala, especially on the Bateke Plateau and along the Lefini River. It was not unusual to hear them at night, although they were rare. Today only a few are found in the Lefini Reserve and their numbers are shrinking.

In 1977 I made a hunting exploration in the Congo to the north of Mbono by the Odzala National Park. In the salt licks located in open spaces frequented by buffalo, I saw fresh lion tracks that indicated they were in the dense forest surrounding the area. This surprised me. Finally, one morning I climbed the hill above the salt licks and watched two lionesses and a lion with a lovely mane for several minutes until they wandered back into the forest. Through the binoculars I could see that they were normal, healthy animals, with their coats darker than usual. They were also quite well fed—probably because of all the buffalo in the area. They were well-known to the local people, as I later found out.

Years ago there were many lions in Chad, especially along the Shari River, in Lai, Melfi, Haraze, Am-Tinam, Aboudela, and Goz-Beida, but particularly in the Abeche area where there were many cattle for them to feed on. I remember well a lady whose hobby was to raise lions and who always had a cub or two around the house. Unfortunately, the situation is very different today. The civil war has battered the territory for many years and has greatly diminished the number of lions throughout the country.

In the Central African Republic there are still many lions in the savannas where there are large numbers of antelope and buffalo to feed on. The highest density of lions are found south of Birao, between Kokab and the Aouk River, which forms the southeastern border of Chad, in Ouada Djalle, Ouada, Adelaye, and throughout the enormous territory that stretches from east of Yalinga to the Sudanese border where every hunting season many fine specimens are taken.

In Zaire, the areas where lions are found are far apart. Some are north of the equator and some south, but none are in the center or west of Zaire. North of the equator lions are found mostly in the northeast in the Garamba National Park and the areas of Niangara, Dungu, Faradje, Watsa, and Adranga. In the Virungas National Park and on the plains abutting the Ruindi River, lions are many and in stable numbers. South of the equator they are now seen in appreciable numbers in the Kabambare, Nyunzu, Manono, Moba, Pweto, and Mitwaba areas and the Upemba National Park. They are also found in other savanna areas but in small numbers.

When I began hunting in the Sudan, lions were all over the southern part of the country. Because they were considered a pest to cattle, lions could be hunted in unlimited numbers and could be found only a few miles from Juba, the capital of the southern Sudan. I still remember when a lion killed a donkey belonging to the veterinary service less than a mile from my home,

A super lion from Zimbabwe, 1993.

and I remember when it was common to see lion tracks near Rejaf, only twenty minutes from the city.

All that is now history, but there are still numerous lions in some places, such as on the eastern bank of the Nile, the area formed by Mongalla in the west, Pibor Post in the north, Kasangor in the east and Torit in the south. No humans live in this huge area, which makes it a perfect habitat for lions. I've hunted many lions in this territory and had the privilege to be one of the first hunters there. I've always found plenty of lions there except for near Torit, which is the easiest area to get to and where certain unscrupulous hunters greatly reduced the lion population.

There were also many lions on the Boma Plateau, in Kurun, and along the Ethiopian and Kenyan borders. West of the Nile, lions were especially plentiful between Terakeka and Yirol and in Minkaman, in the heart of the Aliab-Dinka territory with its great plains full of tiang, reedbuck, and kob, all of which make tasty meals for lions. I traveled this area from 1959 to 1984 and never failed to see lions. The same was true for the area west of Wau and along the Raga and Pongo Rivers, up to the border with the Central African Republic.

Ethiopia is a country where lions have been wiped out in many areas and today they can only be found in small numbers south of Gambela, along the Gilo and Akobo Rivers in Maji, and on the stretch of the Obo River between northern Lake Turkana and Bole, east of Chew Bahir Lake, and the areas of Tertale and Jinca in the southeast of the country. A few remain in the Danakil as well.

Lions flourished in Somalia while it was an Italian colony, but they and other fauna have suffered greatly because of the civil war and very heavy poaching. Today, the only perceptible numbers are found in the province of Jubaland between the Kenyan border and the Juba River. A few are also found west of Kisimaio, north of Dinsor, and west of Garba Harre. Somali lions never have large manes because of the hot climatic conditions there.

Lions are found throughout Kenya with the largest densities in the north ("North Frontier District") and in the Masai area in the south, where in many places they are abundant. In the days when lion hunting was authorized, many beautiful trophies with great manes were taken in Kenya.

The continual wars and general chaos has cost Uganda many wild animals, and the lion is no exception. In Uganda I shot two extremely large lions near Lake Albert with my .416 Rigby, after a horrible trek in which I pursued these wounded animals through tall grass. As the lion is an animal that recuperates quickly if left alone, it is possible that in the near future the situation will be better, and lions will return to their old habitats.

A huge lion from northern Tanzania, 1985.

Tanzania is the No. 1 country in all Africa for lions, and they are found more or less throughout, especially in Loliondo, Ikoma, and Maswa in the north, Moyowosi in the west, in Kizigo and Singida in the center, at the Selous Game Reserve in the southeast, and in Songea and Tunduru in the south. Between 1982 and 1986 in Tanzania, with twenty-eight clients, I took twenty-eight lions, nearly all with big manes. Due to the strict regulations imposed by the government to combat poaching, the number of lions remains constant and has actually grown in many areas.

In Malawi, the old Protectorate of Nyasaland, because of the increase in the human population lions are rare outside parks and reserves, and not very numerous inside them, either.

Zambia, the former Northern Rhodesia, still has a large number of lions. They are especially numerous in the Luangwa Valley, but are found also in Lake Bangweulu, the Kafue Plateau, Barotseland, and the district of Mporokoso. I took fifty-four lions in this country between 1966 and 1974 in the Luangwa Valley, and many of those lions were truly magnificent specimens.

Zimbabwe was also famous for its lions, and many stories by the early hunter/ pioneers like Selous, take place there. Things have changed, and today the growth of farming and the creation of plantations and ranches have reduced the number of lions in many areas. They are still common in the Zambezi Valley, near the border with Mozambique, west of Gatooma, and in most national parks, especially Hwange. They are abundant in nearby areas such as Matetsi, where there are many fine specimens.

Mozambique was always lion country, and despite the civil war that has consumed the country for years, they are still common in some areas such as Marromeu, north and west of Tete, along the Ruvuma, Lugenda, Messalu, and Lurio Rivers, in Macaloge, near Lake Malawi. In southern Mozambique there are also lions with beautiful manes in the zones of Mapai, Saute, Chigubo, and Mabote.

The civil war in Angola had negative consequences for lions when their favorite habitat, Cuando-Cubango in the southeast, became a battlefront. When I was exploring and hunting the area between 1962 and 1964, it was still unknown and marked on maps as "the land at the end of the world." Lions were everywhere then, even in broad daylight, something which I fear is gone forever. Today lions are mostly found in the areas between Serpa Pinto and Cangamba, south of Cazombo, northeast of Gago Coutinho, and between Mulondo and Caiundo.

The old Protectorate of Bechuanaland, now Botswana, had one of the greatest densities of lions in all Africa before abusive hunting reduced the number in many areas. In the Kalahari, many superb lions were taken, but those impressive, long-maned specimens are becoming more and more rare. The general lion population, however, remains high and with strict regulations will remain that way.

The only two countries left in this overview are Namibia and South Africa, where lions are abundant in national parks and few outside of them. It is rare to see one in regular hunting areas.

As we end our journey through the African countries where lions are found, there is a curious conclusion: Ecologists, scientists, and nature lovers have organized movements to ban the hunting of elephants and leopards, which are both ten times more numerous than lions. Of the animals that are disappearing, no one seems to remember the lions. If we forget about them too long, before too long there won't be any left.

Based upon my experience in hunting lions, I'd like to make a general recommendation for those who are planning this kind of hunt: Like all cats, the lion is easily killed by a shot fairly well placed, but it is just as certain that a wounded lion will turn into a formidable enemy and must be treated with the utmost respect. A wounded lion represents great danger—it is not a pussycat.

A projectile from a modern, medium-caliber rifle can kill a lion, but this is not what matters. Always use a caliber sufficiently powerful to kill the animal or put him out of action so that he cannot attack or escape into the grass where he will have to be followed. A wounded lion is very serious business, and it is wise to take whatever measures necessary to avoid being put in the unenviable position of a direct confrontation with him. I recommend the use of expanding bullets of not less than 270 grains with initial energy of not less than 4,000 foot/pounds, which give a good safety margin for hunting lions. Remember that the first shot is the one that decides whether things will go as planned . . . otherwise, things can become horribly complicated in a matter of a few seconds.

LION HUNTERS

Who hasn't dreamed of hunting a lion? I think that nearly everyone in the world, even those who don't hunt, has had this fantasy at some stage of his life. Lion hunting is truly thrilling if you have the steady nerves that allow you to confront this great adversary bravely and gallantly. Nothing is more exciting than a lion roaring, turning that heraldic and majestic face to the hunter and able to cover 100 yards in six seconds. From ancient times it has been the trophy most coveted by kings and emperors. King Amenhotep III offers a classic example. Born 1,406 years before Christ, he took 102 lions with a bow and arrows.

Perhaps one of the most well-known lion hunters of the past century was a French official who took part in the conquest of Algeria. Jules Gerard, of the Third Regiment of Spahis, began hunting in the 1840s and took a total of twenty-five lions, which was a large number in those days. He described his adventures in a book called *Lion Killer*, which was translated into many languages. The book is interesting because it gives us information on where lions were to be found in North Africa in those days (the last was officially killed in 1893, 60 miles south of Constantina). From a hunting perspective, however, it is less a

An Ethiopian lion shot in the high grass near the Sudan border, 1973.

serious work about a hunter's experiences than a mixture of fantasy and reality in the style of Emilio Salgari's adventure tales. Certainly there have been other great hunters in that part of Africa, but they left no records of their exploits and their names have been lost in the passage of time.

Jumping from North to South Africa, around the same period as Jules Gerard, the Boers encountered many lions in their journey from the Cape of Good Hope across the fertile plains that would become the Orange Free State and the Transvaal. A number of their oxen and saddle horses were attacked and the Boers began hunting lions in their own defense. Kotje Dafel and Petrus Jacobs (a famous elephant hunter) became well-known hunters, with each taking more than 100 lions over the years.

Other renowned lion hunters in South Africa were Vaughn Kirby, who between eastern Transvaal and Mozambique took forty-nine; the famous hunter and naturalist Selous, who shot thirty-one; and William Finaughty, who killed seven in a single day but whose total number is unknown. Among the South Africans, the top number was taken by J. Stevenson-Hamilton, who actually was not a hunter but a game warden at the Kruger National Park from the time it was created in 1902, as the Sabi Reserve, until 1942. In those forty years he shot 200 for control purposes. Those he took with the aid of native trackers. Another twenty he took with bait.

In Angola, the Danish elephant hunter Karl Larsen killed seven lions in only two minutes on 20 January 1909. He used a .600 Jeffery Nitro Express and shot thirty-four lions over the course of his life. In what used to be Northern Rhodesia, my old friend Bert Schultz, who was in charge of elephant control in the Luangwa Valley, took twenty-nine lions, most of which had threatened the local population.

The best lion hunting occurred in the fantastic grounds of East Africa, starting with the old British protectorate of Somaliland, which became part of the Republic of Somalia on 26 June 1960. Somaliland was nearly all desert and populated by groups of nomadic Somalis whose herds of goats and camels made frequent meals for lions. Between 1890 and 1902 an estimated 1,000 lions were taken by sportsmen, who would arrive by ship at Berbera and travel to Hargeisa in the interior, which was the starting point for expeditions. Everything was transported by camels which could go weeks or months with little water, even given the high temperatures. During that period the best known hunters were Colonel Curtis, who shot twenty-seven lions in one season, and Lord Wolverton and Colonel Arthur Page, who killed thirty-two between them in five months. Lord Delamere also began his hunting career in Somaliland, shooting sixty lions between there and Kenya. I was in Somaliland a few years before independence and it was still possible to hunt lions with a license that cost less than in any other country. But the lions were very hard to get, and I had to travel nearly to the Ethiopian border to find them.

In the old British East Africa, renamed Kenya in 1922, lions were plentiful, and during my years as a hunter there I had the opportunity to see and hunt a good number of them. Without a doubt my long-departed friend John Hunter had the record number, taking over 600 during a career that began in 1908. In 1924 he was appointed by the government to eliminate lions eating the cattle of the Masai. He hunted and shot eighty-eight in three months. Eighteen of those were taken in a single night using bait. Before becoming a professional safari guide, he hunted lions for their skins, which were sold in Nairobi and Mombasa for the equivalent of £1 sterling each.

The greatest number of lions shot at one time took place in Laikipia, northwest of Mount Kenya in an area infected with cattle-eating felines. In 1921, the Maharaja of Datia, accompanied by the professional hunter Jim Fey and two others—four rifles in all—shot thirty-four lions and two leopards in a single night. This shows how abundant these creatures were until quite recently. The same Jim Fey had a thing against lions. One day in 1922 lions killed four donkeys he used as transportation in Kinganop, not far from Nairobi. In reprisal, Fey used bait and killed fourteen lions in an hour and a half.

Another hunter who shot a large number of lions in a short time was the American Paul Rainey, who used packs of special dogs trained to hunt puma in the United States. Rainey killed 200 African lions. While the lion was distracted by the snarling dogs, it was easy to shoot it. But this had to be done very quickly or the mortality among the dogs would be very high.

Blaney Percival was the first game warden in Kenya and in total shot fifty lions and never a lioness. He always chose animals that threatened a specific area and never hunted for sport. If he had, his number would have been multiplied tenfold. In the old German East Africa, later called the Territory of Tanganyika and today Tanzania, the Baron Bronsart van Schellendorff shot sixty lions over fifteen years. The English aristocrat Sir Alfred Pease, with one of the most impressive hunting resumes in the world, killed more than 100 lions, including fourteen in one day on his farm on the Kapiti Plains between Nairobi and Mombasa. It was on this very farm that ex-U.S. president Theodore Roosevelt began lion hunting under the tutelage of Sir Alfred and the cousins Harold and Clifford Hill. Roosevelt and his son Kermit took seventeen lions between them on this long expedition, which ended in March 1910 in Khartoum, the Sudan.

The Hill cousins were great lion hunters. They were forced to go after these cats because of the frequent and very destructive attacks on their ostrich farm by the lions in their area. The reputation of the Hill cousins grew until local hunters and sportsmen were competing to contract the Hills to accompany them on lion hunts. They are considered two of the greatest figures in East African hunting and they won this reputation fairly, without fancy tricks or special advantages. In total, Clifford took 160 lions and Harold 135.

Many hunters in the 1920s, 30s, and 40s hunted large numbers of lions. Bill Judd, later killed by an elephant, took forty-eight lions. Philip Percival, Andy Anderson, Donald Kerr, Syd Downey, Pat Ayre, R. M. Crofton, and W. H. Hoey each shot at least fifty, and some took double that number. I've read about a Sikh ex-soldier from India who, during the construction of the Mombasa to Kampala (Uganda) railway, formed a team with his son and took ninety lions in nine months. They used a unique system where the father would imitate a goat, and once the lion was in sight, the son would kill it.

Of the most recent generation of hunters since 1950, the champion is undoubtedly my friend the late Eric Rundgren who has taken more than 500 lions. During the years that he was in the game department in Kenya, he was in charge of eliminating animals considered dangerous to humans. He took 434 during that period.

Another great lion hunter is Tony Dyer, who was the last president of the East African Professional Hunters Association until it was dissolved in August 1977. He has shot well over 100, nine in one day on his farm in Kisima, near Mount Kenya. My old friend and companion-in-arms Reggie Destro has killed sixty-five; Freedy Seed sixty; Ronie Babault fifty-two; and David Ommaney over seventy, most of them in Kenya.

I've shot 153 lions, most of which were marauders, and, after elephant, it is my favorite hunt. I remember the days in the Sudan when the lion was considered a varmint and could be hunted freely. Today, we can only dream about such days when the horizon was dotted with the silhouettes of endless lions.

To finish this chapter on lion hunting, I think it would be appropriate to comment on the proper rifle for hunting lion. In general, the lion is easy to kill and never offers the kind of resistance to bullets as does the elephant or buffalo, but the use of an inadequate weapon can turn the lion into a lethal killing machine for the hunter and create a very grave situation. For this reason, never use low-powered weapons or light projectiles. Initial energy should not be less than 4,000 foot/pounds and the bullet's weight more than 270 grains. Naturally, only expanding bullets should be used.

I have had experience with most calibers between .275 and .577 for lion hunting, and I find the 9.3x64 Brenneke with 293 grains (TUG), the .375 magnum with 300 grains, and the .416 Rigby with 410 grains especially effective. Any of the bullets between 400 grains and 500 grains fired by rifles from the .400 Jeffery up to the .475 No. 2 will be satisfactory. I once shot nine lions with eleven bullets from a .416 Rigby without any problems, but I always try to place the bullet in the right spot, and I don't pull the trigger if I can't get a good shot.

The bullet has yet to be invented that kills without being placed properly, and I insist that it is vital to be properly armed when hunting lions. Nothing is more blood chilling than a lion attacking a hunter, with an enormous mouth issuing deafening roars, approaching at the speed of light, and presenting a very difficult target. This is great stuff to impress your friends with but not to experience. I've been through it a number of times, and, as an old hunter, I advise the new generation not to mess with lions. Teasing and games can be deadly.

Never better than here fit the words that were the slogan of the East African Professional Hunters Association: *Nec timur, nec temeritas* (never frightened, never reckless).

THE LIONS OF WEIGA

These events date from 3 March 1962, but what happened then remains as vivid as if it had occurred only yesterday. In those days I hunted in the southern Sudan, based in Juba. The year 1962 had gotten off to a bad start with the Nile floods lasting longer than usual. When the hunting season began at the start of January, roads were still covered with water and mud, totally impassable, and the grass was very green and more than two meters high. In other words, safaris were impossible that year in the Sudan. We had to find a solution, which turned out to be going to Uganda, where the flooding hadn't been so bad.

After a few safaris a German friend arrived who had intended to come to the Sudan for the second time in hopes of repeating our first successful safari. Because of the impossible circumstances in the Sudan, he agreed to come to Uganda, where he arrived with the gamekeeper of his properties, an agreeable fellow and one of the best shots with a rifle I've ever seen in my life.

The safari continued at its normal rhythm. In search of elephants, we arrived at Lake Albert where we camped by the Weiga River. Elephants regularly pass this area on their way to Lake Albert from what used to be Murchinson National Park, to enjoy some of their favorite plants and fruit. The challenge is to check out the entire area, binoculars in hand, looking at every possible elephant with the hope of seeing if one of the park's magnificent specimens has decided to leave his impregnable refuge for a lakeside vacation, but these old elephants know the park better than its director and rarely leave. If they do, it is at night and they don't wander far.

One afternoon, after four or five days of eying hundreds of elephants without finding any with tusks weighing more than fifty pounds each, we decided to change our focus to buffalo, of which there were many a few miles from the border of the reserve. We hopped into the Land Rover and, chatting cheerfully away, headed for the buffalo. My friend was armed with a .416 Rigby with a telescopic sight, the gamekeeper with a .300 Weatherby Magnum, and I had my .416 Rigby and Lang .475 No. 2 Nitro Express double.

We drove around for three-quarters of an hour until Hamisi, my gunbearer and head tracker, hit me on the arm, saying, *Simba, bwana*,"—"Lion, sir."

The lion wounded by a Swiss hunter and finally shot in very tall grass, Tanzania, 1982.

Fifty yards to our right was a beautiful lion stretched out under a tree. He didn't seem very concerned about us, but as soon as we stopped he got up and slowly strolled away. We took our rifles and followed. The lion broke into a casual trot that allowed us to watch him but not to get a good shot. This went on for some time, and then the lion disappeared into thin air. Even in the helpful soil, he didn't leave the tiniest track.

My friend removed his telescopic sight from his .416 in order to fire quickly if necessary, and forming a V shape, we beat the bushes for the lion but found not a sign. Deeply disappointed, we returned to the Land Rover, which was a distance away. There was a dry ravine to our right, quite deep and about twenty-five feet wide. We searched it, but we still found no sign of the lion, which seemed to have evaporated. About fifty yards ahead of us the wall of the ravine had fallen in, forming a gorge between the edge and bottom. This gorge was covered with high grass, which because of its location had never burned. The gully was about twenty-five yards long and five deep, from the embankment where it began to the gash at the bottom of the ravine.

We followed the upper edge of the ravine, heading for a thick tree about seven or eight yards from the edge of the gully when the lion suddenly appeared from behind the tree where he'd been crouching the entire time. It looked as though he wanted to flee again, but we were in the way of his escape route. As we were only twenty yards from his tree, he couldn't wait any longer and sprang out, roaring loudly enough to stop anyone's heart. He was a gorgeous male in his prime with a lush mane more appropriate to a lion in the circus than one in the wild.

After his first jump (imagine coming nose to nose with a roaring, pouncing lion!) we reacted quickly. My friend raised his .416 and shot the lion in the right shoulder. The animal fell with all four paws doubled beneath him. I thought he was dead, but he gathered his forces and leapt into the gully and vanished. I ran after him, and as I got to where he'd disappeared I saw him running through the grass below me to the right. I fired my .416 as fast as I could toward where I imagined his neck to be, but it was hard to tell with that huge mane.

At the sound of my gun, he somersaulted like a shot rabbit and was lost in the tall grass. It was some seconds before the others arrived at my side. I told them I'd hit him but he had run into the grass and I wasn't sure whether he was dead. We stayed silent to listen for some sign of the lion and after a few minutes we heard a deep groan to the right. The lion was badly wounded, but he was still alive.

Almost immediately we heard another groan to the left and then the two together, separated by about twenty yards. We were bewildered and also scared—what if we had two wounded lions out there? That is exactly what had happened, as it turned out. When my friend shot the lion on the edge of the gully, his companion, who must have been napping, was aroused by the shots, roars, and groans and had attempted to escape through the grass. When I saw him running toward the right, I thought it was the wounded lion trying to escape through the bottom of the gully, so I shot him, not knowing it was a different lion.

So, this was a fine pickle—and a lovely Christmas present—for here we had two wounded lions in the gully hidden by thick grass higher than a man's head. I had to resolve this potentially very dangerous problem fast because it was after five, and night fell at six so there was no time for fooling around. We'd try the quickest and easiest thing first. We would stand on the embankment with rifles ready, throwing stones to provoke an attack. This provoked nothing, except a dull roar from one of them. The sun was going down and, desperate measures require desperate remedies. I would have to go down into that grass and find those lions one by one.

Before going down, we crossed to the other side of the ravine to see if we could find anything. There was a dark shape in the grass. I fired at it, but it was nothing. We returned to the other side, and with my friends covering my back, I got ready to enter the tall grass. They wanted to come with me, but I wouldn't hear of it, and they understood. If I went alone, I'd only have myself to worry about, and I'd be able to fire in any direction, but with three people and two injured lions in a small area, someone would be sure to get shot. We shook hands and I jumped down the embankment, loosening some dirt from the three-meter wall. I was completely obscured by the grass.

Only Hamisi came with me, and he stuck to my shoulder like a shadow, his 12-gauge shotgun ready. In following the lion, I had left my .475 double in the Land Rover and had only the .416 now. I have no idea why they brought that shotgun but there it was and it was better than nothing. I have little faith in a shotgun against lions at more than four or five meters but at less than one, if, God forbid, that should be the case, a buckshot load of nine pellets in the face would do the trick. With Hamisi as my Siamese twin, I slowly stepped into the grass to the left, looking for the first lion.

I had the .416 Rigby in my hands, its four expanding bullets ready and my finger on the trigger as I moved forward inch by inch—in the exact meaning of the words—toward where I had heard the lion the last time. I would advance one foot, little by little, winning one scrap of ground without making a sound, and then put the second foot where the first had already been. With the weapon aimed, I parted the grass, looked, and then looked again.

Because I am tall, I could see the others out of the corner of my eye signaling me from atop the embankment. Two or three times they gestured, but I didn't understand what they wanted. My attention was ahead of me, where I expected the lion to come from. What they told me later was that Hamisi had both barrels of the shotgun aimed at the back of my neck, and they were terrified that he would fire and blow my head off. This had happened not long before to another professional in very similar circumstances. He had also been going after wounded lion in the grass.

I think I covered the ten yards toward the lion in five or six minutes, although to me it seemed like years. I finally saw something in the grass, and that something was slowly taking the form of a lion, lying on his side but still breathing. He didn't make a peep when I shot him. I saw that one of the bullets fired from the other side of the ravine had hit him in the mouth and broken a tooth. I fired still again, even though the animal was virtually dead. I wasn't taking anything for granted, figuring it would be easier for a taxidermist to patch up the lion's skin than it would be for a surgeon to patch up mine.

With the killing of this lion, half the work was done. I heaved half a sigh and went toward the thicket where I calculated the other to be. I covered those twenty yards toward the other end of the gully where I had last heard him very slowly. Bit by bit we crept closer while Hamisi stuck to my back like a band-aid. Where we had expected to find a lion, we found nothing. I made a little circle, and the result was the same—negative. I figured that I must have become disoriented in the grass, so I decided to go back to the embankment to reorient myself.

As I started to the right, I saw something move ahead of me on the ground. It was the tip of the lion's tail. He was sitting like a dog with his back to me and with his head leaning forward. My bullet to the neck had left him stunned, so he hadn't heard me approaching. We reacted at the same time. As I pulled the trigger, the lion turned toward me with a really impressive roar. The end of the barrel was now smack in the center of his chest. The expanding bullet stopped his attack and knocked him on his side, where he lay roaring and clawing the ground with his paws, his tail twitching violently. I quickly shot him twice more, and he was dead. I kept my rifle aimed, the last cartridge in the chamber, just in case.

Then the others came and embraced me. I told them what happened while they looked the lion over and then examined the other. Once this problem was solved, there remained the question of how we were going to get the lions out of the ravine since they were huge as well as heavy. I truly thought they weighed a ton. We managed to get them to the edge of the embankment by dragging these two immense bodies through the grass. Then the fun began. The walls of the embankment were ten feet high as well as being nearly vertical, so our effort began to take the characteristics of a Greek drama. Since it was nearly dark, I ran to get the Land Rover so that we could use the headlights, and with some ropes we began the adventure of hauling the lions out of the ravine. We all pitched in and after what seemed hours, we heaved the lions up, one after the other, our efforts punctuated by grunts. As a perfect ending, we got lost on the way home and finally arrived there after eleven at night. We were dirty, tired, and hungry, but we were damn happy. After all, we had taken, on an unforgettable hunt, two fantastic lions at Weiga, near the legendary Lake Albert.

MORE ABOUT LIONS

I had two clients from Spain, and I was sharing camp with an old friend and colleague who also had two Swiss clients. We'd taken a lion that afternoon after an exciting chase where we had followed him wounded, so things were going well. One Swiss hadn't gotten a lion and was very concerned because he had to leave early. He was annoyed at not taking a lion, especially since he'd

Two large Zambian lions. One has a black mane and the other none at all, even though both are mature males.

been on safari before in Botswana and hadn't gotten one then, either. We said good-bye to him and his young son after dinner. We wouldn't see them again because we'd be getting up early, and they would be gone on the charter plane by the time we got back.

I called my clients at five, and, after a light breakfast, we headed off in the direction of a place where we'd heard lions, in hopes of finding them. As we got close, however, the lions dived into the bushes and disappeared. We tried to flush them out and when this didn't work, we decided to take a ride in the Toyota to where that road crossed the one to the camp, about 600 yards to the east. There were no fresh tracks. It was now eight A.M., and we decided to go someplace else. As we doubled to the left, I saw a car with the others on top, waving furiously. We were quite surprised to see them because I was under the impression that they'd decided not to go hunting in order to prepare their things to leave. Curious, we pulled up and found the following scenario:

After we'd left, they remained in bed, snoozing away until about seven, when a lion began roaring near camp in a gully. Because this represented their very last chance, they decided to go see what would happen. At the instant they got there, the lion stepped into the clearing, and stood about eighty yards away looking at them. The Swiss fired, hitting the lion in the chest. The wounded animal leapt down into the gully and vanished in the thick grass. We appeared at the moment they were about to begin the search for the injured lion, so we joined forces to help resolve this bad turn of events. We sent the two Swiss and my clients back to the cars because, despite their good intentions, they were more of a hindrance than a help.

I entered the gully armed with my .375 magnum and followed by my gunbearer Kiribai, while my friend covered our backs with his .470 Nitro Express from several yards behind. We moved slowly. Suddenly the lion sprang in front of us, fled the gully, and took refuge in a thicket about 100 yards toward camp—without giving us time to fire. Because of the marshy soil, the thick brush had survived the fires that usually clean the land during the dry season. What remained was an impenetrable wall of grass almost ten feet high. Once the lion entered this haven, he disappeared from sight.

Our problem was now aggravated. A wounded lion in that kind of terrain is bad news! We had the cars brought over and parked between the grass and the gully to block off this avenue of escape, while Kiribai and I poked through the grass trying to find the lion or provoke a charge. We

An unusual heavy maned lion from Ubangi-Shari, 1967.

wanted to lure him out of the grass and into the clearing. We threw clods of dirt and sticks toward where we thought the lion might be hiding while I kept my .375 magnum at the ready. Slowly we traveled around but found nothing. To relieve the tension, we joked as a way to relax, fundamental in these compromising situations.

We weren't getting the desired result, so we decided to go into the grass where the blasted thing was hiding. It had yet to make a sound or give some sign of life, so we could hope for the best. We fought our way for six feet into the wall of grass before giving up, realizing that we couldn't go a step farther. We tried in another place but the outcome was the same. There was no human way to get through it—it was just like a solid wall.

The only viable solution was to use one of the four-wheel-drive vehicles to open a path through that mass of vegetation. I explained the plan to our clients, and we got to work. We put the clients in one car and took my Toyota. We decided to make a run for the lowest part with Kiribai and I on top to see if we could spy the lion. My friend closed the windows and with a smile asked me not to leave him to the lion for breakfast. That wall of grass was so incredibly dense that he could see nothing from inside the car. On our first try the car couldn't break through. We put it in four-wheel-drive and in first gear, bit by bit, it pushed into the thick grass. I kept the .375 magnum ready, but we drove from one end to the other with no sign of the animal. We were surprised and confused because we knew it had to be there.

We combed the grass again. In the middle, Kiribai said he thought he saw something, but try as I might, I couldn't. He insisted that we get down and take a look, which we did, separating the grass with the barrel of my rifle. Crouching, I inched toward the point that Kiribai had indicated. He tugged at my arm and pointed ahead of us, but I, like a mole, could see nothing but grass and more grass, until that instant when I was nose to nose with the lion. His mouth was open, but he didn't make a sound, something very unusual because they always announce an attack with a big roar.

I fired once and then twice more, but the lion slid away, completely silent. I could almost see a dark mass stretched out on the ground, so I fired the .375 magnum again. This time there was a soft sighing roar. We strained our ears to hear something, anything, until we heard the unmistakable sound of an animal dying. Nobody can imagine how relieved we were to hear this. We hacked open a tunnel with a machete, and because there was no possible way to move the lion we tied a rope to its neck and pulled it to a clearing with the Toyota. It was a beautiful animal in the prime.

We called the others, who came with tragic faces, but once they tunneled into the grass and saw the lion there was much grinning and back slapping. What started badly ended well. The Swiss took those longed-for photos and barely had time to get back to camp and pack before catching the charter plane to start his journey home.

We returned to camp amid the joyful songs of the African staff. I was starving after so much activity on an empty stomach and wolfed down two fried eggs, cheese, toast, and coffee. I noticed something strange about my client who hadn't yet taken a lion. He was the only one who hadn't wanted to see the lion, nor had he wanted to take part in the brief festivities that always follow such an event, but I figured he was jealous. As diplomatically as I could, I explained the obligation I had to help a fellow hunter in distress,

Lion doublette, Zambia, 1970.

which is also part of a hunter's duty. I also explained the danger that a wounded lion presents. He finally understood why I had left his hunt to help the others. Calm returned. It's difficult to understand how some people can put their own desires ahead of serious and pressing events like this, but I guess that's human nature.

Saturday finally ended and on Sunday we took a buffalo in the morning and, if I remember correctly, also a Grant gazelle. After lunch we headed again for the valley near the Serengeti Park, and, after crossing a muddy gulch, we decided to follow it to see if we could find something. After a few kilometers, the Toyota gave a few gasps and jerked to a stop, the sign that there must be, once again, water in the carburetor. No one can imagine the amount of junk found in

Two huge Masai lions, Tanzania, 1985.

the gasoline in those days, but since this happened every other day or so we had enough practice in removing and cleaning the carburetor to challenge the skill of the mechanics at Le Mans. We carefully removed everything and put all the little screws and springs (the Japanese are really devilish with those springs) in a hat so as not to lose them, which would have meant the immediate death of the vehicle. The tireless Kiribai asked if he and Charles, the other gunbearer, could go ahead and check things out on the road. They disappeared from sight 100 meters down the road and we focused on the carburetor, which was full of all sorts of strange things. . . .

It was a mess, and we lovingly remembered the gas jockey who had pumped that junk into the car, casting grave doubts as to his heritage as we huffed and puffed like bellows into the carburetor to clear it out. Charles suddenly came running full speed around the bend. He could barely gasp out the word *"simba, simba,"* which means lion, several times. When he caught his breath a little he managed to tell us that there was a huge lion stretched out ahead, along with a lioness and a nearly grown cub. Kiribai had stayed behind, hiding and watching while Charles ran to tell us. We grabbed our rifles and followed Charles to the point where Kiribai waited, who signaled us to advance slowly and quietly.

We crept like shadows to his side and I looked where he was pointing. An enormous lion was sitting like a dog about 200 yards away. Beside him

One of the largest lions I've ever seen, Loliondo, Tanzania, 1982.

were a lioness and a large cub sitting on the slope of a hill near the gully, perfectly visible in the short grass. As we approached within ninety yards, we saw that the male was perfectly placed to take a shot in the center of the chest. I asked my client if he was certain he could kill him with the first shot. Of course he said yes, but he was so terribly nervous that I reminded him of the mess the day before and asked him not to make me go after another wounded lion. He swore that it was a done deal and like a fool, I let him shoot from there.

He put his Winchester .375 Magnum on the tripod we used for long shots, and I saw the lion take a hit in the lower stomach, jump up and head for some bushes. Without missing a beat, the lioness charged at us, jaws wide, roaring fiercely. The last thing I wanted to do was kill a lioness even in self-defense, so I ran toward her, shouting and hoping to scare her off. The others followed, not knowing why, as they later told me, but this wide defense did serve to stop her. She stopped when she was about twenty-five yards away, just at the point when I feared I might have to kill her. She fell back, roaring and lashing her tail about before deciding to leave. The cub ignored us. We formed a semicircle and pitched some rocks after the lioness. This did the trick, and both she and the cub disappeared. Even in this open territory, there was no sign of the wounded lion.

It was already five in the afternoon, so there wasn't anything to smile about. We ran to where the lion had been hit in hopes of finding a trail of blood, but there wasn't any. It was an open area with only a few bushes, cut through by the wooded gully. The lion had to be in there. I tried to flush him out by having Kiribai throw stones at the bushes while I waited with the .375 magnum ready. Nothing happened, and we began eliminating various groups of bushes in a systematic manner.

This was too nerve-wracking for the clients who waited behind, chattering and making our job more difficult until I yelled at them "to shut the hell up." Like an apparition, Ali drove up at that moment, so I loaded the clients and Charles in to watch the action from a higher elevation where they could see if the lion tried to escape from the gully. Only Kiribai and I were left to beat the last bushes.

We again had no luck, which meant the lion had to be down in the gully. We then decided to climb to the highest part and go down the right side. From the distance we could hear the others squawking like parrots in the car, even though I had told them to be quiet. As we began our descent, the sun was

The lion that pushed me down, eastern Transvaal, 1991.

The author and his gunbearer, Kiribai, with a lion shot on the open plains, Tanzania, 1983.

already very low and I estimated that we had twenty minutes of light left. In the tropics, evenings are short and night comes in minutes. My preoccupation grew as we slowly, very slowly, went down the side of the gully, as had happened to me many years before in Uganda. We saw nothing. The gully twisted into a sharp "S" shape, and as we came around the last curve there was the lion, crouched in front of us. He sprang with a great roar and I got him in the middle of the chest, which stopped him and flung him back into the gully. I shot him again, just in case. When Kiribai and I reached the body, we saw that it was absolutely enormous, the biggest lion I had ever seen in my life and a super trophy worth all the trouble we had had to face.

We called the others to come over with the Toyota, all their nerves now steady, and there was once again celebration, photos in industrial quantities, dreams of glory, and a triumphant return to camp where everyone was astonished at the size of the trophy. This was an unusual trophy as well because the dark mane dragged on the ground, something you don't often see in a wild lion, which usually has tangled locks.

Everything came out okay again, thanks to Uncle Tony, whose name, I doubt, is ever mentioned when the happy owners of these trophies tell their friends at home about the terrible trials they had to go through to get them. The satisfaction Kiribai and I got could not be erased. Nor could my affection for the .375 magnum and the results it gave me. A little mistake on the part of my rifle or its bullets, and the scales could have tipped out of my favor. Three lions wounded and three lions taken in three consecutive days is no joke!

DON'T MESS WITH LIONS

I hope this adventure will never be repeated. It happened on 7 August 1991 at 9 A.M. in eastern Transvaal, near the edge of the Kruger National Park. On the sixth of August, we had seen a lion with a huge mane that was nearly black, the kind of exceptional animal that is every hunter's dream. It had escaped by a hair, so we decided to use bait to see if we could get it the next day. We shot two impalas, the only thing we could find around there. These we hung in a tree, high enough to be out of the hyenas' reach and high enough to make the lion work, too. We set everything and returned to camp commenting on this impressive animal, which was as large as the lions from the Masai district in northern Tanzania.

The next morning we left camp early in a bitter cold to see if the lion had gone for the bait. It was a long trip, nearly twenty miles, but when we arrived the first thing we saw was the lion about thirty yards away, eying us though the grass. It was a difficult shot, but my friend is a good shot and I told him to fire before it was too late, as had happened the day before. He had to guess at the

The lion remained dead on top of a stone, Tanzania, 1982.

Lion from northern Tanzania with an exceptional mane.

location of the middle of the animal's chest through the grass, and at the moment he pulled the trigger of the .375 magnum the lion lowered his head. The bullet struck him in the lower jaw, so it didn't reach its desired point. The lion jumped on impact and fell over. We thought he might be dead, but he gathered his strength in an instant and raced off into the thick bush to his left.

We had gotten a good enough look to realize that he was extraordinarily large, so to have a wounded monster on the loose was serious trouble. My friends, Japie and Tim, young Mosi, who was shooting a video of the hunt, and I began following the trail of blood. I carried my .500 Jeffery with 535-grain expanding bullets; Japie had his Westley Richards .470 Nitro Express; Tim, a .458 Winchester; and Mosi a big .44 Magnum revolver with a six-inch barrel, which he carried in his left hand while he handled the video camera with his right.

With all four senses on maximum alert, we followed the trail for about 200 yards when we saw the lion lying on the ground. At the moment I pointed the rifle toward him, he leapt up and ran almost out of sight. I fired blindly at him, but made no hit. As I reloaded I saw that the empty cartridge of the .500 hadn't ejected and was still in the chamber. I tried to get it out but the extractor was broken. I was disarmed.

I sent Mosi to where the others were waiting to get a rifle, so I could continue the chase. He quickly returned with a double Holland & Holland Royal .375 magnum and some cartridges. I loaded it, and we got on the trail again, moving step by step through the increasingly dense and wooded terrain.

We crossed a dry riverbed where the lion's blood still glistened on the rocks. We hadn't gone twenty-five yards after climbing the bank when we heard the lion's great roars and Japie shouting, "There he goes!" At the same time I heard two shots and saw the vanishing hindquarters of the lion as he fled. It

A big Masai lion from northern Tanzania, 1985.

was only the matter of half-a-second before the lion turned and without hesitating launched a fierce and violent attack. In the formation, I was first to the left, then Mosi, Japie, and Tim. The shots were still ringing in my ears when I saw the lion coming at me, snarling and bounding at lightning speed. He covered the short distance between us in the blink of an eye.

Mosi, on my right, fired his revolver and thanks to the agility of a twenty-three year old, leapt behind some bushes. I only had time to raise the double rifle and shoot the animal in the chest, which didn't stop him for a moment. I fired the second barrel just as the animal was on me, but the lion was so close that the momentum from his charge knocked me down. It is simply not possible to describe the horror of that moment. I thought I was dead. The lion had taken the bullet from the left barrel over the left eye, stunning him, thank God. Luckily Japie had the chance to put another bullet into the lion before he recovered from my second shot.

My jacket was smeared with blood, but fortunately it was the lion's. As I fired the second shot with the barrel almost touching him, I was splashed with his blood. I checked my arms and legs to make sure everything was still in one piece. If the lion had gotten me with his teeth and claws, 7 August 1991 would have been a day of mourning for my family. After the shock was over, I had to laugh at my friends whose faces were ghostly white and whose tongues were speechless. I don't know who was the more terrified—them or me! They'd given me up for dead when they saw the lion on me, for they had thought that the second shot had come too late to stop him.

Everything came out fine, but I will never forget how grand and terrifying that lion looked as he closed, that magnificent mane standing on end and filling every corner of my sight. I've hunted many lions and I think it was my experience that enabled me to survive the attack, so my advice—even to the seasoned hunter—is to be careful of lions because you never know how they'll respond. The same can be said for all dangerous game. These animals must be treated with extreme respect. Never turn your back on them. This was the 145th lion I had taken, and he was nearly my last. It was only by a miracle that this episode didn't end tragically.

•••

CHAPTER XVI

The Leopard

Years ago there was a huge uproar worldwide about leopards, which, it was claimed, were practically extinct in Africa. The Greens went crazy with their protection campaigns, without, of course, ever having been to the areas where leopards are found. Their enthusiasm went to the extreme end of flinging paint onto the leopard coats worn by innocent women, who got the shock of their lives. Meanwhile, in the United States, Congress prohibited U.S. sportsmen from bringing leopard trophies back from their safaris, and in London, a brochure given out at customs featured a drawing of a battered leopard and a beautiful woman adorned with its skin. The caption under this picture read, "The leopard needs its skin more than you do." On the street the lady who wore her coat was insulted by seemingly ordinary people who have it in their brains that they must save the poor leopard from immediate extinction, a worse crime than the murders committed by the infamous killer Charles Manson.

While the world spun in pro-leopard hysteria, we professional hunters in Africa were aghast at the outcry because if any animal is safe it is the leopard. I don't know who the "expert" was who started the fuss, but it lasted for many years and was felt by the safari industry. In 1986 a leopard census was done in twenty-three African countries, with a number of animal protection groups picking up the tab. In charge of the project were two respected specialists Rowan Martin, Chief Ecologist for Zimbabwe's national parks; and Belgian biologist Tom Meulenaer. They spent months on a detailed study of the leopard population, helped by the wildlife and nature protection departments of the different African countries that participated in the study. When the project ended in 1989, they had found that there were more leopards than anyone ever imagined, with official figures of between 700,000 and 850,000. What's noteworthy here is that there are ten times as many leopards as lions in Africa, and no one is raising an outcry about lions, which continue to be hunted everywhere as usual.

The leopard is not, nor has ever been, in danger of extinction. It is able to adapt perfectly to changing conditions where the intrusion of man is felt most deeply, finding a lair in any forest, hill, or mountain and often coexisting successfully with humans without one bothering the other. So overwhelmingly positive was the leopard count that even many leopard-loving biologists have recommended that the skin trade be reopened under strict controls. This would cut down on poaching and pour millions of dollars into various governments to create new reserves and improve existing ones. Countries such as Ethiopia and the Central African Republic, which had banned leopard hunting for years, authorized it again.

In some places, there is one leopard every three square miles, with the greatest number in the equatorial forests that cover the northern parts of Gabon, Congo-Brazzaville, and the central-northwest of Zaire, where at some places there is one leopard per two square miles. These are areas where the habitat has not been degraded, where there is little human contact, and where leopards can live quiet lives with plenty to eat, protected by the great forests.

The leopard's adaptability permits it to live in a variety of different terrains, from the bone-dry sub-Saharan zones to the humid equatorial forests, from savannas to steppes and mountains where they can live at altitudes up to 9,000 feet. On Ruwenzori and Kilimanjaro, their tracks have been found as high as 13,000 feet, and on Kilimanjaro the body of a leopard was found preserved by the eternal snow at 19,000 feet, the same place that gave Hemingway the basis for his famous story *The Snows of Kilimanjaro*.

Unlike lions, leopards are territorial and don't have to seek food from the large migrating animals such as antelopes, buffalo, and zebra. Their smaller size permits them to live off the small and medium animals that are always present in their various habitats as well as the domestic dogs and goats brought by man. Because of their eating habits, the only places a leopard cannot live are sandy deserts and swampy areas like the Sudd in the southern Sudan, where the Nile turns into a labyrinth of canals cutting through impenetrable masses of vegetation and papyrus.

It is impossible to give concrete statistics about how many leopards exist in each country. I can only report whether there are few or many in each territory, dividing the African continent into different geographic zones beginning with West Africa. This offers a general idea of the leopard's situation in 1994.

MAURITANIA: Very few, and those only in the mountains of Assaba, in the southern part of the country near Mali.

SENEGAL: Leopards are frequently seen in the Niokolo-Koba National Park in the southeastern part of the country and along the Casamance River in the south, near Ferlo in the northeast and on the left bank of the Senegal. Although their hunting is prohibited, the leopard is a common animal in Senegal.

GAMBIA: In the smallest country in Africa, few leopards survive due to the degree of human intrusion into their habitat.

GUINEA BISSAU: Only a few leopards remain along the Curubal River and east of Cabuca.

REPUBLIC OF GUINEA: In the old French Guinea there is still an important population of leopards, especially in Kiffaya, Bara, Gadaundu, Bone, Maleya, the mountains of Tamgue, and along the Bating and Tinkisso Rivers, all of which is in the northern part of the country. In the east, leopards can be found along the Djon, Kurai, Milo, and Sankarani Rivers; and they can be found in the forests of Macenta, Pela, Nzerekore, and Gueasso in the southeast.

SIERRA LEONE: Due to the destruction of their habitat by humans, there are few leopards remaining in Sierra Leone, and those are limited to the Koinadugu district, Bendugu, the Loma Mountains, along the Sonfon River, and the Wang and Tingi hills.

LIBERIA: I remember that the first time I visited Monrovia, the capital of Liberia, in 1955 I was amazed at the number of street stalls offering leopard skins and elephant tusks brought by people from the interior. The marketplace was as wild looking as anything in an adventure novel. I was twenty-five then and this "exotic Africa" impressed me greatly, especially the ridiculously low prices of $10 per skin and $2 for a pound of ivory. Unfortunately, these marvels in the style of "true adventure tales" are gone now, as are the leopards. Only a few remain in the northern areas of Pendembu, Kolahun, and along the Mano and Loffa Rivers. In the eastern part of the country, there are leopards in Gboyi, Tobli, Tchien, north of Jarzon, north of Paluke, northwest of Webo and on the Cess, Sangwin, and Nipue Duaba Rivers and along the right side of the Cavally where it forms the border with the Ivory Coast.

IVORY COAST: Because of the exploitation of forests and the development in agriculture and mining, fauna outside parks and reserves has been negatively impacted. The leopard has been no exception, and its habitat has been reduced to the most remote and inaccessible areas. In forest areas it is found mostly in the southwest areas of Grabo, Tai, Giglo, Tulepleu, Buyo, Subre, Mount Nienokue and near the Hana, Nzo, San Pedro, and Sassandra Rivers. They can also be found in the wooded savanna areas of the northwest like Bako, Djiboroso, Gueleban, Gulia, Tienko and Madiani. Outside the Bouna Reserve, leopards can be found in Tehini, Kong, Varale, Lenkio, and Kotuba districts, along the border to the reserve.

GHANA: As in most West African countries, the increase in population has forced leopards into the most remote corners of the country, especially in the northwest. They are found in the Mole Reserve and Damango, Sawia, Bulinga, Yala, Fian, Han, Wiasi, and Tumu. I used to be offered leopard skins when I was elephant hunting in Tumu, when it was still the Gold Coast.

TOGO: This densely populated country has few habitats favorable to leopards and only a few are found in the Fazao Mountains, Mount Togo, Mount Kamina, and near the Mono and Ogu Rivers.

NIGERIA: With a huge human population packed into every corner of the country, little space is left for leopards. There are a few in the far northwest between Sokoto and the Niger border, Argungu, and on the Zamfara and Ka. At the other end of the country there are also some leopards in the northeast corner, south of the Komadugu River, on Lake Chad, and the Gubio, Marte, Kala, Gulumba, Gwoza, Dumboa, and the Mandara Mountains.

MALI: Most of the small leopard population is found in the west, especially in the Fina Reserve and the National Park of the Boucle de Baoulé, as well as in Faraba, Kurukoto, Fore, Dialafara, Kussane, Demeke, and Sefeto. There is also a leopard population in the central-south part of Mali in Bura, Mandjakuy, Diallassagu, Bandiagara, Dinaguru, and Bumbum.

BURKINA FASO: Leopards are found throughout the former Upper Volta in variable numbers. The highest concentrations are in the east in Pama, Fada-N'Gurma, Matiakoali, Diapaga, on the Sirba and Tapoa Rivers, in the Arly, and in the "W" National Park, which extends into Niger, Benin, and Burkina Faso.

NIGER: Due to the desert conditions of the country, leopards can only be found in any number in certain zones. One of these areas is the corresponding part of the "W" National Park; leopards are also found in the areas of Sabongari, Liddo, Gumbi, Keita, Kornaka, and Tarka. There is a diminished number of leopards in the mountainous region of Air, north of Agades, and along Lake Chad.

The smallest number of leopards on the continent is found in West Africa, but at least there are still some. In North Africa, specialists say the last 200 or so survivors are in Morocco. I remember many years ago a number of articles were published about hunting leopards in what was then Spanish Morocco, and if I remember correctly, the specimens shot were very big animals.

Unfortunately I haven't been able to get any recent information about the so-called "Barbary leopards," which are only found in the most inaccessible areas of the High Atlas mountain range in Morocco, between the El Abid and Dades Rivers.

Let's move on to Central Africa, which is the part of the continent where the majority of leopards are to be found. The kind of terrain, the wooded area covered by large and dense equatorial forests, make the hunting of leopards difficult. Only occasionally are some taken with traps and more rarely with the bullets of European hunters.

CAMEROON: This country has two kinds of terrain. The north is covered by wooded savanna, what we could call "open terrain," and the south by equatorial forest. Leopards are found throughout with most living in the southeastern part of the forested region and in abundant numbers between Yokaduma and Molundu. I remember that in 1986, while pygmies helped me in hunting duikers by calling them, a beautiful leopard appeared. He was as surprised as we were and left faster than he came. In northern Cameroon leopards live in the mountainous areas such as the Adamaua as well as by the Faro and Rei Rivers, and in the Sora Bum district, east of Bandjuki, north of Belel, and south of Tuboro where I saw some more than thirty years ago.

EQUATORIAL GUINEA: In the old Spanish Guinea, the leopard population was impressive, but today it is almost impossible to calculate how many are left since there is nothing even remotely like a game department. When I was hunting there, the greatest number were found in Evinayong, Acurenan, and Nsoc. As if it were yesterday, I remember leopard skins sold for virtually nothing in Bata, trapped and brought from the interior. Once as I leapt onto the trunk of a fallen tree near the Teguete road, I saw a leopard stretched out in the sun. He paid me no mind until I tried to grab my rifle, then he disappeared like a shadow.

GABON: There are many leopards in the northern part of the country and they are found throughout. They are especially numerous in southern and eastern Minvul, eastern Oyem, western and eastern Mitzic, in the Chrystal mountain range, northwestern Belinga, between Mekambo and Okanja, eastern Booue, northern Anguma, northern Eteke and west of the road between Mokoku and Okanja. I saw one of the largest leopards in my life in Gabon, taken by a local hunter with a decrepit 12-gauge, single-barrel shotgun.

CONGO (Brazzaville): Due to the increase in the human population in the southern Congo, only a few leopards can be found in such places as the Lefini Reserve. But they are plentiful in the central and northern parts of the country except in the marshes crossed by the Sangha and Likuala Mossaka Rivers and except also in the territory south of the administrative post at Impfondo. Good areas for leopards are in Kelle, Mandzala, Sembe, Bellevue, Bolozo, and Lengue in the central-west part of the Congo. There are many in the extreme north of the country from the left side of the Motaba River to the border with the Central African Republic, where I have seen pygmies adorn themselves with leopard skins.

CENTRAL AFRICAN REPUBLIC: Except for a small portion of the country covered by equatorial forest in the far southwest near the borders with Cameroon and Congo-Brazzaville, the rest of the country is covered by wooded savannas with clearings in some areas alternating with gallery forest. The clearings are called "*bakos*." Leopards exist throughout the country, in the forests as well as the savannas and are particularly abundant in Nola, Bigene, Bandoka, Salo, Bayanga, Lidjombo, and Bambio in the forest region. In the savannas, northern Buar, northern Crampel, southeastern Ndele, northern Ippy, western Muka, and the areas of Dongolo, Birao, Uadda, Uanda Djalle, Adelaye, Yalinga, Yakossi, Barrua, and Djema and along the Mbari, Chinko, Uarra, Kerre, Mboku, and Upper Mbomu River are all good. They are also to be found in the last place I hunted leopards many years ago near Mount Uada, south of what later became the Andre Felix National Park. It was named for an old game warden in Birao who was killed by a buffalo. I had the satisfaction of knowing him and supplying him with ammo for his .416 Rigby. If I'm not mistaken, when poor Felix was killed by the wounded buffalo he was armed with a Mauser 9.3x62, but I don't know all the details of the accident.

CHAD: Of all the countries in Central Africa, this is the only one that doesn't have forested areas. In fact, more than half is desert or semidesert. Leopards are found in the savanna areas of Chad that have some forests such as Bessao, Moissala, Kumra, Guidari, Busso, Korbol, Melti, Kunguri, Singako, Haraze, Am-Timan, Mongororo, Goz-Beidam, Am-Dam, Hilleket, Molu, and Guereda, with a small nucleus in the desolate Ennedi Mountains in the northeast.

It is very difficult to get a precise idea about the status of leopards (or anything else) in Chad because of the two wars the country has been fighting: the civil war and the one against Libya. There is no game department with effective methods of controlling the territory. But if leopards are enjoying the respite afforded them by the wars, given the speed with which they reproduce, the number of these felines in Chad must have increased considerably, possibly surpassing the figures from before 1975.

ZAIRE: This large country that covers all of the center of Africa has the most leopards, especially in the 500,000 square miles of equatorial forest that extends from west to east like a green mantle. In some places the density of leopards is none less than one per two square miles, which guarantees their survival, especially considering the complete protection they enjoy. They are common throughout the forest areas, especially in the districts of Kiri, Monkoto, Dekese, Lornela, Katako-Kombe, Opala, Djolu, Basoko, Businga, Buta, Bafwasende, Angumu, Walikale, and Mambasa. In 1989 I made a survey in the northern part of Zaire as a guest of the government and through their fresh tracks I was able to confirm the existence of leopards, even in areas they might not generally favor. Although they are found throughout the savannas of southern Zaire, even with the large amount of mining and farming done there, they are only numerous in Katanga (in the southwest) and Kabambare (southeast) and near the Luama, Lukuga, and Luvua Rivers, and on Lake Tanganyika and in the Marungu Mountains in the extreme southeast of Zaire near the Zambian border.

RWANDA: A small, densely populated country with a very small leopard population. I would be surprised if there are 200 leopards in Rwanda, and those live mostly in the Kagera National Park.

BURUNDI: Also very densely populated, with a small number of leopards, especially in the southern part near the Tanzanian border as well as in the Makamba, Rutana, and Cankuzo areas. Burundi is the last of the countries that together make up Central Africa; we now will turn our attention to East Africa.

SUDAN: This is the largest country in Africa and one with every kind of terrain imaginable, from the northern deserts to the thick tropical forests of the southwest, including endless plains, savannas, wooded savannas, and marshes. Leopards exist in all of these except for the deserts and marshes. When I began hunting in the Sudan, leopards were so common that one was captured near my home in Juba with a trap. A few months later, as I was heading toward the Hellenic Club one evening with a friend, a leopard sprang out in front of us from a hedge, and after scaring us out of our wits, vanished between some houses. The game department told me that they came to eat stray dogs that wander all over the city.

In those days a general hunting license allowed four leopards with no extra charge. Later, for no understandable reason, their hunting was prohibited altogether, only to be reopened several years later with the exorbitant price tag of $3,000. And so it went on until the civil war put an end to hunting altogether in 1984. In general leopards have been numerous in the Sudan despite the poaching, quite active as the number of skins available for sale attest. The numbers do not seem to have been affected by poaching, and it remains a common animal from the border with the Central African Republic in the west to Ethiopia in the east and from Nimule in the south (on the border with Uganda) to Malakal in the north. The leopard is well represented in the southern parts of the provinces of Darfur, Kordofan, and the Blue Nile. I still have some of the skins of leopards I took during my twenty-five years in the Sudan.

ETHIOPIA: The number of leopards in this country must have once been incredible, since 1,741 skins were exported to the United States in 1968 alone. I remember that souvenir shops in Addis Ababa carried huge numbers of them at fantastically low prices. In 1973 the government ordered all Ethiopian merchants to register all the skins in their possession. Three thousand appeared. Leopards are abundant or very abundant in certain areas such as Maji, Mizan-Teferi, Godare, Gambela, Bonga, Jimma, Waca, Gota, Baco, and Giarso as well as on the Baro, Gilo, Akobo, Omo, and Dawa Rivers. In Mizan-Teferi, Arussi, and Bale, black leopards are frequently found, but I know of no European hunter who's taken one. These skins were generally from animals caught in traps.

SOMALIA: The leopards in this part of Africa have always had the bad luck—for them—to have the reputation for the most beautiful skins on the continent. For this reason they've been hunted almost to extinction in most parts of the country to meet the furriers' demands. In 1960 official export numbers reached 800, with quite a few more illegally exported. Today the Somali leopards are in a precarious position and are only found in very small numbers in the southwestern part of the country, north of Afmadu, east of Dugiuma, west of Saco Uen and south of El Uach, east and west of Garba Harre, Uegit, Totias, and Ted.

UGANDA: Before the disaster that befell this beautiful country during Idi Amin's reign, leopards were everywhere, and it was common to hunt them while on safari. Today, it is impossible to know their status, but like Chad, it is possible to imagine that the wars have left them alone and that with their excellent adaptability they remain in good numbers in the least populated areas of the country, such as northern Karamojo province, north and east of Kingum, north and south of Patonga, near the Aswa River, and between Atiak and the Albert Nile. When I

A giant Loliondo leopard which charged the author, Tanzania, 1984.

A nice leopard from Barakitabu, Kenya, 1974.

hunted in Uganda, I took leopards in the Semliki Valley and in the foothills of the impressive Ruwenzori Mountains, the mythical Mountains of the Moon.

KENYA: Leopards are common in most of Kenya and abundant in some areas. When we did safaris in Kenya, leopards were one of the traditional animals taken. I can remember the magnificent examples hunted in the green hills of Barakitabu, in the Masai zone, and in the arid North Frontier District where they shared their habitat with huge elephants, now been eradicated by poaching. Leopards are found about everywhere, from the hot coast of the Indian Ocean to the humid and cold forests that cover Mount Kenya and the Aberdares. Some of the main areas where leopards are found are Maralal, Isiolo, Garissa, Marsabit, the Mathew Range, west of Kinango, the Nguruman Range, Mau Escarpment, and Tukai.

TANZANIA: Like Kenya, leopards are abundant everywhere. I've hunted many leopards in this country, finding them especially numerous in the area of Loliondo north, near the Kenyan border, in Maswa south of the Serengeti National Park, in Nyonga, south of Tabora, south of Manyoni, east of Isoke, Lake Rukwa, north of Mbeya, along the Kilombero River, in the Selous Reserve, south of Liwale, and in the areas of Songea, Tunduru, and Newala along the border with Mozambique. Thanks to the anti-poaching patrols, effective hunting control, and a genuine effort on the part of the government, the leopard population is the same as it was years ago. I believe it will remain so in the future. Tanzania is one of the few countries in Africa where I've hunted leopards in the middle of the day.

Finally, on to southern Africa where we finish our rundown of the entire continent, beginning the final phase with:

ANGOLA: Conservation efforts in many parts of this country have been negatively impacted by the war that has devastated Angola, uncontrolled poaching, and every kind of imaginable abuse by foreign soldiers. But, in general, leopards have come out better than other species and are still common in areas where there are few humans. When I had the great luck to travel, hunt, and explore the extreme southeast of Angola in 1962-1964, I found leopards even in daylight. This is a thing of the past because the area was turned into a battlefield between rebel and government troops. There is nothing left of that marvelous land; it has been razed. Information from Angola is generally unreliable, but I have been told that leopards are now to be found in the following locations: north of Mavinga, west and east of Cangombe, north of Cangamba, Tempue, Muangai, south of Serpa Pinto, Cazombo in the far eastern part of the country, Lumbala, Macondo, along the Zairian border from Texiera de Sousa in the south to Forte Nordeste in the north, Fort Carumbo and along the Chicapa, Luele, Luxico, Luangue, and Cuilo Rivers, all in the north between Cacolo and the Zairian border.

ZAMBIA: Except in the mining area of the northern part of the country (Ndola, Mufulira, and so on), leopards are more or less found throughout Zambia, with a good number in some areas such as the Luangwa Valley (eastern Zambia) and the Kafue National Park in the southwest. I saw many leopards when I was hunting in Zambia and although I was concentrating on elephants, I did shoot a few of them. Besides the places already mentioned, other areas rich in leopards are the Mporokoso district, Chiengi, Iago Mweru, Kasama, west of Mpika, south of Luwingu, along the Kabompo and Lunga Rivers, and the Zambezi Valley.

MALAWI: The former Nyasaland has one of the largest populations of people in Africa, which is bad news for wild animals. The habitats of the animals have been greatly reduced in recent years, especially the large animals such as elephants and buffalo, which have also been plagued by poachers. Leopards, however, have adapted to new circumstances, which is typical of their nature. Although they have vanished in areas of intense agriculture, there are still a good number of them in the north: Nyika Plateau, Kaporo, Chisenga, Rumpi, and Katumbi. There are many leopards in the Kasungu National Park and in the Lengue National Park, which is in the extreme southern part of the country.

MOZAMBIQUE: Before 1975 the leopard population in Mozambique had to be one of the largest in Africa. It was a rare safari that didn't return with its trophy—and this in spite of the organized poaching that took more than a thousand skins annually out of the country. After independence and the following political, economic, and social chaos that has reigned until the present day, the number of leopards has been greatly reduced in battle areas, but in isolated districts of the far north their number has increased and is perhaps greater now than in 1975. Leopards are abundant between the Ruvuma River in the north and the Lurio in the south, which has the administrative post of Marrupa in the center of this large territory and which is crossed by the Lucheringo, Lugenda, and Messalo Rivers. There are also leopards in the upper Zambezi, in Fingoe, Tembue, Chioco, and Tambara, in the Gorongosa National Park, east of Inhaminga, on the Sabe River, areas of Mabote, Machalla, Mapai, Chigubo, and the Lembombo Mountains near the South African border and the Kruger National Park.

ZIMBABWE: Leopards are common throughout the country except in highly populated areas, with the greatest number found in the western part (Matabeleland) between Bulawayo and Victoria Falls. This area includes the Hwange National Park. Leopards are also found south and west of Gwanda, Lake Kariba, Zambezi Valley, along the border with Mozambique, east of Zaka, and in the Gona-Re-Zhou Game Reserve. In August 1988, a gigantic male was shot in Tundamela, 80 miles north of Bulawayo, which weighed 200 pounds when weighed shortly after being shot; it was a truly splendid trophy. In general, the number of leopards in Zimbabwe remains steady despite the numbers shot every hunting season, year after year. The species does not appear to be affected.

BOTSWANA: In the former Bechuanaland, leopards are found throughout the northern part of the country. They are considered common in such places as the periphery of the Okavango Swamps, Lake Ngami, north of Ghanzi, west of Tsau, south of Shakawe, north of the Kalahari, along the border of the Caprivi Strip (Namibia) and Zimbabwe, in the Chobe National Park, in the Makgadikgadi Hunting Reserve, around the Makarikari, and the Nxai Pan National Park. Leopards continue to be one of the traditional trophies of Botswana safaris.

NAMIBIA: Due to the desert terrain of this country, leopards are found in few areas, most of which are in the zone known as "Bushman Land" in the northeast of the territory that has Tsumkwe as its administrative center. They are also found in the area of Grootfontein, the Etosha Reserve, in the Kaoko Veld, Damara Land, and throughout the mountain range that parallels the Atlantic.

SOUTH AFRICA: Thanks to the excellent protection given to wild animals in the last fifty years, the leopard population has recuperated so that in many areas they are again common animals and their hunting has been authorized. Outside the famous Kruger National Park, where they are abundant, they can be found in good numbers in the mountainous area of the northern Transvaal. In the Cape Province there are a few leopards in the mountain ranges that run parallel to the ocean, in the district of Namaqualand, on the Molopo River, west of Mafeking, and in Transkei.

LESOTHO: This tiny country carved in the middle of South Africa has a small population of leopards, mostly in the Maluti Mountains. The former Basutoland has never been a popular hunting area because of its small size and large human population. This is our last stop on this trip through Africa checking out the leopard.

With very few exceptions, their number is above the line of risk, assuring their survival for an appreciable length of time. But no one can foresee what will happen in the next twenty or thirty years as there are a thousand factors at play. If things continue as they are now, we can at least say that leopards will continue to roam peacefully for many years to come in the remote parts of the equatorial forests where few humans live.

Let's look at some points of interest for the hunter who wants to get this beautiful trophy, which is, without a doubt, the most beautiful of the felines. I have taken fifty-seven leopards and have helped my clients hunt sixty-nine, which means I've been present at the deaths of 126 of them, so I feel that I've got a reasonably good idea about how they behave. I also feel that my experience qualifies me to offer the following advice:

I will say that when wounded, they are very dangerous. When the leopard is on his own turf, he is jumpy, wary, and so frightened of humans that he will flee at the smallest opportunity. If he is wounded or cornered, however, expect a 180-degree change. Then the shy leopard becomes a fury, and it is necessary to treat him with the maximum caution, or the hunter will find himself embroiled in a very dangerous and threatening situation before he knows it. Many is the hunter who has suffered damage to his anatomy as he tries to take a wounded leopard without giving the animal the respect he deserves! Without proper caution, the hunter can very easily become the hunted.

I remember that my old friend John Hunter considered the leopard the most dangerous animal when wounded. Leopards stay crouched and silent until the moment they jump onto their persecutor, leaving no time for anything. I agree entirely with John Hunter. I have to confess that chasing a wounded leopard is the activity I hate most in the world, and one I've had to engage in many times, unfortunately. Thank God I've never been touched by one of their snarling charges, although I've found myself in dicey situations more than once. One time in Zambia I did stop a leopard when I was practically touching him with the muzzle of my rifle, which for me is a bit too close.

This happened in 1968 when an incompetent assistant-hunter wounded a male, which then sprang at me. I only had time to half raise my .465 Nitro Express and shoot the animal point blank in the chest, which left me drenched in blood without me even realizing it. I hadn't allowed anyone else to come with me into the high grass where the leopard had fled, and, when I shouted at

A very big leopard from Tanzania, 1983.

them that the leopard was dead, my gunbearer, Didion, was the first to my side. He took one look at me and began to scream and covered his face. I, of course, was completely perplexed. When the others came, they repeated this strange behavior until I realized that I was so covered by the leopard's blood that I seemed to have been sprayed with red paint. Didion and the others thought I'd been clawed and badly wounded, but fortunately I never got a scratch.

Like all cats, the leopard is easy to kill. I never tire of insisting that a bullet should never be fired unless it is sure to hit its mark. Just shooting to see what happens . . . well, what can happen is that things will turn out badly, and you'll find yourself in a situation you wouldn't wish on your worst enemy. I'm against the kind of macho posturing found in adventure novels, but in the case of the leopard I particularly want to warn future hunters not to fool around and to be certain when they pull the trigger. To have to chase a wounded leopard through dense bush is no fun, and many accidents have happened in these circumstances. You don't have to fear them, but you shouldn't act like an idiot, either.

The average weight of a mature male leopard is 130 to 150 pounds, reaching 200 on rare occasions. This means that they can be easily hunted with medium-caliber weapons. My experience is that any projectile between 175 and 270 grains is adequate for a leopard, including the 7x57 Mauser, 7mm Remington Magnum, .300 H&H Magnum, .300 Winchester Magnum, .300 Weatherby, 8x68, .30-06, .388 Winchester, 9.3x62 Mauser, 9.3x64 Brenneke, and .375 H&H Magnum. Larger calibers and heavier bullets are not necessary, which reminds me of a story.

This story took place in Tanganyika in 1958, when it was still part of British East Africa under the federation of Kenya, Uganda, and Tanganyika. One day, on my way to camp about 2 P.M., a leopard sprang out of a tree and sat watching the car, which was about sixty yards away. We jumped out and went after him, and, of course, one of my clients shot and wounded him. Cursing the client between my teeth, I changed my solids for expanding bullets with hollow tips, which were the only ones available then for the .416 Rigby. Advancing slowly, I saw the animal at the exact moment that he sprang at me from behind a fallen log. This was his fatal mistake, for, as he leapt his chest made a perfect target in the air. As he took the bullet from the .416, he seemed to have collided with an invisible wall and fell to the ground like a rag. I approached cautiously and was astonished to see that the bullet had passed through the entire animal, exiting above the tail and leaving a king-sized hole. When the client arrived and saw this "half-a-leopard," he almost had a seizure, but I still think that it was better that the hole was in the leopard's skin rather than mine.

When looking for a wounded leopard, it's a good idea to have a 12-gauge shotgun loaded with buckshot. This will only work for short distances up to fifteen feet or so; for longer distances the pellets will lose energy and density for a sure kill. Keep this in mind. I've hunted leopards with a multitude of calibers and the one I have the most faith in is the .375 H&H Magnum with a 270-grain Winchester Power Point bullet. Thanks to it, I can write these lines even after some hairy adventures with wounded leopards in the tall grass.

THE IMMORTAL LEOPARD

What I'm about to tell happened because of the poor conduct of a projectile. One cool and lovely morning in the month of May 1987, I was on safari in an area between the Wankie National Park and Gwaii in Zimbabwe's west Matabeleland. With me was my friend and companion of many African hunts, Pablo Galvez. We were looking for a superfine example of sable antelope, which were abundant in the area, and we were hoping to surpass the ones Pablo had taken years ago in Mozambique and Tanzania.

The afternoon before, we had taken a look around and seen so many sable we didn't know which one to choose. We counted eleven males, all of which easily beat 44 inches. With so many to choose from, we decided not to rush ourselves and to take another look around the area, so we started with a valley that teemed with all sorts of animals. As well as sable, we saw eland, tsessebe, zebra, reedbuck, and some excellent greater kudu. All the time we were looking, we had high hopes of sighting our "monster." We found him after several days of searching. He was an old male with long and very thick horns that went 45½, a magnificent trophy.

One morning Pablo, a hunter named Deon, another young apprentice-hunter, two Matabele trackers, and I piled into the Toyota. The sun appeared in the east, and it was icy cold to the point that the apprentice, who was wearing shorts, began to turn blue. We had to stop and build a fire to keep him from freezing until the sun could warm everything up. On the road again, we decided to take a shortcut in order to come out at the beginning of the valley. We were all riding along happily and enjoying the beautiful scenery.

As we came around a curve, we saw a leopard sunbathing beside a pond, sitting there like a huge house cat. Deon, who was driving the Toyota, slammed on the brakes, and Pablo and I jumped out with his .300 Weatherby and my .375 magnum. The leopard remained motionless throughout, only turning his head to give us a withering glance as he continued his sunbath. Covering ourselves with bushes, we crept within forty yards of him without the leopard seeming to notice us, which showed how rarely animals in that area were ever shot at. As I pointed at a branch to use as support, Pablo aimed his .300 Weatherby loaded with 180-grain bullets. Because the leopard was seated with his flank toward us, he presented a perfect target and Pablo hit him perfectly in the shoulder.

Dr. Pablo Galvez and author with the leopard that refused to die.

The shot sent the leopard into the air and I could see that the bullet was perfectly centered. I was so sure the leopard was a "total victim" that I had left the safety on my .375 magnum.

The leopard recovered and took off like the devil toward a thick strand of tall grass on the other side of the pond. Pablo was speechless with surprise. I was as well. After all, that shot had been perfect. While we howled the proper curses for the situation, Deon shouted that the leopard was going from one clump of bushes to another, so we returned to the Toyota to try to cut off his retreat. We climbed onto the back of the vehicle trying to see something but all we saw were bushes and dry grass. Pablo craned his neck trying to spot something while I took up my .375 magnum loaded with 270-grain softpoints.

As we couldn't see anything, we decided to comb the area in the Toyota with Deon at the wheel and the rest of us serving as lookouts. We'd covered about 200 yards and were entering a patch of tall grass when the leopard charged out and raced ahead of the car. He had been crouching until the instant we'd come upon him. Deon braked hard, and I slammed my 200 pounds against a piece of iron, using my leg as a bumper and getting a gash that bled like crazy. It didn't stop me from firing away, together with, Pablo at that spotted thing. We saw it and didn't see it, like something in a circus magic show. I had the good luck to hit the left back paw, as we saw later, but that leopard carried on as if nothing had happened.

When he vanished again into a clump of bushes, I realized that my leg was covered with blood down to my boot and that I had an impressive hematoma. I managed to reduce it a little by pressing with my free hand while I tried to staunch the flow of blood with a moist handkerchief. For better or worse, I patched myself up well enough to head toward the bushes where the leopard had disappeared. The thorn got thicker every minute as did our anxiety about what was awaiting us. A wounded leopard is nothing to laugh about.

We left the Toyota, and after finding blood we very cautiously followed the trail. My main worry was the young apprentice who had situated himself behind me. He was breathing hard and had eyes like saucers. He was also carrying his rifle—directly behind my back. I felt sandwiched by trouble—the leopard that was waiting to disembowel me from the front and the apprentice who could shoot me from behind.

Deon was armed with a 12-gauge shotgun loaded with 00 buckshot, and so we four advanced trying to spot something. We hadn't gone 300 yards when the apprentice gave me a whack on my shoulder that nearly knocked me over. There, under a tree and nearly hidden by bushes was the leopard. Forgetting, for a moment, the pain in my leg, I raised the .375 magnum and fired without thinking more about it. Pablo and Deon were a little to the left covering that flank and I didn't see them. As the bullet hit, the leopard groaned, ran six or seven yards in our direction, and then, as if he changed his mind, he turned and tried to go back into the bushes. He had only managed to get his head into the cover when he died.

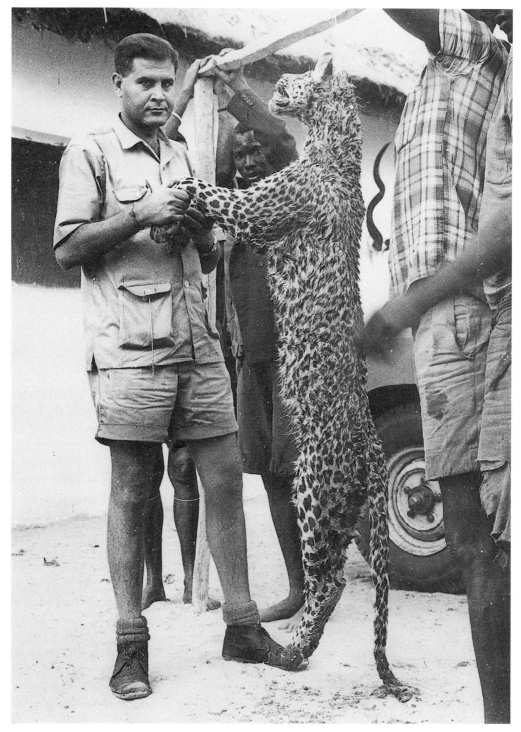

The "Water Leopard," Angola, 1962.

At that second, the situation changed. Pablo was smiling from ear to ear, the apprentice's face lost its green hue and went back to its usual color, Deon returned to his usual habit of swearing, and I, at last, could look at my leg. What I saw made my hair stand on end, for my leg looked as though the leopard had used it as a chew toy.

We took the animal to a clearing and were able to see what had happened. Pablo's bullet had hit its mark, but due to the initial speed of those projectiles, 3,245 feet per second, it had disintegrated upon hitting the leopard. In that short forty-yard distance, it had produced only a large superficial wound. Because of the spectacular way the animal reacted, we had assumed that he was seriously wounded when, in fact, he wasn't. He recovered and took off with only a superficial flesh wound—nothing more. Luckily one of the desperate shots had fractured a back leg, or this story might not have turned out as it did. More than one of us could have ended up wrapped in gauze and covered with iodine. The .300 Weatherby, which is an excellent caliber for long distances, doesn't have the same effect at short ones. The ammunition isn't designed for it, and I'm more than certain that if the leopard had been hit with a larger projectile at slower speed, he would not have thumbed his nose at us—especially after receiving that well-placed bullet from Pablo.

A UNIQUE WAIT FOR A UNIQUE LEOPARD

This happened in 1984 on the northern end of Tanzania, a few miles from the Kenyan border. A lot of time has passed since then, but the events remain in my memory. After having taken so many leopards, nothing like this had ever happened to me.

I was on safari in the Loliondo District with my friend of more than thirty hunts, Armando Bassi. We were out after lion and leopard, which were many in that part of Tanzania, the heart of Masai country. On the second day of the safari we took an immense lion with a great blond mane. We baptized him "the Scandinavian lion," and he certainly looked odd enough to make a unique trophy. I've never seen another one like him in my life.

Once we'd gotten the lion, we turned our minds to putting bait for the leopard in the places where we'd seen fresh tracks or where the terrain was the kind they preferred. One morning, while doing the traditional rounds from bait to bait to see what had been eaten, we found a leopard stretched out on the branch where the bait, a Thomson's gazelle, hung. He looked as though he was considering when to take a bite. The bait was on a solitary tree next to a gully with a small stream and a lot of grass, which was about twenty-five feet below. When he saw us, the leopard jumped to the ground and quickly disappeared. He was a big, strong male, who had scarcely touched the bait even though he must have been hungry. When we found him eying the gazelle it was nearly noon, a strange hour to be sniffing at bait.

Trying not to scare him, we made a blind, which is a camouflaged hut of grass, leaves and branches where we could sit and wait. He would return. To whet his appetite, we left an impala as an extra snack and got our battle plan ready for the afternoon. We returned to camp about three miles away, ate, and returned with folding chairs, books, and magazines to entertain us during what we suspected would be a long wait. I played the old trick of arriving at the blind in the Toyota, making all sorts of noise. While the natives whooped and hollered, we slipped silently into the little hut. Once we were situated, the Toyota roared away, leaving the leopard to imagine that danger was gone and that no one was left. The Toyota waited at a prudent distance, ready to return at the sound of a shot or when it got too dark to fire.

There were three of us in the blind: Armando Bassi and his .300 Weatherby, Antonio Cervera with the cameras, and myself, armed with my .375 magnum. It was still early, so we leafed through magazines while keeping an eye on the bait through a hole disguised by green leaves. Twenty minutes hadn't passed when a lion came by and sat underneath the branch watching the meat hanging above him. He was only fifty yards away and completely unobscured. We were enchanted at the sight and waited to see what he would do.

After a while, he jumped up to try to nab the meat, but he had no luck. He tried a few running jumps, but he couldn't quite reach the meat. Finally, he tried climbing the tree to get out on the branch. The first part of the plan worked fine: He could get up the trunk with no trouble. It was the branch that caused the problem, swinging wildly under his weight until he lost his balance and fell on his head. He tried leaping again, but all was in vain. We, his audience, peered through every little nook and cranny in our hut so as to not miss a second of this performance. The lion spent another ten minutes leaping and grunting, leaping and grunting until he casually turned his head in our direction.

Immediately his belly hit the dirt, his ears pinned back, and his tail lashed from left to right—in other words, he had assumed the hunting position. We realized right away that we were the objects of this hunt. Perhaps in craning our necks to see the show, we'd given ourselves away. The fully alert animal, tense, began his approach, planning to get closer before the final leap and attack. It was an impressive thing to see him slinking closer, trying to blend in with the terrain, and licking his chops at the thought of his theoretical snack. We were not laughing. The lion kept slithering toward us, and things began to look bad, so I decided to kill him if he came closer than a burnt tree, which was about fifteen yards away. As he got there, I stood up, ready with the .375 magnum. The lion reacted by staying quiet for a second, and then, with a leap and a ominous growl, he sprang down the gully to his left and was out of sight.

We had just simmered down again, hoping the leopard hadn't heard the lion, when Armando signaled me with his eyes. Following his glance, I saw the head of a huge leopard appear in the fork of a tree about twenty yards behind the bait, eyes fixed in our direction. Without blinking so as not to startle him, we stood like three statues waiting for him to approach the bait. But time went on, and on, and he didn't move a muscle. He simply stood there, staring, with his ears cocked. The animal was sitting on the ground on an elevated promontory behind the tree, which allowed him to see the terrain. From our position, his body was covered by the tree trunk, and we could only see his neck and head through the crook in the tree, which gave the mistaken impression that he was actually sitting in the tree.

We waited as long as we could, with the leopard never blinking. The newest problem was that the sun was starting to set. Armando whispered that he was sure he could get him, even at seventy yards and even though the head and neck presented such a small target. Because I know Armando to be a very fine shot, I gave him the go-ahead, adding that he should take all the time he needed to be sure of the shot in order to avoid the fun and games that a wounded leopard provides. Armando calmly aimed, placed the crosshairs of his Zeiss scope at the leopard's throat, and slowly pulled the trigger. At the sound of the .300 Weatherby, the leopard's head disappeared, and through the binoculars we could see that his body had been thrown across the tree trunk.

There was no movement whatsoever from the animal, so we approached. As a precaution, I went first with the .375 magnum ready because I knew that if the animal were only wounded he would surely attack. Armando and Antonio followed ten feet behind, as instructed. We kept our eyes pinned on the leopard and as we got to the side of the gully, a huge roar tore the air, and there was the lion just steps away. Apparently he had been there all the time, and that was why the leopard wouldn't approach the bait. Because of the angle, we thought he was looking at us, but in fact he was staring at the lion. Leopards are terrified of them.

The lion scared us to death, so we fired off a couple of shots into the air, at which he turned and scampered away in a rather undignified fashion. After blessing the lion's family in Spanish and Valencian, we got to the leopard, which was indeed dead with a bullet through the throat which had fractured the neck as well. The skin was undamaged and it made a beautiful trophy. That day remains in my memory because of the range of emotions we experienced in such a short time. When Armando and I get together to fight old battles, that one is one of our favorites.

THE SWIMMING LEOPARD

This unusual story happened long ago, at the beginning of August 1962. At the time I was in charge of opening a new hunting area, which was also a virgin area to safaris, located in the Cuango-Cubango in the southeast of Angola. This remote, unknown, and beautiful area was a real hunter's paradise, the virgin Africa of our childhood dreams, like something out of the Jules Verne novel, *The Adventures of Three Russians and Three Englishmen in Southern Africa*.

Naturally, I was thoroughly enjoying my double role of hunter and explorer, and I took full advantage of the opportunities offered by that marvelous, lost corner of Africa, which was only attached to the rest of the country by a single, devilish road. Our camp was located about five kilometers south of Luiana, the only administrative center for thousands of square miles. There lived the *chef do posto* with his family. He was a little Portuguese fellow who wore white outfits with epaulets, had a deadpan face, and was always friendly and ready to do whatever favors he could. He was lonely in his outpost at the edge of civilization. More often than not, he felt himself to be the prisoner of Zenda rather than the king of the castle. I think he viewed his position as a sentence rather than an honor, since he was terribly isolated and did not see anyone for many months.

I traveled back and forth marking new roads, looking for places with special concentrations of animals and getting to know the place little by little. I'd just arrived back at camp after a trip to distant Luengue when the following occurred. One of the professional hunters in the area was on safari with an American client, and everything was going well. In those days it wasn't difficult to please a client because it was like hunting in a reserve. I was relaxing in camp talking with the *chef do posto* who had come for a visit and a cold beer, when the other hunter appeared with a worried look. His American client who was with him looked very, very concerned.

It seemed that they had wounded a leopard with a .270 Winchester bullet to the belly and the animal had disappeared into the tall, thick grass by a large pond. They'd tried to find him but had had no luck. They had heard the leopard's threatening snarls, but they had been unable to get to him, so they decided to come back and seek help. I at once offered a hand and we discussed a plan of action. To our surprise, the *chef do posto* offered to come and help, claiming to have a machine gun ideal for this kind of hunting. To our added discomfort, he offered to bring it from the car to show us.

It was a really sinister-looking tool. The last thing in the world I wanted was to have an excited person with no hunting experience, armed with a machine gun, following me as I tracked a wounded and angry leopard. His generous offer created quite a dilemma. Did we tell him absolutely not and run the risk of offending him and thus complicating all our future transactions with him? Or did we say okay and possibly get a "rat-a-tat-tat" in the back? In a moment of inspiration, I told the *chef do posto* that we would not go after the leopard that day but that we would leave the animal to bleed and weaken. That way, we assured the kind man, the leopard would be easier to hunt the next day. He thought this was a good idea, and we said that in the morning we would come by to get him when we were ready to go after the wounded cat. He said good-bye, and heroically grasping his machine gun went back to his post. As soon as his dust had settled, we tore off in the opposite direction to check on the wretched leopard, figuring we'd come up with something to tell our benefactor later.

The American offered, with suspicious rapidity, to stay in camp so as not to be a bother. So, off to the party went—the hunter, about half-a-dozen natives to serve as beaters, and I, armed with a 12-gauge shotgun and buckshot, which I consider the best to use on leopards hidden in thick vegetation. When we got to the big pond, we found the two trackers who had stayed to watch the leopard. They assured us that the animal had not moved and had to still be in the thick grass.

This grassy area was about thirty yards long and a dozen wide, and it ran parallel to the water. At the beginning, things looked better than I imagined. The eight Angolans would be able to beat the area perfectly, sending the leopard right at us. We organized a simple plan, hiding behind some bushes with each of us covering half the clearing through which our trophy would have to come. The beaters took their positions and began whooping and hollering to force the leopard our way. With my shotgun ready I kept an eye on where I expected the leopard to emerge, but time went on, and as noisy as the beaters were there was no sign of our presumed victim. The beaters caught up to us and we stared at each other like idiots. There was nothing, not even a stupid rat, nothing. There was no way the leopard was dead because the eight beaters moving elbow to elbow would have seen the body. It seemed as if the wounded leopard had evaporated, and this was very worrying.

We decided to go back over the entire area very slowly to see if we could find blood or some sign that would help us find him. Considering the agony the animal must be suffering, we couldn't leave him on the loose. Before we started combing the area again, the natives asked if they could stop and refresh themselves in the pond. They were very sweaty after going through the grass and after making such a ruckus. Two of them kept hold of their spears as they got into the cool water and began to bathe. They moved six or seven yards from the shore to where the water was up to their waists and there they stood, peacefully soaking while the two of us chatted about what had happened.

There we were, peacefully chatting when suddenly quietness of the landscape was shattered by some huge roars followed by the natives' shouts. In a second I saw the leopard emerge from among the grass and water plants. He was only a few meters from the bathers, and he was swimming like a dog—but a very fast and angry dog—splashing and roaring his displeasure. In an instant he reached the scared and surprised natives, who raced for the shore. One of the natives, however, faced the leopard and put his spear in the animal's chest. The man held on to his spear, thus enabling himself to keep that distance away from the claws and teeth, and he shouted like a lunatic begging for help. I jumped into water and as fast as I could slog through the muddy pond I fired the first barrel of the shotgun just as the leopard had jumped the spear. The animal was nearly drowned from the water he had swallowed trying to escape the spear, and I was at no real risk in my rescue attempt. All I needed to do was to stay away from those claws.

When he took the nine pellets from the buckshot, the leopard simply somersaulted over himself and half-floated, motionless.

We dragged him by a paw and his tail to the place on shore where the others were calming down. The fears of a few moments ago had been transformed into expressions of joy. My buddy's face was lit up. Everything had come out well and there was the leopard to satisfy his client.

The animal, without anyone noticing, had fled the start of the beating by taking refuge in the only place he wouldn't be seen—among the thick water plants and grasses. He must have been quite bothered by the wound to do something so contrary to a leopard's habits as to go into the water and stay there. It was only due to the natives' decision to take a bath in the pond that we found him. It certainly had never occurred to us to look for a leopard in a pond. He probably thought that the bathers had come for him and, thinking himself in danger, decided to attack them. Fortunately for us, this meant his end.

With everything in order and the leopard loaded onto the Land Rover, we remembered the *chef do posto* and what could have happened to the eight bathing natives if he'd had that machine gun along. To the *chef do posto* we later told a string of pious lies that partially convinced him, and so everything ended happily, especially when we took a photo of him and his beloved machine gun beside the leopard. So ended the adventure of the swimming leopard, the only one I've ever seen to seek refuge in the water. That's the way hunting is: No matter how much experience you have, every day you learn something new.

•••

CHAPTER XVII

Epilogue

Many things have changed since I first set foot in Africa forty-two years ago. More has changed on that continent than on any other, with the consequent negative effect on its incomparable fauna. The abuse these creatures have suffered through the agonies that came with independence, through the advance of so-called progress, through the lamentable incompetence of some authorities, and through the lack of vision many had in not appreciating the value of wild animals until too late has led to the critical state that the fauna of Africa is in today and the even more uncertain one of tomorrow.

Exotic Africa of the children's books, full of herds of wild animals and natives with feathers on their heads and painted faces, is gone forever. Today, I am left only with memories of those romantic and happy days in which the hunters were kings of the tall bushes, and our presence was a reason for celebration for the primitive and hospitable villagers.

In 1952 my dear friend John Hunter, one of the most famous professional hunters in East Africa, published a book called *Hunter*, which offers a vision of what those old and golden days of hunting in Africa were like. That was the year I began hunting on the Dark Continent, and I had the fortune to hunt with great intensity in the final stage of this *belle epoque*. I continue to this day tramping the forests and savannas of Africa with a rifle on my shoulder . . . still looking for elephant, bongo, and so on.

Before beginning this epilogue, I would like to confess and clarify my position on the field of hunting: I don't care to play two-fistedly, in order to later choose the most convenient hand. Now the fashion is for everyone to pretend to have always been a passionate conservationist/hunter and that before anything else their main concern has been the safety of these species and their happy existence. This reminds me of the Roman proverb *Excusatio non petita acusatio manifesta* ("excuse not the small; accuse the great"). I'm sorry to have to say that, considering what I personally have seen and with a few honorable exceptions, most of these "apostles" are nothing more than butchers who heedlessly fire at any of the unfortunate animals that have the bad luck to come within range of their insatiable rifles.

I am nothing more than a hunter and will be as long as I live. I have nothing to hide and nothing to be sorry for, for the simple reason that I have always conducted myself as a gentleman. I always gave every chance to each animal I hunted, and I never used any tricks in bagging the game. I like to hunt, but with moderation, and I never pull the trigger in a crazy manner just to shoot at something. I always choose the trophy in a way so as to allow me to sleep peacefully.

I don't want to be too destructive to the traditional tales of the dangers of the safari, but I think we should put aside those fabrications and not forget that envy and vanity play important roles in the hunting world. Let's look at those deeds as they really are and feed a piece of humble pie to that hero we all carry inside ourselves.

The truth is that animals considered fierce in general are less aggressive than they pretend, creating a threat more theoretical than real for human beings on safari. In most cases the animal will avoid the hunter, sometimes even if they've been wounded, and I can count on two hands the number of times in forty-two years I've been in serious danger. I'm sick of seeing animals' hindquarters vanishing into the grass at top speed, and anyone who has hunted in Africa will honestly admit that the real difficulty is to get close enough to an animal without it running away. Except in very rare occasions, they never offer a serious risk.

I believe that something in between is the truth, distancing ourselves from extremism on both sides, remembering that the so-called brutes react out of their instinct for self-preservation like all irrational animals. Sometimes hunting becomes complicated due to circumstances, sometimes created by the incompetence of the hunter, but with common sense along with the minimum experience required for the sport, there shouldn't be anything to dramatize. Sometimes there are fatal accidents, but this doesn't mean anything. It also happens in other activities such as driving, mountain climbing, horseback riding, or water sports, yet nobody feels that he or she must stay at home hiding under the bed because of it. There's risk in every activity, but that's all part of the game.

It's too bad that some authors spice their hunting stories up with horrifying adventures that make it obvious—at least to me—that they don't know what they're talking about. The hunt can be easy or difficult, dangerous or not. Only the hunter has it in his power to make sure everything goes well or ends in disaster. Rare are the cases when things are outside of one's control.

Hunting is not a war waged on animals, but a noble, passionate sport where the hunter uses his skill to try to take a trophy by overcoming its fear and wariness in its own habitat. It is not a military operation where all enemies must be

A leopard from western Matabeleland, Zimbabwe, 1989.

exterminated; indeed, I've never considered any animal I've hunted an enemy. To me they've all been more like noble opponents.

It is sad to see the change in mentality of many sporting hunters today. It used to be that clients who came years ago to Kenya, the Sudan, Tanganyika, or French Equatorial Africa were hunters in every sense of the word, people willing to put up with discomfort and the necessity of putting a lot of effort into getting the desired species, which they were very selective about. Today, comfort is the top priority . . . with the minimum effort expected for the maximum result. These butchers only know how to pull the trigger, and if they don't get at least fifty animals on safari they go home in a snit and later write to magazines about how everything was a disaster, the professional hunter inept, and the organizer a thief. It is also unfortunate that certain complacent guides allow decadent clients to commit hunting atrocities, clients whose only merit is that they are loaded with money and empty of the least understanding of the hunter's ethics or sportsmanship.

I think that my forty-two years of crossing all the corners of Africa allow me to offer some friendly advice to the future hunter: When starting along your African road, forget all those stories about safaris. Abandon preconceived ideas and arrive there completely fresh. This way everything you see and experience will be something completely new, and in this way you will enjoy the entire safari experience up to the last moment of your stay. The old times are gone forever and cannot come again. If you hope to take trophies like mine or those of Hunter and Percival, you will only be frustrated and disappointed. You must hunt for hunting's sake, taking, of course, the best trophy possible. Don't let one inch more or less ruin your pleasure as a hunter. Not seeing your name in the trophy book is nothing to be depressed about. What is important is the satisfaction you gain from being out in the wild, pitting yourself against nature and beast. No record book in the world could begin to make a category out of satisfaction to be gained in pursuit of the challenge. The challenge comes in how the game is taken, by hunting it in a sporting way, not by murdering it from the seat of a Toyota.

Don't try to compete with anyone, but instead try to make the most of the hand you've been dealt. No matter what size trophy you take, you can still enjoy the wonderful hunting fields of Africa. Don't try to compete with the likes of John Hunter since those times belong to hunting history and are gone forever. The main thing is never to forget the hunter's ethic and to keep in mind the old saying, "There are many hunting gentlemen but very few gentleman hunters."

•••